Violence in
the Black Family

Violence in the Black Family

Correlates and Consequences

Edited by
Robert L. Hampton
Connecticut College

Lexington Books
D.C. Heath and Company/Lexington, Massachusetts/Toronto

Library of Congress Cataloging-in-Publication Data

Violence in the Black family.

Includes index.
1. Afro-American families.   2. Family violence—
United States.   I. Hampton, Robert L.
E185.86.V56   1987   306.8'7   86-45897
ISBN 0-669-14584-X (alk. paper)

Published simultaneously in Canada
Printed in the United States of America
Casebound International Standard Book Number: 0-669-14584-X
Library of Congress Catalog Card Number: 86-45897

The paper used in this publication meets the minimum requirements
of American National Standard for Information Sciences—
Permanence of Paper for Printed Library Materials, ANSI
Z39.48-1984. ⊗ ™

87 88 89 90 91 8 7 6 5 4 3 2 1

To four generations of support:

Mary and Charlie Hampton
Reverend T.L. Hampton and Anne A. Williams
Marcellus and Lauretta Melson
Cathy M. Hampton
Robyn M. and Conrad R. Hampton

Contents

Preface

In September 1984 the Attorney General's Task Force on Family Violence submitted its final report to the president. The task force found that although the problem of family violence has existed for generations, only recently has it begun to receive the attention it deserves. Task force members conceded that family violence is a widespread problem that occurs among families in every social and economic class (Attorney General Task Force 1984).

Almost a year later, another high-level government task force issued its final report. The Secretary's Task Force on Black and Minority Health was a landmark effort in analyzing and synthesizing current knowledge of major factors that contribute to the health status of blacks and other minorities. Among its many findings was that after heart disease, homicide accounts for more excess mortality among black Americans than any other cause of death. The task force reported that most homicides in the United States involve relatives and acquaintances, and more than 65 percent were not related to criminal events. Many homicides were preceded by nonlethal conflicts and violence that frequently came to the attention of police or were the occasion for visits to hospital emergency departments (U.S. Department of Health and Human Services 1985).

Although each task force examined different issues, one can easily see areas of common interest and concern. It was clear to both committees that violence is not a problem just for blacks. The disparity in rates of violence between blacks and other groups, however, suggests a need for more research and discussion of violence within this population. Each task force recognized the need for more research and major preventative efforts. They also recognized that the public must become aware of the problem and its obligations in combating it.

The purpose of this book is to promote thought and discussion about violence in black families: its prevalence, correlates, and consequences. Although there has been an increase in the literature on family violence, substantial deficits remain in our knowledge in general and specifically in our knowledge about ethnic and cultural factors associated with family violence.

Sexual abuse, physical child abuse, family violence, and homicides are arguably among the most serious social problems in the black community and thus justify the current level of public and professional concern. Although there are some similarities between domestic violence in the black and nonblack community, there are some significant differences. These patterned differences in rate, nature, severity, and consequences are created in part because of historical and contemporary factors in the social ecology of black family life.

Research on the origins of family violence appears to favor an ecological perspective, which focuses on the multiple levels of individual and familial characteristics that interact with characteristics of the broader social environment (Garbarino 1982). Within this framework, one would not focus exclusively on individual psychiatric disturbance among perpetrators as a cause for family violence. This approach stresses the need to examine individual histories, as well as institutional and societal factors involved in the violence process.

Individual and institutional racism are important contextual variables for the study of all aspects of the black family in the United States. The distinctive visibility, if not vulnerability, of poor, socially marginal, and black families cannot be separated from a substantial bias, which at times results in the application of onerous labels and unequal treatment. One cannot argue, however, that family violence among blacks is caused exclusively by racism; a number of important variables simultaneously mediate the effects of racism and other external factors on families.

This book is intended to raise a number of questions concerning the external environments and internal operations for black families victimized by the violence process. The chapters show that responsibility for violence in black families resides as much in the society as in the relationships among family members.

This book does not provide complete answers for the questions it raises. Indeed it is the intention of the chapters to raise many questions and speculate upon them. The issues addressed are of interest to professionals who study black family life and family violence, as well as to professionals who provide services to families.

The contributors were carefully selected from a variety of disciplines and reflect different approaches. Although they differ in professional training and orientation, they share a common concern of extending knowledge beyond negative stereotypes and in a small way contributing to the reduction of family violence among blacks in the United States.

Acknowledgments

Many people have been involved in the process of developing this book. The contributors are the major actors. My students in Methods of Social Research and Analysis and Family Violence who asked countless questions that required answers provided an important incentive to me to pursue further research in this area.

I thank the following for their special contributions to this book: Eli H. Newberger, a pediatrician at Children's Hospital Center, Boston, who directed the Training Program on Family Violence and who served as a mentor, co-investigator, and supportive colleague; and my other colleagues associated with the Research Training Program on Family Violence, who patiently and thoughtfully worked with me in seminars, journal groups, conferences, and clinics around issues of research and practice: William Bithoney, Richard Bourne, Roy T. Bowles, Jessica H. Daniel, Howard Dubowitz, Lisa Gary, Richard J. Gelles, Thomas Marx, Daniel Kessler, Mitch Katz, Sylvia Krakow, Joanne Michalek, Carolyn M. Newberger, Steve Shirk, Betty Singer, Jane Snyder, Marti Straus, and Kathleen White.

I want to express my thanks to my colleagues in the Department of Sociology at Connecticut College, Francis Boudreau, Arthur Ferrari, and Jerry Winter, who encouraged me to develop a course on family violence and to pursue my research interests in this field; R. Francis Johnson, dean of the faculty, who saw the importance of reaching audiences beyond the classroom and provided support toward this end; the many research assistants who helped with data acquisition, review, and library work: Laura Coleman, Larry Pellegrino, Andrea Saltzberg, Fran Smith, Joannie Spitz, and Michelle de la Uz; my primary typist, Donna K. Temple, who quietly suffered through countless drafts of several chapters; and department secretaries Anita L. Fernald and Regina B. Foster, who provided essential backup support. I would like to thank Margaret N. Zusky, my editor at Lexington Books, who believed in this project and encouraged its completion, and Karen E. Maloney, also of Lexington Books, for their cooperation and support. Finally, I want to thank Cathy, Robyn, and Conrad, my wife, daughter, and son, who have sustained me through the many challenges of working in this field.

I acknowledge with appreciation grant support from the Connecticut College Faculty Study, Research and Travel Fund, National Research Council, Rockefeller Foundation, Center for Studies of Violent and Antisocial Behavior of the National Institute of Mental Health, and the National Center on Child Abuse and Neglect in the U.S. Department of Health and Human Services.

I
Child Maltreatment

1
Violence against Black Children: Current Knowledge and Future Research Needs

Robert L. Hampton

I t has been suggested that Americans are more violent than the citizens of any other developed country in the world. And black Americans as a group are considered more violent than white Americans (Comer 1985).

Although the media and the public have shown an increasing interest in child maltreatment in recent years, relatively little attention has been given to violence against black children. The few studies that have examined child abuse and neglect in black families have done so only in passing. Few researchers have attempted to develop a more precise conceptual or empirical understanding of the nature, type, and severity of family violence experienced by black children.

This chapter draws on data from the National Study of the Incidence and Severity of Child Abuse and Neglect (U.S. Department of Health and Human Services, 1981) for two purposes: to ascertain whether ethnic differences exist within the population of maltreated children, specifically among cases of physical abuse, and to examine intraracial differences among black physical abuse and other black abuse cases.

Prevalence

The true prevalence of child abuse is unknown, although the number of nationally reported cases has increased 158 percent since 1976 when 416,033 child maltreatment cases were reported to the child protective services system (CPS). The number of reported cases increased annually to a total of 1,024,178 in 1984, the last year for which data are available. This increase can be attributed to a number of factors, but we must remember that it is impossible to determine to what extent the increase in reporting is associated directly with an increase in the number of maltreated children. Individual states continue to modify reporting legislation to encompass new reportable conditions, such as emotional abuse (American Humane Association 1986). It is likely that the increase in reporting is due to increased public awareness and to improved accountability on the part of state reporting systems.

The total number of reports is a general indicator of the level of activity on the part of CPS. The number of reports, however, is not equivalent to the number of children involved. In 1984, for example, slightly more than a million reports were made representing more than 1.7 million children. The rate of reporting was estimated at 27.3 children per 1,000 in the U.S. child population (American Humane Association 1986.)

According to the 1980 census, black children accounted for about 15 percent of all children in the United States. From 1976 to 1980, the proportion of child abuse and neglect reports involving black children remained fairly constant at about 19 percent, but national data for 1982 showed that black children were the victims in 22 percent of all child maltreatment reports. In 1984, black children accounted for 20.8 percent of CPS cases (American Humane Association 1986.)

Race and Child Maltreatment

An assessment of the impact of race on violence toward children must be based on careful examination of the previous research on case reports, the reporting process, and attitudes toward child abuse.

Examinations of the relationship between family violence and race have yielded mixed results. In the first large-scale summary of national reporting, Gil (1970) concluded that families reported for abuse were drawn disproportionately from the less educated, the poor, and ethnic minorities. Black children were overrepresented as victims of abuse. A more recent compilation shows a similar picture: whites were underrepresented in reported cases of maltreatment, and lower-income families in general were overrepresented (Jason et al. 1982).

Lauderdale, Valiunas, and Anderson (1980) computed annual rates for the occurrence of validated cases of abuse and neglect in Texas from 1975 to 1977 for whites, blacks, and Mexican-Americans. Without controlling for social class, they found that blacks had the highest rates for all forms of maltreatment, followed by Mexican-Americans and then whites. In a follow-up study using the same data, Spearly and Lauderdale (1983) extended their earlier study by controlling for social class and community (county) characteristics. Once again their results indicated that a higher rate of child maltreatment existed among blacks. The study also found that a greater proportion of high-risk families in a given area is not responsible in itself for increased rates of maltreatment, but when this higher proportion is combined with a highly urban environment, it may yield particularly high rates for blacks relative to the majority population.

Jason et al. (1982) reported similar findings in their analysis of data from the Georgia Department of Protective Services. They found that blacks accounted for a higher than expected proportion of confirmed cases of child maltreatment and suggested that this high rate indicated that the results were not the product of reporting bias.

In a study of 4,132 cases of child abuse reported to the Los Angeles County Sheriff's Department from 1975 to 1982, Lindholm and Willey (1983) reported a number of significant differences attributed to ethnic status. Physical abuse was highest in black families, with discipline given most often as the reason for the abuse. The children also suffered different types of physical injuries as a result of the abuse. Black children were more likely to be whipped or beaten and to receive lacerations or scars, whereas white children were more likely to receive bruises.

Although blacks constituted only 9.8 percent of the Los Angeles County population, they accounted for 23.8 percent of abuse victims. These data also showed that among whites and Hispanics, males (especially fathers) were the most frequent perpetrators. Among blacks, however, mothers were identified most frequently as alleged perpetrators. Given the number of female heads of household in the sample, this finding is not surprising. The results indicated that females in single-parent homes and males in stepparent (consensual or legal) families were most likely to be the abusers.

Other evidence in the literature suggests that blacks are overrepresented in case reports. In an analysis of case records of 616 children seen by the child abuse team in a metropolitan children's hospital, Johnson and Showers (1985) found that black children were reported disproportionately more often than white children. They also found significant racial differences in the causes of injury: black children were more likely to be struck by a belt, strap, or cord than were white children. A marginally significant difference existed between blacks and whites for injuries incurred by a switch or stick; blacks were struck more frequently with these implements.

Black children were also knifed more commonly and burned by an iron more offten than white children, who were more commonly struck with a board or paddle or hit with an open hand (Johnson and Showers, 1985). The researchers speculated that black children suffered more lacerations and more erythema or marks because of a higher use among blacks of knives, cords, straps, and belts. They also believed that because black children were abused more often with belts and cords, while white children were hit more frequently with boards or slapped with the hand, strong subcultural or racial differences in approaches to discipline might exist.

In a recent study of 78 cases of child abuse conducted at Children's Hospital, Columbus, Ohio, in which electric cords were used to discipline children, black children over the age of 5 years were most often the victims (Showers and Bandman 1986). Although black children constituted only 39 percent of the entire sample of 616 abused children, they made up 91 percent of the cord-injured subsample. The researchers concluded that black children are at significantly higher risk than white children for abuse with cords. Perpetrators are most frequently poorly educated black mothers who are single and raising more than one child; many of these mothers report striking out at their offspring because they want them to perform better in school and to have better lives than they themselves have had (Showers and Bandman 1986).

Newberger and his colleagues (1977) believe that children from poor and minority families are more vulnerable to receiving the label "abused" than children from more affluent households, who are more likely to be classified as victims of accidents. Support for this proposition, particularly with respect to abuse cases seen in medical settings, comes from several sources. In research conducted among physicians, Gelles (1982) found that when the physicians made a report of child abuse, they considered not only the child's physical condition but also the caretaker's occupation, education, race, and ethnicity. Five percent of a group of 157 physicians surveyed stated that the caretaker's race and ethnicity were so important that they would file a child abuse report on the basis of those characteristics alone.

Using a case vignette model, Turbett and O'Toole (1980) found that recognition of child abuse by physicians was affected by the severity of the child's injury and by the parents' socioeconomic status and ethnicity. When children were described as having a major injury, black children were nearly twice as likely as white children to be recognized as victims of abuse. Physicians were 33 percent more likely to report black children suffering from a major injury than children identified as white who were described in identical vignettes. Children described as lower-class whites suffering from major injuries were more likely to be classified as abused than white children with the same injury who were presented as members of an upper-class group.

Additional empirical evidence exists to show that racial factors are associated with child maltreatment reporting as strongly as or more strongly than the nature and severity of the child's injury. Hampton and Newberger (1985), using a sample of cases from the National Study of the Incidence and Severity of Child Abuse and Neglect (U.S. Department of Health and Human Services 1981), have shown that hospitals tend to overreport blacks and Hispanics and underreport whites. For black and Hispanic families, recognition of alleged child maltreatment almost ensured reporting to child protective services.

Data from the National Survey of Family Violence (Straus, Gelles, and Steinmetz 1980) indicate little difference between black and white families in the rates of abusive violence toward children (15 percent in black families, 14 percent in white families). Although wife abuse was nearly 400 percent more common in black than in white families and husband abuse was twice as common in black families as in white families, blacks in this sample were not more violent toward children. This finding was quite similar to an earlier observation made by Billingsley (1969).

In a more detailed examination of the national survey data, Cazenave and Straus (1979) concluded that aid and support, especially child care provided by black extended-family kin, seemed to reduce the risk of abusive violence toward children. They found that when income and husband's occupation are controlled, blacks were less likely to engage in child abuse. Because these data included only two-parent families, some caution must be made in interpretation.

In the most complete attitudinal research to date on the topic of ethnicity and violence, Giovannoni and Becerra (1979) explored how the various ethnic and professional groups within a large city define child maltreatment. They presented a series of case vignettes that described specific incidents of child maltreatment, representing a range of behaviors that might be considered maltreatment and that varied in degree of severity. Respondents included professionals and lay people in the metropolitan Los Angeles area.

The respondents were asked to rate each vignette according to the "seriousness of its impact on the welfare of the child." The sample population comprised 12 percent blacks, 17 percent Hispanics, 65 percent white (Anglo), and 7 percent "other." The study sought to test the idea that ethnic minorities and people of lower socioeconomic status are "more tolerant of mistreatment and likely to have a higher threshold for considering actions as mistreatment" (Giovannoni and Becerra 1979). The results, however, showed just the opposite: in 94 percent of the cases, blacks and Hispanics gave more serious rating to the vignettes than did Anglos. Contrary to the authors' expectations, education and income (the prime indicators of socioeconomic status) were related inversely to ratings of seriousness: the higher was the education and income level of the respondent, the lower was the seriousness rating. Ethnic differences among respondents were not merely a product of social class differences; they persisted even across educational levels. Blacks at all educational levels, for example, rated categories of neglect as more serious than did others. The results of analysis by income show similar but less consistent trends.

This research suggests that poor and nonwhite families may hold attitudes toward maltreatment different from those held by white and more affluent families. Nonwhites and people of lower socioeconomic status tended to evalute the vignettes as more serious (Giovannoni and Becerra 1979).

Thus, as Hampton (1987) points out, many questions about the dynamics of ethnicity and family violence have been raised, but the evidence to date has made the relationship difficult to determine. Similarly, there has been selective inattention to intraracial patterns of family violence among blacks. The present study represents an attempt to further discussions of ethnicity and violence and to examine more closely the patterns of physical abuse among blacks.

Methodology

The National Study of the Incidence and Severity of Child Abuse and Neglect (NIS), conducted from April 1979 to May 1980, was a large, systematic effort to gather information on cases of child abuse and neglect in the United States. The study collected family-level data for each suspected case of child abuse or neglect received by the county CPS agency during the study period.

In addition to CPS caseworkers, professional staff in other agencies were asked to participate in the study. The agencies included those with statutory authority to investigate or treat situations involving child abuse or neglect (for example, juvenile probation departments and juvenile courts) and those whose staff might encounter abused or neglected children (such as schools and hospitals). The NIS collected case data from agencies located in twenty-six counties throughout the United States; the counties were chosen by stratified random sampling. To compensate for unequal probabilities of selection and to provide a basis for computing national estimates, each case was weighted by the product of four weighting variables. Three of these variables compensated for variations in probabilities of county selection, agency selection rate, and nonparticipation by designated agencies. In addition, an annualization weight was included. Overall, 17,645 cases of child abuse and neglect were reported to the study. Once the appropriate weightings were applied, the investigators estimated that for the United States as a whole, professionals suspected 1,151,600 cases of child abuse and neglect for the year May 1979 through April 1980 (U.S. Department of Health and Human Services 1981).

This analysis is based on the assumption that an investigator's classification of a case as substantiated or nonsubstantiated is a better assessment of whether maltreatment occurred than is the suspicion of someone who reported the case to the system. Consequently only substantiated cases were included in this analysis.

For the purpose of this study, maltreatment was defined as a situation in which "through purposive acts or marked inattention to a child's basic needs, behavior of a parent/substitute or other adult caretaker caused foreseeable and avoidable injury or impairment to a child or materially contributed to unreasonable prolongation or worsening of an existing injury or impairment" (U.S. Department of Health and Human Services 1981 p. 47). This study included not only the traditional areas of physical and sexual abuse and neglect but also problems in the areas of educational neglect and emotional maltreatment. The scope of these concepts was generally consistent with the National Center on Child Abuse and Neglect (NCCAN) Draft Model Child Protection Act and with many recent state reporting statutes.

Results

Interracial Differences

The NIS data set includes an estimated 4,170 (unweighted) substantiated cases of child maltreatment. Whites constitute 77.4 percent of this sample, blacks 15.8 percent, and Hispanics 4.2 percent. Approximately 2 percent of the sample had an ethnic classification of "other" and are excluded from this analysis.

The calculation of percentages and cross-tabulations used the weighting procedures described already. The procedures enabled the researchers to estimate the percentage and distribution of cases in the general population on the basis of the sample. When tests of significance are reported, they are calculated conservatively from unweighted cases.

Previous analyses of these data have shown that in comparison to whites and Hispanics, substantiated maltreatment cases among blacks included families who were poorer, more likely to be on public assistance, and in father-absent households (Hampton, 1987). Three-quarters of the black families had incomes of $7,000 or less compared to 50 percent of white families. Three-fifths of black families but only one-third of white families received public assistance.

Physical neglect was the most frequently diagnosed form of maltreatment for all groups, followed by physical abuse (table 1-1). Almost 40 percent of the sample were reported to have experienced physical neglect, in contrast to the 25 percent who experienced physical abuse. There was a high proportion of black families in both categories. Black children were less likely to be classified as victims of emotional injury, however.

Table 1-1 shows several other important differences in this sample of maltreated children. Nonwhite children were younger than whites; nonwhite parents had fewer years of formal education; and black mothers in particular were more likely to be unemployed. Nonwhite mothers were also younger (Hampton, 1987).

Table 1–1
Selected Demographic, Maltreatment, and Injury Variables for All Substantiated Cases, by Ethnicity

Variable	White	Black	Hispanic	Total
Age of child				
0–5	31.5%	34.5%	45.5%	32.8%[a]
6–12	50.4	49.3	40.8	49.7
13–17	17.8	14.4	13.7	17.0
Sex of child				
Male	50.5	48.9	42.8	49.7
Female	49.5	51.0	57.2	50.2
Mother's education[b]				
0–8 years	13.6	27.1	34.7	16.7
9–11 years	47.2	51.5	40.4	47.7
12 years or more	39.6	21.4	24.9	35.7
Number of children in household				
1	19.0	14.8	20.2	18.6
2	28.3	23.7	30.2	27.5
3	22.9	19.5	27.5	22.3
4	14.8	14.6	10.8	14.8
5 or more	15.1	27.4	11.3	16.8
Father in household				
Yes	56.1	27.0	56.0	51.5
No	43.1	73.0	44.0	48.5
Family income[c]				
Less than $7,000	50.1	74.6	47.0	53.7[a]
$7,000–14,999	39.9	18.7	41.0	36.8
$15,000–24,999	7.5	4.5	10.5	7.2
$25,000 or more	2.5	2.1	1.5	2.3
Receiving AFDC[d]				
Yes	34.8	62.7	30.0	38.8
No	65.2	37.3	70.0	61.2
Type of maltreatment				
Physical abuse	25.2	29.1	25.0	25.7
Sexual abuse	7.9	7.0	12.4	7.9
Emotional injury	11.9	4.0	8.1	10.4
Physical neglect	36.7	45.8	34.6	38.4
Other	18.3	14.2	17.1	17.5
Severity of maltreatment				
Serious	9.7	8.1	9.9	9.4
Moderate	25.8	19.3	27.4	24.8
Probable	64.5	72.6	62.8	65.9
Role of mother in maltreatment				
Perpetrator	70.0	76.8	64.1	70.6
Nonperpetrator	23.8	18.6	32.1	23.6
Don't know	6.1	4.6	3.8	5.8

City size				
SMSA over 200,000	32.6	47.9	83.8	38.2
Other SMSA	23.6	17.5	13.0	21.9
Non-SMSA	43.8	34.6	3.2	39.9
Unweighted N	(3,183)	(746)	(224)	(4,153)
Weighted N	(364,697)	(74,503)	(20,008)	(459,203)

[a]Percentages are based on weighting and may not add to 100 percent because of rounding.
[b]Excludes 1,330 women for whom data were missing.
[c]Excludes 139 cases for whom data were missing.
[d]Excludes 166 cases for whom data were missing.
[e]Excludes 215 cases for whom data were missing.

Because physical abuse receives the most emphasis by professionals, the media, and the general public, a separate analysis of physical abuse cases by ethnicity was conducted. Compared to whites, black victims of assaultive maltreatment were more likely to be in the 6–12 age group, live in urban areas, have mothers who had not completed high school, and suffer more serious injuries. There were more children and more victims in black households.

Table 1–2 shows a number of other important ethnic differences within this subsample. A relatively small number of black cases were reported to CPS by law enforcement agencies (7.9 percent black versus 14.5 percent white). Schools and medical sources, however, reported a fairly high proportion of black children to CPS.

The data in table 1–2 contain information concerning the caseworkers' assessments of any caretaker problems associated with abuse. These are, of course, subjective evaluations grouped into very large categories, but they nevertheless provide some valuable insights.

Caseworkers reported that caretaker stress was associated strongly with physical abuse in general and to an even greater extent in nonwhite families. Child-rearing difficulties, which included poor child-rearing and homemaking skills, were cited as a problem for 17 percent of the families. Emotional problems ranked third on the list for black families, and substance abuse ranked third for white families.

More than half (52 percent) of the black victims of physical abuse received injuries from weapons (knife, gun, stick or cord). In comparison, 27.4 percent of white and 44.4 percent of Hispanic assaultive violence victims suffered injuries inflicted by weapons.

Together the ethnic comparisons for all forms of maltreatment and for physical abuse suggest some similarities in distributions across several variables. These data also suggest that there may be some important differences among these groups.

Table 1-2
Demographic Distribution of Physical Abuse Cases, by Ethnicity

Variable	White	Black	Hispanic	Total
Age of child				
0–5	36.3%	21.6%	41.6%	33.8%[a]
6–12	45.8	59.9	53.4	48.6
13–17	18.0	18.5	5.0	17.5
Sex of child				
Male	55.2	42.9	41.8	52.4
Female	44.8	56.9	58.2	47.6
Mother's education				
0–8 years	4.8	17.5	12.6	7.2
9–11 years	40.7	50.1	62.3	43.1
12 years or more	54.5	32.4	25.2	49.7
Mother's employment				
Employed full time	30.1	36.9	20.0	30.8
Employed part time	63.4	53.9	67.7	61.9
Unemployed	6.5	9.3	12.3	7.3
Mother's age				
19 or less	4.0	2.7	7.3	3.9
20–24	18.4	16.1	7.6	17.5
25–29	23.5	18.1	12.9	22.1
30–34	21.8	33.6	47.3	24.9
35 or older	26.2	20.0	11.1	24.5
Don't know	6.1	9.5	13.9	7.0
Number of children in household				
1	23.0	14.3	17.9	21.2
2	32.4	17.5	24.0	29.2
3	20.4	21.1	19.7	20.5
4	14.3	15.6	30.6	15.2
5 or more	9.9	31.5	7.8	13.7
Number of victims				
1	54.2	43.7	74.3	53.1
2	22.3	10.9	6.1	19.5
3	12.8	13.9	1.4	12.5
4	7.3	11.3	18.2	8.5
5	3.4	20.2	0.0	6.3
Father in household				
Yes	68.7	48.7	83.7	65.7
No	31.3	51.3	16.3	34.3
Family income				
Less than $7,000	36.4	43.7	31.2	37.5[a]
$7,000–14,999	48.5	37.8	39.4	46.2
$15,000–24,999	10.5	11.5	24.6	11.3
$25,000 or more	4.6	7.0	4.8	5.0
Receiving AFDC				
Yes	25.5	38.4	23.9	27.7
No	74.5	61.6	76.1	72.3

Role of mother in abuse				
Maltreator	50.5	51.9	22.3	49.6
Not involved	44.3	38.1	72.5	44.3
Don't know	5.2	10.1	5.1	6.1
Severity of abuse				
Serious	9.2	11.7	9.3	9.7
Moderate	57.6	42.8	75.7	55.6
Probable	33.2	45.5	15.1	34.7
Caretaker problems associated with abuse				
Alcohol/drugs	16.8	12.0	8.2	15.6
Physical disability	5.0	0.9	0.0	1.2
Child rearing	16.0	23.1	15.1	17.1
Emotional	9.1	13.1	6.3	9.6
Stress	32.3	40.3	51.6	34.5
History of abuse	11.0	3.3	12.5	9.8
Other	9.9	7.4	6.3	9.3
Source of report to CPS				
Law enforcement	14.5	7.9	17.4	13.4
Medical sources	12.2	22.4	12.7	14.1
Schools	20.3	25.2	52.2	22.6
Other	53.0	44.5	17.6	49.9
City size				
SMSA over 200,000	36.5	59.6	80.6	42.6
Other SMSA	26.9	18.4	16.8	24.9
Non-SMSA	36.5	22.0	2.6	32.4
With implement				
Yes	27.4	52.0	44.4	32.6
No	72.6	48.0	55.6	67.4
Unweighted *N*	(734)	(205)	(37)	(967)
Weighted *N*	(92,008)	(21,654)	(5,008)	(118,671)

aPercentages are based on weighting and may not add to 100 percent because of rounding.

Intraracial Differences

There is little question about the importance of comparative analyses within the field of family violence. It is equally important to address differences that may exist within an ethnic group. Clearly an ethnic community contains considerable variation in the nature, type, severity, and scope of child maltreatment.

In a comparison of all black cases substantiated by primary allegation, several important differences emerge, (table 1-3). Physical and sexual abuse are associated positively with the age of the child; physical neglect is related inversely to the age of the child. This is illustrated more clearly by the fact that 45 percent of the sample were victims of physical neglect, but 65 percent of the 0–5 year olds, 37 percent of the 6–12 year olds, and 27.5 percent of the 13–17 year olds fell within this category of maltreatment.

Table 1–3
All Black Cases Substantiated by Allegation

Variable	Physical Abuse	Sexual Abuse	Emotional Injury	Physical Neglect	Other	Total
Age of child						
0–5	18.2%	2.5%	4.5%	63.0%	11.9%	35.1%
6–12	35.3	9.5	3.1	37.3	14.8	50.2
13–17	37.3	10.0	6.2	27.5	19.0	14.7
Sex of child						
Male	25.5	5.6	2.6	52.6	13.8	48.9
Female	32.4	8.4	5.3	39.4	14.5	51.0
Mother's education						
0–8 years	17.1	7.3	1.8	50.6	23.2	27.1
9–11 years	25.9	5.8	5.0	47.8	15.4	51.5
12 years or more	40.4	8.7	6.2	31.5	13.2	21.4
Mother's employment						
Employed full time	54.8	5.3	4.1	34.7	1.0	18.5
Employed part time	21.0	7.8	4.4	49.7	17.1	70.5
Unemployed	23.2	6.6	2.6	50.1	17.5	11.0
Mother's age						
19 or less	10.0	0.2	3.2	70.1	16.5	7.4
20–24	23.3	5.1	2.6	58.3	10.6	19.1
25–29	27.0	13.6	6.0	37.6	15.8	18.4
30–34	31.6	3.7	1.7	49.7	13.2	29.3
35 or older	28.6	13.0	7.3	30.2	20.9	19.3
Don't know	39.9	2.3	1.5	53.8	2.5	6.6
Father in household						
Yes	52.4	13.6	2.6	22.0	9.4	27.0
No	20.4	4.6	4.5	54.6	15.9	73.0
Family income						
Less than $7,000	17.3	6.8	4.5	53.2	18.3	74.6
More than $7,000	65.4	7.1	3.0	21.5	3.0	25.9
Receiving AFDC						
Yes	17.4	5.0	3.2	57.0	17.4	62.7
No	46.9	10.2	4.7	29.4	8.8	37.3
Role of mother in maltreatment						
Maltreator	19.6	2.7	3.7	56.6	17.4	76.8
Permitted	42.5	26.3	14.6	12.8	3.7	6.0
Not involved	67.4	24.6	2.1	5.2	0.7	12.6
Don't know	64.2	4.9	0.0	20.5	10.4	4.6
Severity of injury						
Serious	40.0	11.2	4.2	38.7	5.9	8.1
Moderate	62.5	7.0	6.5	14.3	9.8	19.3
Probable	17.7	6.6	3.1	56.3	16.3	72.6
Source of report to CPS						
Law enforcement	20.7	13.2	2.2	51.3	12.6	11.9
Medical sources	35.5	10.9	2.7	42.1	8.9	19.7
Schools	43.8	6.5	5.2	29.7	14.8	18.0
Other	27.6	5.4	4.5	50.1	12.4	50.4

Caretaker problems associated with maltreatment						
Alcohol/drugs	13.1	18.0	0.8	56.7	11.4	22.3
Physical disability	4.1	1.2	8.5	35.9	50.3	6.0
Child rearing	25.8	0.8	5.2	54.9	13.2	23.7
Emotional	28.1	3.0	9.5	14.6	44.8	12.3
Stress	45.0	2.7	4.2	34.2	13.8	23.8
History of abuse	16.9	4.9	4.0	74.2	0.0	5.2
Other	29.1	2.2	0.0	68.8	0.0	6.4
City Size						
SMSA over 200,000	36.2	6.2	4.5	37.6	15.6	47.9
Other SMSA	30.6	5.5	4.8	51.1	8.0	17.5
Non-SMSA	18.5	9.0	2.8	54.5	15.2	34.6
Total percentage	29.1	7.0	4.0	45.8	14.2	100.0

Weighted *N* = 74,503
Unweighted *N* = 753

^aPercentages are based on weighting and may not add to 100 percent because of rounding.

Higher than expected proportions of females, families with incomes over $7,000, families not receiving public assistance, and father-present households fell into the physical abuse category. Physical and sexual abuse cases accounted for a higher than expected proportion of serious injuries, and they occur in two-parent families. These data indicate that stress is a caretaker problem most frequently associated with physical abuse, while alcohol-related problems are associated more frequently with sexual abuse.

Physical abuse cases were likely to occur in families residing in urban areas and in households in which the mother was employed full time. Mothers, however, were not usually the perpetrators of this abuse. Females were overrepresented among the victims of physical abuse.

One factor often related to the severity of abuse is the use of an implement. These implements may include common household items ranging from brooms, hairbrushes, and belts to potentially lethal weapons. One cannot assume, however, that an implement is used with the intent of causing a more serious injury. The severity of injury should be viewed in most cases as a consequence. It comes as no surprise that severity of injury is related to implement. In the sample, 59 percent of the serious injuries occurred in situations involving an implement (table 1–4).

Within the subsample of physically abused children, younger children and females were most likely to be victimized by an implement. Implements were used in the maltreatment of 59 percent of the physically abused females.

No relationships exist between use of an implement and Aid for Dependent Children status, family income, mother's employment, or mother's education. Implement use was more common in situations where the mother was the maltreator and in urban areas. Both caretaker

Table 1–4
Substantiated Black Physical Abuse Cases by Use of Implement

Variable	Implement	No Implement	Total
Age of child			
0–5	56.1	43.5	21.6
6–12	51.1	48.9	59.9
13–17	49.3	50.7	18.5
Sex of child			
Male	42.3	57.7	43.1
Female	59.0	41.0	56.9
Mother's employment			
Employed full time	57.1	42.9	36.9
Not employed	56.8	43.2	53.9
Don't know	57.2	42.8	9.3
Mother's education			
0–8 years	56.9	43.1	17.5
9–11 years	48.3	51.7	50.1
12 years or more	53.0	47.0	32.4
Father in household			
Yes	46.3	53.7	47.7
No	58.1	41.9	52.3
Family income			
Less than $7,000	47.9	52.1	43.7
$7,000–$14,999	68.9	31.1	37.8
$15,000–24,999	47.7	52.3	11.5
$25,000 or more	0.0	100.0	7.0
Receiving AFDC			
Yes	50.0	50.0	51.5
No	52.5	47.5	48.5
Role of mother in maltreatment			
Maltreator	61.3	38.7	51.9
Permitted	50.6	49.4	8.8
Not involved	53.5	46.5	29.3
Don't know	0.5	99.5	10.1
Severity of injury			
Serious	59.3	40.7	11.7
Moderate	54.1	45.1	42.8
Probable	44.0	56.0	45.5
Caretaker problems associated with abuse			
Alcohol/drugs	30.3	69.7	10.1
Child rearing	53.6	46.4	23.1
Emotional	45.7	54.3	13.1
Stress	63.8	36.2	40.3
History of abuse	78.3	21.7	3.3
Other	51.2	48.8	7.4

City size			
SMSA over 200,000	67.3	32.7	59.6
Other SMSA	29.1	70.9	18.4
Non-SMSA	29.4	70.6	22.0
Total percentage	52.0	48.0	100.0

Unweighted N = 205
Weighted N = 21,654

Note: Percentages are based on weighting and may not add to 100 percent because of rounding.

stress and history of abuse suffered by caretaker were associated with the use of an implement.

Discussion

Research on child abuse and violence toward children has failed to examine issues of ethnic differences or aspects of violence in the minority community. This analysis has identified several variables in which ethnic differences exist within a sample of substantiated child maltreatment cases and some differences within the sample of black children.

The findings of this study suggest that differences exist among blacks, whites, and Hispanics in regard to family income, age of victim, perpetrator, and type and severity of abuse. These data also suggest that ethnic differences exist within the category of physical abuse cases. There are important differences between black and nonblack cases with respect to family demographics, sources of report to CPS, and problems associated with maltreatment. Although differences across variables are important, the primary issue here is that the differences need to be explored in greater detail in future empirical studies and addressed more closely in service delivery programs.

This study not only explores differences among groups but also suggests that differences exist among the maltreated children within a single ethnic group. This phenomenon was observed readily when black children who were abused physically were compared with black children who suffered other forms of maltreatment.

This study has attempted to provide some information concerning differences between and within groups. One difficulty with these data, however, is that they rely on caught cases. We can only speculate as to the actual number of abused children. In addition, the data do not permit a discussion of differences between abusing and nonabusing parents. For that purpose, case control comparisons are needed.

Although the study has limitations, its advantages must be considered. First, the study used a national probability sample and as such is more representative of the population than samples used in other research based on small clinical samples or agency referrals. In addition, the samples of substantiated maltreated children (4,153) and black children (753) were much larger than those used in most previous studies.

This study has provided some useful estimates and descriptions, but many questions remain. The following list specifies some of the issues and research strategies that need to be addressed:

1. Ethnic, cultural, and subcultural variations in the prevalence, distribution, correlates, and consequences of violence toward children are among the areas in need of further research.

2. Studies on the effects of family violence intervention of victims, perpetrators, and families. It has been suggested that families as a unit of analysis have often been neglected in this area. This research should also be sensitive to differential effects by race, class, and community.

3. Factors that might naturally work within a family or community to extinguish violence. This process, called natural desistance, would focus on critical events or processes that reduce or eliminate family violence. Although there is evidence to support the intergenerational transmission of violence, there are a significant number of individuals who either experienced or witnessed violence who are not violent.

4. Cohort studies of abused children and high school graduates. The former would be prospective and would provide insights on the effects of alternative interventions, as well as no interventions, on the cycle of violence. The latter, also a prospective study, would identify a cohort of high school graduates and follow them prospectively in order to study the developmental process by which young adults become violent adults.

5. The institutional processing of victims, perpetrators, and families. Research in this area would address the different effects of the processing of family violence cases and of different types of cases, by different public and private agencies and systems.

6. Different community definitions of abuse. Do communities differ with respect to what acts they define as abusive and how they respond to such acts?

7. Existing service delivery models and alternatives. An empirical evaluation would assess the role of the services within communities not only by measuring the extent to which they achieve their stated objective but also by measuring the preferences of those who use the services.

Conclusions

In a sense, this chapter discusses yesterday, today, and tomorrow in the field of violence toward black children. Past and present research have greatly contributed to knowledge, answering many questions while raising many more. Future research must include many studies similar to those described. These studies must be sensitive to the needs, experiences, and realities encountered by black families. In the development of knowledge about violence toward black children and violence in black families, it is necessary and important to pursue these issues and to refine the empirical evidence and theoretical perspectives.

Note

1. Many of items listed were generated by discussions at the National Institute of Justice Conference on Family Violence as a Crime Problem, Washington, D.C., October 1984. They are of general interest to all who study family violence.

References

American Humane Association. 1986. *Highlights of Official Child Abuse and Neglect Reporting: Annual Report, 1984.* Denver: American Humane Association.

Billingsley, Andrew. 1969. *Black Families in White America.* Englewood Cliffs, N.J.: Prentice-Hall.

Cazenave, Noel, and Murray A. Straus. 1979. "Race, Class, Network Embeddedness and Family Violence." *Journal of Comparative Family Studies* 10:281–300.

Comer, James. 1985. "Black Violence and Public Policy: Changing Directions." In *American Violence and Public Policy.* Edited by Lynn Curtis. New Haven: Yale University Press.

Gelles, Richard J. 1982. "Child Abuse and Family Violence: Implications for Medical Professionals." In *Child Abuse.* Edited by Eli. H. Newberger. Boston: Little, Brown.

Gil, David. 1970. *Violence against Children: Physical Abuse in the United States.* Cambridge: Harvard University Press.

Giovannoni, J.M., and R.M. Becerra. 1979. *Defining Child Abuse.* New York: Free Press.

Hampton, Robert L. 1987. "Race, Class, and Child Maltreatment." *Journal of Comparative Family Studies* 13:113–126.

Hampton, Robert L., and Eli. H. Newberger. 1985. "Child Abuse Incidence and Reporting by Hospitals: Significance of Severity, Class and Race." *American Journal of Public Health* 75, no. 1:56–60.

Jason, Janine, N. Ambereuh, J. Marks, and C. Tyler. 1982. "Child Abuse in Georgia: A Method to Evaluate Risk Factors and Reporting Bias." *American Journal of Public Health* 72, no. 12:1353–1358.

Johnson, Charles F., and Jacy Showers. 1985. "Injury Variables in Child Abuse." *Child Abuse and Neglect* 9, 2:207–216.

Lauderdale, Michael, Al Valiunas, and Rosalie Anderson. 1980. "Race, Ethnicity, and Ethnic Maltreatment: An Empirical Analysis." *Child Abuse and Neglect* 4:163–169.

Lindholm, Kathryn J., and Richard Willey. 1983. "Child Abuse and Ethnicity: Patterns of Similarities and Differences." *Spanish Speaking Mental Health Research Center.* UCLA Occasional Paper No. 18.

Newberger, E., R. Reed, J. Daniel, J. Hyde, and M. Kotelchuck. 1977. "Pediatric Social Illness: Toward an Etiologic Classification." *Pediatrics* 60:178–185.

Showers, Jacy, and Rosalyn L. Bandman. 1986. "Scarring for Life: Abuse with Electric Cords." *Child Abuse and Neglect* 10:25–31.

Spearly, James L., and Michael Lauderdale. 1983. "Community Characteristics and Ethnicity in the Prediction of Child Maltreatment Rates." *Child Abuse and Neglect* 7:91–105.

Straus, Murray, Richard J. Gelles, and Suzanne Steinmetz. 1980. *Behind Closed Doors.* Garden City, N.Y.: Doubleday.

Turbett, J.P., and R. O'Toole. 1980. "Physician's Recognition of Child Abuse." Paper presented at the annual meeting of the American Sociological Association, New York.

U.S. Department of Health and Human Services. *National Study of the Incidence and Severity of Child Abuse and Neglect:* Study Findings, Publication (OHDS) 81-03026. Washington, D.C.: Government Printing Office.

2
The Significance of Ethnic and Cultural Differences in Child Maltreatment

James Garbarino
Aaron Ebata

Professionals in the United States "discovered" child abuse in the last twenty years (Pfohl 1977) and have gone on to concern themselves with a variety of research, policy, and clinical issues. One of these issues concerns cultural and ethnic differences, and the obvious question is this: Are some cultural and ethnic groups more prone to abuse and neglect their children than are others? We note that while social-class differences have been actively studied (e.g., Pelton 1978), cultural and ethnic differences have received a treatment that we may describe as benign neglect—with some notable exceptions (e.g., Giovannoni and Becerra 1979; Korbin 1977, 1979, 1980, 1981; Rohner 1975; Rohner and Nielsen 1978). Our goal here is to review the evidence and state the research issues more clearly.

To get a good grasp on child maltreatment, we can adopt the intellectual tools of a perspective that is both cross-cultural (Glick 1975; LeVine 1980) and sociobiological (Barash 1977; Gould 1978; van den Berghe 1979). These tools help us to see what is universal and what is particular in human experience, which of our axioms about human reality reflect only local conditions, and which have general application (Korbin 1980; Olmedo 1979). This perspective is a necessary precondition for dealing with cultural and ethnic factors in child maltreatment because any conclusions about *who* abuses and *how much* they abuse depend upon a culturally validated definition of *what* abuse is (Garbarino and Gilliam 1980). What is more, the temptation to embrace an ethnocentric perspective is difficult to resist, particularly when those in positions of social and economic power judge those who are relatively powerless (Ogbu 1981; Tulkin 1972). We need transcultural as well as intracultural standards.

Reprinted with permission from the *Journal of Marriage and the Family* (November 1983): 773–783.

The emerging field of sociobiology serves a useful purpose in this by reminding us that we spent more than 90 percent of our history as a species in technologically simple, hunting-gathering communities and by suggesting that some forms of social organization and personal values are better suited to what biological predispositions we may have (Barash 1977; Rossi 1977; van den Berge 1979). For example, the greater biological investment of females in their infants (Trivers 1972) may make it easier to maintain social arrangements emphasizing maternal child care than paternal child care—easier but not predetermined. Also, children may be at greater risk for abuse in stepparent relationships because of this same principle of investment (Burgess and Garbarino 1982). The value of a sociobiological orientation is that it alerts us to the *possibility* that some social forms are more in tune with our evolutionary history than others, that we make our individual and collective choices with respect to social arragements in counterpoint to our species' traditional answers to these questions, and that the nature of the human being does more than just set limits. It may establish universal needs and set developmental agendas (Garbarino 1982). This can help us identify principles for understanding child maltreatment across cultures and ethnic groups.

Research suggests that modal or normative perceptions of and response to particular temperaments and activity levels of children can vary across cultures (Caudill and Frost 1975; Thomas and Chess 1977). These differences can decrease or increase the risk of maltreatment for particular children. For example, Puerto Ricans may evaluate a very high activity level positively, while Anglos negatively evaluate such a child and may label him or her "hyperactive."

Biological differences among groups may even represent a stimulus for cultural adaptation. As Freedman (1974) suggests, this stimulus produces adapation in the form of socialization practices as well as values and norms. However, the time frame for cultural evolution is much longer than the conventional time frame of modern social change. Therefore, we must be particularly concerned about rapid changes in the social environment of previously stable groups, and we must be concerned with short-term effects—short-term here meaning decades. This is particularly important in the case of specific physiological characteristics that interact with changed social circumstances in an adverse way—such as inability to metabolize alcohol efficiently—and that may precipitate child maltreatment (Wolff 1977).

In our efforts to identify and illuminate these cultural and ethnic differences in child maltreatment, we face methodological challenges. First, these terms represent "packaged variables" (Whiting 1967). That is, they are intricately and often indirectly and ambiguously linked to specific, observable behaviors (Ogbu 1981). Second, they are usually associated with socioeconomic differences. Social class and cultural differences often are confounded when ethnic groups occupy socioeconomically marginal positions in society (Lewis 1965) and when there is inadequate participation and integration of the poor in the major institutions of the society (Tulkin 1972). This applies with special force to child maltreatment, where socioeconomic deprivation is a highly significant factor (Garbarino 1977; Pelton 1978).

When class and ethnicity are confounded, we always run the risk of confusing legitimate ethnic differences in style with the deleterious effects of socioeconomic deprivation (at the lower end of the spectrum) and of elevating the values of the economically privileged to the status of universal standards (at the upper end of the scale). Also, it is incorrect to assume that environments that are economically impoverished are also, inevitably, socially improverished (Garbarino and Crouter 1978). The goal of our analyses should be to detect genuine and legitimate stylistic (and, thus, comparable) differences, as well as adaptations to deleterious social conditions (and, thus, appropriately defined as nonnormative in a larger sense). With this in mind we turn to the evidence concerning cultural and ethnic differences in child maltreatment. We can organize this pursuit in terms of three tasks.

1. Document differences in rates of child maltreatment by group, separately for each form of child maltreatment.

2. Identify changing or changed social conditions that have altered or will alter the environmental basis for specific child-rearing practices. The adaptiveness, appropriateness, and normativeness of a group's practices depend upon circumstances, and changed circumstances are an important stimulus to maltreatment. We need to ask how groups are changing in relation to each other, particularly when immigrant groups are in the process of bridging between old and new cultures.

3. Identify values and group characteristics that increase or decrease risk for both specific types and overall incidence of maltreatment and develop countervailing or alternative norms that build from existing values.

Documenting Differences in Rates of Child Maltreatment

Almost none of the existing compilations of incidence data present ethnic and cultural groups unconfounded by social class. This makes it difficult to draw any but the most tentative conclusions. Furthermore, the typical pattern of aggregating all differences into white, black, and "other" is generally inadequate for the kind of analysis that needs to be done. However, we can make the best of the evidence that we have.

In the first large-scale summary of national reports, Gil (1970) concluded that families reported for abuse were disproportionately drawn from the less educated and the poor and from ethnic minorities, with black children overrepresented as victims of abuse. A more recent compilation of reports shows a simliar picture: whites are underrepresented in reported cases of maltreatment. The study also shows that lower-income families are grossly overrepresented (American Humane Association 1980).

The most recent comprehensive attempt to document the "true" incidence of child maltreatment in the United States is the National Incidence Study conducted for the National Center on Child Abuse and Neglect (Bergdorf 1981). It sought to identify cases known to any professional in representative communities across the country. The results are flawed, though useful for our purposes.

The only "ethnic" comparisons contained in this study are "black" versus "white" (Anglo, Hispanic, and other). Using this gross dichotomy, the Incidence Study reports clear and very significant social class effects that correspond to the general pattern: much higher incidence rates among low-income families than among affluent families. However, the study reports an interaction between income and race. Whereas blacks and whites have equal and low rates of maltreatment among the affluent population, among the low-income population whites have substantially higher rates of child maltreatment than blacks have (Bergdorf 1981). This suggests ethnic differences in the ability to respond to socioeconomic stress in adaptive ways that help protect children. Certainly Stack's (1974) account of black coping tactics supports such a notion. In any case, we come away from the National Incidence Study with qualified evidence in support of the hypothesis that ethnic differences in child maltreatment are very small when all groups have adequate socioeconomic resources and larger when groups experience impoverishment. We need to explore the hypothesis that it is under conditions of socioeconomic deprivation and stress that cultural differences are most significant.

Lauderdale and his colleagues (1980) computed annual rates of occurrence (per 1,000 under 18 years old, adjusted for population size) for validated cases of abuse and neglect in Texas between 1975 and 1977 for Anglos, Mexican-Americans, and blacks. Without controlling for social class, total annual rates for all forms of maltreatment (abuse, neglect, abuse and neglect) were highest for blacks, followed by Mexican-Americans and then Anglos. Analysis by type of maltreatment yielded variations according to ethnic groups, with blacks having the highest rate for all types, Anglos with the lowest neglect rates, and Mexican-Americans with lowest rates for both abuse and for abuse and neglect (but not for neglect).

In looking at frequency of types *within* groups Anglos showed the highest proportion of abuse (33.5 percent of all Anglo cases) compared with blacks (29.4 percent) and Mexican-Americans (25.2 percent). Mexican-Americans and blacks showed a greater proportion of neglect (65.6 percent and 61.2 percent of the cases, respectively) as compared with Anglos (55.4 percent).

While the authors recognize the potential biases of differential labeling in accounting of ethnic differences in reported rates, they suggest cultural factors that may influence differences in rates for particular types of maltreatment. For example, they suggest that the lower abuse rates among Mexican-Americans suggests "less manifest aggression and violence toward children," which may reflect socialization patterns producing a "more passively and internally-oriented style of coping with problems and challenges of life" and a personality type that is "more accepting of life's conditions and perhaps less aggressive in interpersonal relations" (Lauderdale et al. 1980). We must view this explanation with caution, of course, because it is easily construed as merely restating a simplistic stereotype. What is more, it can lead to obscuring differences *within* Spanish-speaking groups (Laosa 1979, 1981).

In analyzing abuse and neglect data for Hawaii during 1976–1977, Dubanoski and Snyder (1980) found that Japanese-Americans (representing 27 percent of the total population) were highly underrepresented in reported cases of maltreatment—accounting for 3.5 percent of abuse and 4.7 percent of neglect, while Samoan Americans (making up 0.8 percent of the population) accounted for 6.5 percent of all abuse and 2.6 percent of all neglect cases. Of course, here too we have a serious confounding of class and ethnicity. The Japanese in Hawaii are a much more affluent and powerful group than are the Samoans. Nonetheless, the role of neglect versus abuse differs for the two groups (and between Hawaiian- and European-American residents as well, according to another study by Dubanoski 1981). These results suggest cultural differences. Among Japanese the ratio of abuse to neglect cases was 1:3, while for Samoans it was 3:1. This leads us to consider the role that values and attitudes play in releasing child maltreatment in the presence of social stress. The few existing studies of values and attitudes concerning types of child maltreatment help us to do this.

Polansky and Williams (1978) developed the Childhood Level of Living Scale, describing specific child-rearing conditions in the home, in order to rate physical and cognitive-emotional care. They designed the instrument to identify conditions that could be regarded as neglectful, and they tested the instrument in a study comparing a sample of Caucasian lower- and middle-class mothers with social workers. The authors found much agreement in ratings of items among lower-class mothers, middle-class mothers, and professionals. In addition, there were great similarities between lower- and middle-class mothers, with the significant differences (43 of 214) all of degree, not of direction of evaluation. These few differences, however, consistently showed that working-class mothers placed greater "evaluative emphasis" on matters of physical care, while middle-class mothers valued cognitive-emotional care more highly. This suggests that one of the most important cultural aspects of the child maltreatment problem is the "cultural" differences associated with social class.

In the most complex work to date on the topic, Giovannoni and Becerra (1979) sought to explore further how the various ethnic and professional groups within a large city define child maltreatment. They presented a series of vignettes depicting specific incidents of child maltreatment, representing a range of behaviors that might be considered maltreatment, and varying the degree of severity, to professionals and lay people in the metropolitan Los Angeles area. Respondents rated each vignette according to the "seriousness of its impact on the welfare of the child."

The sample population comprised 12 percent blacks, 17 percent Hispanics, 65 percent white (Anglo), and 7 percent "other." Whites had higher mean education, income, and occupational status than the other groups, while Hispanics had the largest families and whites the smallest.

The study sought to test the idea that people of lower socioeconomic status and ethnic minorities are "more tolerant of mistreatment and likely to have a higher threshold for considering actions as mistreatment" (Giovannoni and Becerra 1979). However, the results point to just the opposite—blacks and Hispanics were found to give *more serious* ratings to vignettes than Anglos were, in 94 percent of the cases.

Contrary to the authors' expectations, it was found that education and income (the prime indicators of socioeconomic status) were inversely related to ratings of seriousness—the higher were the education and income level of the respondent, the *lower* was the seriousness rating. That ethnic differences were not merely the effect of social class differences was shown in the findings of persistent ethnic differences *within* educational levels. Blacks across all educational levels rated "failure to provide" and "supervision" categories as more serious than did others, while Hispanics rated "drugs/sex" and "physical injury" as more serious than did others. Results of the analysis by income show similar though less consistent trends.

Analysis of differences *within* each ethnic group provides an even clearer picture of ethnic differences in perception patterns of specific kinds of mistreatment, although, like Polansky's data, these results show no real disagreement on direction of evaluation, only on degree. Among the black respondents, there were no differences according to education, income, or gender, suggesting that responses were influenced primarily by ethnicity rather than class membership, a finding consistent with the results of the National Incidence Study. Blacks across all socioeconomic status (SES) levels showed greater concern for failure-to-provide and supervision and "unlike the other ethnic groups, demonstrated greater consensus as a group without regard to social class." This is not the first study to question the utility of traditional social class categories when applied to blacks (Bronfenbrenner 1979).

Among whites the levels of education made significant differences in seriousness ratings, with more highly educated respondents giving less serious ratings to each category of incidents. Income was related to ratings for failure-to-provide and physical injury in the same manner as education.

As a total group all Hispanics rated matters of physical injury, sexual abuse, and drugs/sex as more serious than ratings of others. When separated into English-speaking and Spanish-speaking groups, the Spanish-speaking groups rated the above categories as more serious than did the English-speaking groups. Among Spanish-speaking Hispanics, higher income was related to lower ratings of sexual and physical abuse and drugs/sex. Income was unrelated to the ratings of English-speaking Hispanics. Sex of respondent and, more important, education were important factors in ratings of physical injury, sexual abuse, and drugs/sex. Again, the higher was the education level, the less serious was the rating for each category.

Ironically, Giovannoni and Becerra's study is most useful in establishing that, for the most part, it is *not* attitudes and values about abuse and neglect per se that differentiate ethnic groups in the United States. In general, we can say that all groups share some common definitions of what constitutes maltreatement, albeit with differences in emphasis. The problem is threefold.

First, the link between attitudes and behavior is notoriously weak, as demonstrated by decades of social-psychological research. What is more, people often seem to compensate for their behavioral problems by exaggerating their beliefs (Festinger 1957). Thus, if a behavior is particularly problematic for a group (a tough issue they have trouble resolving), they may increase the intensity of their attitudes about it. This is one explanation offered for some class differences in child-rearing values. Middle-class parents take for granted that their children will achieve some characteristics (for example, following rules in organized groups) and, thus, do not explicitly value them so highly, while for working-class parents those achievements are problematic and thus are valued explicitly and highly (Kohn 1977).

Second, Giovannoni and Becerra's findings highlight the importance of the social conditions of life in producing behavior. Given the relative uniformity of condemnation for maltreatment, we should expect actual behavioral differences to be attributable to the balance of social stress and support; and this is what our own research indicates (Garbarino 1977; Garbarino and Crouter 1978; Garbario and Gilliam 1980).

This leads to a third point—namely, that the critical ethnic differences may be in values, attitudes, and practices that only *indirectly* concern child rearing. For example, it may be in ethnic differences in the use and maintenance of social-support networks for families (for example, neighboring styles and kinship) that we will find the differences of greatest importance (see Korbin 1980; Whittaker, Garbarino, and Associates 1983).

Towards an Ecological Analysis of Ethnicity

Although the studies by Lauderdale and his colleagues (1980) and Dubanoski and Snyder (1980) go beyond what has previously been done in exploring subcultural differences, in both studies they did not succeed in disentangling the effects of socioeconomic status and ethnicity. Neither study takes into account possible differential effects of occupying different social positions in terms of education, power, and income, despite the fact that the populations they studied represent clear differences on these dimensions. The Japanese in Hawaii occupy a socioeconomic role resembling the Anglos in Texas, just as the Samoans in Hawaii are as much a part of an underclass there as the blacks are in Texas. We believe that the most profitable route for assessing the significance of ethnicity requires a complete ecological explication.

In studying parental values, Kohn (1977) claims that social class (primarily conditions of occupational life) is the primary influence on parental values, with other factors adding little. Attempting in part to replicate Kohn's work with a national sample of mothers and fathers, Wright and Wright (1976) report that although indicators of social class do explain a significant proportion of variance (10–14 percent), the addition of ethnicity and geographic location into the analysis accounts for an additional 8 percent to 11 percent of the total amount of variance. These results reinforce our belief in the need for contextually specific analyses; but the question remains, "How does one best characterize these groupings of neighborhoods, communities, or regions?" Straus, Gelles, and Steinmetz (1980) report small but significant differences in the level of domestic violence in the United States as a function of region, as well as the urban-suburban-rural dimension. However, our own research suggests that for most issues, the best targets are neighborhoods within communities or communities themselves (Garbarino and Crouter 1978; Garbarino and Gilliam 1980).

This community orientation is important, of course, in dealing with the general child maltreatment problem, but it is of special importance in considering ethnic differences. We can expect acculturation to proceed most rapidly and thoroughly when communities have diverse and dispersed ethnic groups and to move slowest and be least profound in areas that are ethnically homogeneous and dense (Harwood 1981). Thus, cultural differences may be differentially relevant as a function of the geography of ethnicity—the more concentrated is the group, the more relevant will ethnic influences be for understanding child maltreatment (Weisner 1981). Ethnicity, then, does not have the same meaning or influence on all people or a particular group, nor does it have the same significance for behavior and ideology (Greely 1974; Harwood 1981).

If there is a relatively small degree of "fit" between cultural patterns of the group and the host culture, the amount of stress acting upon that group may be mediated by the composition of the more proximal or local region or community. Rabkin and Struening contend that if "a given ethnic group constitutes a smaller proportion of the total population in a particular area, diagnosed rates of mental illness increase in comparison both to the rates for other ethnic groups in that area and to the rates of the same ethnic group in neighborhoods where its members constitute a significant proportion of majority" (1976, p. 1019). Thus, the extent to which ethnicity is a factor for an individual's behavior and attitudes is mediated by region of residence ("ethnic density") and length of residence with the host culture. We must move in the direction of measuring or inferring amount or degree of ethnic influence to know its significance for specific instances of child maltreatment.

Different groups appear to demonstrate different patterns of specific types of maltreatment, reflecting different social and environmental conditions, or differences in the ways groups perceive, evaluate, and act on these conditions based on a shared sense of beliefs, goals, and values. Few, if any, of these differences are so large, however, as to present non-overlapping ranges. Indeed, Minturn and Lambert (1964) report that in most cases *intra*cultural variability exceeds *inter*cultural variability.

Whether one impoverished group will exhibit more maltreatment than another is likely to depend upon the special *social* resources each possesses—for example, values that place caring for children above all else or social arrangements that deflect stress away from children. This is probably one of the most significant aspects of the entire story of ethnic and cultural differences in child maltreatment. It is the values, practices, and institutions for dealing with material stress that count most heavily in the child-maltreatment equation.

Korbin (1981) identified four general factors that may affect the incidence of child maltreatment, three of which highlight more directly child-relevant values: cultural value of children, beliefs about special categories of children (for example, physically handicapped or illegitimate), and beliefs about age capabilities and developmental states. The fourth factor is the embeddedness of child rearing in kin and community networks—the more, the better.

Rates of particular types of maltreatment seem to be affected by factors that influence the beliefs, goals, and values of a people concerning child rearing. Ethnicity is one indicator of "prior experience" that mediates current functioning. However, ethnicity is an influence that varies in relevance for day-to-day functioning from being almost negligible among some groups to being highly influential in others. All have ethnic heritages, but some are amalgamated into the national culture while others are still largely alien. Thus, acculturation is a key issue. Even here, however, things are not simple. Greeley's research (1974) on European ethnic groups in the United States demonstrates pockets of relatively unacculturated enclaves in some cities.

Olmedo (1979) defines several dimensions of acculturation, based on research that explores the salience of contrasting patterns of behavior and belief in day-to-day life. These dimensions assess the interplay of diversity within a common environment:

1. Differential knowledge and behaviors in culture-specific domains, including language proficiency, preference, and use, as well as traditions, customs, and cultural identification.

2. Culture-specific attitudes and value orientations.

3. Socioeconomic status.

A group's status on all these dimensions counts, but change itself is also important.

The Role of Changing Conditions in the Etiology of Child Maltreatment

Studies of community mental health suggest that rapid change in any direction—either "boom" or "bust"—can set off serious problems (Parker and Saski 1965). The most dramatic examples of how changing conditions can alter the reality basis for child-rearing patterns come from migration and radical technological development (Werner 1979). For example, Nigeria has never had formal adoption or foster care laws because children in need of care were always adopted informally through kin and community networks. With the advent of rapid urbanization, however, the number of neglected and unclaimed urban children has risen dramatically (Ajenifuja 1982). Modernization has been accompanied by similar problems of child maltreatment in other Third World areas as well—for example, Polynesia (Ritchie and Ritchie 1981) and Sri Lanka (deSilva 1981). In most cases the problems are increasing, along with the "baseline" conditions of malnutrition associated with societal improverishment—as in the case of India (Bhattacharyya 1981).

Another example comes from Taiwan. To be an adopted daughter in China and Taiwan meant being "at risk" for being sold into slavery or prostitution, for beatings or death. This "culturally institutionalized abuse" resulted in higher mortality rates for adopted as compared with biological daughters. Government and popular movements were organized in the 1960s to discourage maltreatment of adopted daughters, and in 1976, when the first child welfare law was passed in Taiwan, "the main concern was adoption and the rights of adopted daughters" (Wu 1981). Although no statistics have been kept, surveys of a leading newspaper showed "almost no stories" about mistreated adopted daughters during 1976–1980—stories that were numerous during the 1950s. The massive and widespread improvements in the welfare of children on the Chinese mainland in the last thirty years is also well known (Korbin 1981).

A third example comes from transplanted Samoans. As Samoan families immigrate to Hawaii and the mainland United States, their children are exposed to an educational system that may disassemble traditional Samoan family patterns. One result seems to be an outbreak of physical abuse as traditional discipline (corporal punishment) escalates without really providing social control (Dubanoski 1981).

> They are using the Samoan approach of discipline on kids who aren't really Samoans. I feel concerned for these kids who are born here. . . . They're not really Americans and they're not really Samoans. (Alai-lima 1979, p. 1)

Finally, as Japanese family size has rapidly decreased in the post–World War II era, observers have noted an increase in what might be termed emotional abuse, as parents focus all their highly motivated attention on one or two children (Hoshino 1982). The intense achievement pressures placed on these children appear to be emotionally harmful, and the Japanese use the the term *monster-mother (mamagom)* to refer to mothers who are particularly hard driving in this respect. These kinds of developments give credence to those who worry that emotional maltreatment has been increasing in the United States for similar reasons (Garbarino 1980).

Conclusions

Perhaps the most important aspect of basic research that can shed light on group differences in risk for abuse and neglect is the study of factors creating either special vulnerability or resistance to particular *forms* of child maltreatment. These can include *values* (for example, the American belief in privacy and individualism as a growth medium for social isolation versus the Japanese belief in interdependence), *practices* (for example, the Samoan belief in corporal punishment versus the Japanese belief in emotional punishment), and *biological predispositions* (for example, the higher neonatal activity level of Anglos versus Chinese). We should be alert to the mix of risk *and* countervailing forces within groups. This can lead to a better understanding of how to prevent the expression of a group's special "vulnerability" in child maltreatment.

For example, the rate of neglect was highest among Mexican-Americans in Lauderdale et al.'s (1980) study of maltreatment cases in Texas. This may reflect what other researchers describe as a preference for indirect means of control and disdain for physical aggression (Holtzman 1975). Indeed, Hispanics in Giovannoni and Becerra's (1979) Los Angeles samples rated depictions of physical injury as more serious than other forms of mistreatment and rated them as more serious than did either blacks or Anglos.

Wagatsuma reports that the absolute rate of abuse and neglect among the Japanese is relatively low as compared with rates in the United States. However, maltreatment takes on different forms when it occurs. "Japanese parents, especially mothers, tend to abandon or kill their children more often than they . . . abuse them. Further, the . . . parent-child joint suicide (*oyako shinju*), in which a child is killed by the parent or parents, may very well be a uniquely Japanese phenomenon" (1981, p. 121).

These differences of form contrast with the differences in overall incidence reported on cross-national comparisons. Thus, reports from Sweden (Tietjen 1980) and from Chinese authorities (Korbin 1981) indicate a very low overall incidence of maltreatment because of the favorable balance of social support versus socioeconomic stress. We suspect that overall incidence of maltreatment is primarily a matter of social conditions, while form is heavily influenced by the content of basic values concerning children. However, this can be only a hypothesis at this point.

Cultural differences seem to demonstrate that gross differences in values, practices, and perhaps even biological predispositions can have a significant and even dramatic effect on the risk for different types of child maltreatment. Ethnic differences within societies also appear to be associated with differences in the risk of child maltreatment, although the frequent confounding of social class with ethnicity obscures the picture, as does the possible link between culture and biological predispositions hypothesized by Freedman (1974) and others. We see two major implications for prevention arising from what we know already.

First, we need to identify the special risks and strengths of cultural and ethnic groups. Some groups appear to be more susceptible to maltreatment in general because of their problems on the four dimensions cited above in Korbin's analysis and because of their adverse position in the socioeconomic system. Prevention, therefore, should address these four dimensions where and when they present problems, as well as address the issue of socioeconomic adequacy. In addition, however, prevention programs should look for the special vulnerability of some groups to particular forms of maltreatment. We do not yet have a good accounting of these vulnerabilities, but those responsible for areas that are ethnically diverse should be alert to such differences when they become apparent in information-management systems that monitor case characteristics. Multicultural analysis teams may be helpful in verifying and explaining such patterns of difference when they occur. They should look for different ratios of abuse to neglect, and physical to psychological maltreatment in both categories for different groups. What is more, they should look for different responses to the same stimuli—for example, to poverty on the negative side and to family-centered childbirth on the positive side. This demands more than cultural sensitivity; it calls for "cultural competence" (Green and Tong 1978) and "cultural translation" (Spradley 1979). One example comes from efforts to assess and harness Hawaiian peer orientations to achieve conventional mainstream academic goals (Jordan and Tharp 1979). In these efforts the motivation-behavior paradigm common to Anglos (individual orientation) is translated to the Hawaiian context (peer orientation) with success.

Second, models for prevention need to adapt to cultural and ethnic differences in terms of "how" as well as "what." The routes of influence may differ significantly from group to group—for example, through elders in one group but through peers in another. Several points must be taken into consideration, however. First, patterns of influence identified as being "traditionally" influential may not be in operation or may be modified in the present context in which the group is situated. This highlights the point about community ethnic density made earlier. Traditional resources are more *likely* in an ethnically dense community, but we cannot allow group trends and stereotypes to overcome the needs of specific individuals.

Furthermore, the interpersonal and family dynamics in different cultural groups may not follow patterns that have been identified in control and abusive samples studies to date. Although there is some research among ethnic groups, less is known of father-child, husband-wife, and sibling relationships among these groups. A case in point might be where kinswomen are the preferred birthing companion-helpers and where extended kinship networks are still functional and operating. In such a setting, enlisting fathers as birthing coaches might not be an efficient and effective tactic (Korbin 1981).

In addition, even less is known of "second-order effects" (Bronfenbrenner 1979) in which a dyadic relationship or interaction pattern may be modified in the presence of another person, such as when the presence of the father affects mother-child interaction (Belsky 1981). This is particularly important since the identity and role of such a person may vary from group to group—for example, in one group it may be a grandmother; in another an aunt. These second-order effects may be particularly susceptible to disruption by rapid social change. For example, in traditional Samoan culture, a community is led by a system of chiefs and elders (*matai*) that mediate, oversee, and otherwise govern community life and economic transactions within and between villages. Vestiges of this system remain among many first-generation Samoan immigrants living in Hawaii. However, the role of the chief is often more symbolic and ceremonial, or one consisting of indirect influence only. Similarly, among the Japanese, elders were the traditional influences. However, in present-day Japan, emphasis on loyalty and commitment to an employer may point to the workplace as a starting point for preventive programs. Finally, among families in a rural Hawaiian community, men were found to have deep commitment and attachments to peers, particularly workmates, which seemed to rival or supersede family relationships (Howard and Scott 1981). Prevention programs have different "significant others" to contend with or to utilize in each case. Attending to such matters may permit us to strengthen and support families indirectly—for example, through the tribal milieu among American Indians.

All of these suggestions for intervention flow from the hypotheses we have developed. However, the paucity of reliable evidence is noteworthy. The process of adequately studying the nature and significance of ethnic and cultural differences in child maltreatment has really only begun. The confounding of class and ethnicity cries out for further attention. The notion of special strength and vulnerabilities demands explicitly empirical attention. The search for a research-based and appropriate mix of cross-cultural and sociobiological perspectives is an important task facing students of child maltreatment in particular and family relations in general.

References

Ajenifuja, H. 1982. "Formal Adoption in Nigeria." In *International Symposium on the Child and the City*, pp. 64–69. Edited by N. Kobayashi. Tokyo: National Institute for Research Advancement.

Alailima, F. 1979. "Education Conflicts Here Seen by Samoan Scholar." *Honolulu Advertiser,* May 13.

American Humane Association. 1980. *Annual Statistical Report: National Analysis of Official Child Neglect and Abuse Reporting.* Denver: American Humane Association.

Barash, D.P. 1977. *Sociobiology and Behavior.* New York: Elsevier.

Belsky, J. 1981. "Early Human Experience: A Family Perspective." *Developmental Psychology* 17(January):3–23.

Bergdorf, K. 1981. *Recognition and Reporting of Child Maltreatment: Findings from the National Study of the Incidence and Severity of Child Abuse and Neglect.* Washington, D.C.: National Center on Child Abuse and Neglect.

Bhattacharyya, A.K. 1981. "Nutritional Deprivation and Related Emotional Aspects in Calcutta Children." *Child Abuse and Neglect* 5, no. 4:467–474.

Bronfenbrenner, U. 1979. *The Ecology of Human Development: Experiments by Nature and Design.* Cambridge: Harvard University Press.

Burgess, R., and J. Garbarino. 1982. "Doing What Comes Naturally? An Evolutionary Perspective on Child Abuse." In *Issues and Controversies in the Study of Family Violence,* pp. 88–101. Edited by D. Finkelhor, R. Gelles, R. Hotaling, and M. Straus. Beverly Hills: Sage Publications.

Caudill, W., and L. Frost. 1975. "A Comparison of Maternal Care and Infant Behavior in Japanese-American, American, and Japanese Families." In *Influences on Human Development,* pp. 139–150. 2d ed. Edited by U. Bronfenbrenner and M.A. Mahoney. Hinsdale, Ill.: Dryden Press.

deSilva, W. 1981. "Some Cultural and Economic Factors Leading to Neglect." *Child Abuse and Neglect* 5, no. 4:391–406.

Dubanoski, R. 1981. "Child Maltreatment in European- and Hawaiian-Americans." *Child Abuse and Neglect* 5, no. 4:457–466.

Dubanoski, R.A., and K. Snyder. 1980. "Patterns of Child Abuse and Neglect in Japanese and Samoan-Americans." *Child Abuse and Neglect* 4, no. 4:217–225.

Festinger, L. 1957. *Cognitive Dissonance.* Stanford, Calif.: Stanford University Press.

Freedman, D.G. 1974. *Human Infancy: An Evolutionary Perspective.* Hillsdale, N.J.: Erlbaum.

Garbarino, J. 1977. "The Human Ecology of Child Maltreatment: A Conceptual Model for Research." *Journal of Marriage and the Family* 39(November):721–735.

———. 1980. "Defining Emotional Maltreatment: The Message Is the Meaning." *Journal of Psychiatric Treatment and Evaluation* 2:105–110.

———. 1982. *Children and Families in the Social Environment.* New York: Aldine.

Garbarino, J., and A. Crouter. 1978. "Defining the Community Context of Parent-Child Relations: The Correlates of Child Maltreatment." *Child Development* 49 (September):604–616.

Garbarino, J., and G. Gilliam. 1980. *Understanding Abusive Families.* Lexington, Mass.: Lexington Books.

Gil, D.G. 1970. *Violence against Children: Physical Child Abuse in the United States.* Cambridge: Harvard University Press.

Giovannoni, J.M., and R.M. Becerra. 1979. *Defining Child Abuse.* New York: Free Press.

Glick, J. 1975. "Cognitive Development in Cross-Cultural Perspective." In *Review of Child Development Research,* vol. 4. Edited by F. Horowitz. Chicago: University of Chicago Press.

Gould, S. 1978. Biological Potential versus Biological Determinism." In *The Socio-biology Debate*, pp. 343–351. Edited by A. Caplan. New York: Harper & Row.

Greeley, A. 1974. *Ethnicity in the United States: A Preliminary Reconnaissance.* New York: Wiley.

Green, J., and C. Tong. 1978. *Cultural Awareness in the Human Services.* Seattle: Center for Social Welfare Research, University of Washington.

Harwood, A. 1981. *Ethnicity and Medical Care.* Cambridge: Harvard University Press.

Holtzman, W.H. 1975. *Personality Development in Two Cultures.* Austin: University of Texas Press.

Hoshino, A. 1982. "Environment and Personality Formation of Children." In *International Symposium on the Child in the City*, pp. 54–55. Edited by N. Kobayashi. Tokyo: National Institute for Research Advancement.

Howard, A., and R.A. Scott. 1981. "The Study of Minority Groups in Complex Societies." In *Handbook of Cross-Cultural Human Development*, pp. 113–152. Edited by R.H. Munroe, R.L. Munroe, and B.B. Whiting. New York: Garland.

Jordan, C., and R.G. Tharp. 1979. "Culture and Education." In *Perspectives on Cross-Cultural Psychology.* Edited by A.J. Marsella, R.G. Tharp, and T.J. Ciborowski. New York: Academic Press.

Kohn, M.L. 1977. *Class and Conformity: A Study in Values.* 2d ed. Chicago: University of Chicago Press.

Korbin, J.E. 1977. "Anthropological Contributions to the Study of Child Abuse." *Child Abuse and Neglect* 1, no. 1:7–24.

_____ . 1979. "A Cross-Cultural Perspective on the Role of Community in Child Abuse and Neglect." *Child Abuse and Neglect* 3, no. 1:9–18.

_____ . 1980. "The Cultural Context of Child Abuse and Neglect." *Child Abuse and Neglect* 4, no. 1:3–13.

_____ .ed. 1981. *Child Abuse and Neglect: Cross-Cultural Perspectives.* Berkeley: University of California Press.

Laosa, L.M. 1979. "Social Competence in Childhood: Towards a Developmental, Socioculturally Relativistic Paradigm." In *Primary Prevention of Psychopathology*, vol. 3: *Social Competence in Children*, pp. 253–279. Edited by M.W. Kent and J.E. Rolf. Hanover, N.H.: University Press of New England.

_____ . 1981. "Maternal Behavior: Sociocultural Diversity in Modes of Family Interaction." In *Parent-Child Interactions: Theory, Research, and Prospects.* Edited by R.W. Henderson. New York: Academic Press.

Lauderdale, M., A. Valiunas, and M. Anderson. 1980. "Race, Ethnicity, and Child Maltreatment: An Empirical Analysis." *Child Abuse and Neglect* 4, no. 3:163–169.

LeVine, R.A. 1980. "Anthropology and Child Development." *New Directions for Child Development* 8:71–86.

Lewis, O. 1965. *La Vida: A Puerto Rican Family in the Culture of Poverty.* New York: Random House.

Minturn, I., and Lambert, W. 1964. *Mothers of Six Cultures: Antecedents of Child Rearing.* New York: Wiley.

Ogbu, J.U. 1981. "Origins of Human Competence: A Cultural-Ecological Perspective." *Child Development* 52(June):413–429.

Olmedo, E.I. 1979. "Acculturation: A Psychometric Perspective." *American Psychologist* 34(November):1061–1070.

Parker, S., and Saski, T. 1965. "Society and Sentiments in Two Contrasting Socially Disturbed Areas." In *Approaches to Cross-Cultural Psychiatry*, pp. 329–359. Edited by J. Murphy and A. Leighton. Ithaca, N.Y.: Cornell University Press.

Pelton, L. 1978. "The Myth of Classlessness of Child Abuse Cases." *American Journal of Orthopsychiatry* 48(January):569–579.

Pfohl, S. 1976–1977. "The 'Discovery' of Child Abuse." *Social Problems* 24(3):310–323.

Polansky, N.A., and D.P. Williams. 1978. "Class Orientations to Child Neglect." *Social Work* (January):397–401.

Rabkin, J.G., and E.L. Struening. 1976. "Life Events, Stress, and Illness." *Science* 194 (12):1013–1020.

Ritchie, J., and J. Ritchie. 1981. "Child Rearing and Child Abuse: The Polynesian Context." In *Child Abuse and Neglect: Cross-Cultural Perspectives*, pp. 186–204. Edited by J. Korbin. Berkeley: University of California Press.

Rohner, R. 1975. *They Love Me, They Love Me Not.* New Haven, Conn.: Human Relations Area Files Press.

Rohner, R., and C. Nielsen. 1978. *Parental Acceptance and Rejection: A Review of Research and Theory.* New Haven, Conn.: Human Relations Area Files Press.

Rossi, A. 1977. "A Biosocial Perspective on Parenting." *Daedalus* 106(Winter):1–31.

Spradley, J.P. 1979. *The Ethnographic Interview.* New York: Holt, Rinehart and Winston.

Stack, C. 1974. *All Our Kin: Strategies for Survival in a Black Community.* New York: Harper & Row.

Straus, M., R. Gelles, and S. Steinmetz. 1980. *Behind Closed Doors.* Garden City, N.Y.: Doubleday.

Thomas, A., and S. Chess. 1977. *Temperament and Development.* New York: Bruner-Mazel.

Tietjen, A.M. 1980. "Formal and Informal Support Systems: A Cross-Cultural Perspective." In *Protecting Children from Abuse and Neglect*, pp. 15–36. Edited by J. Garbarino and S.H. Stocking. San Francisco: Jossey-Bass.

Trivers, R.L. 1972. "Parental Investment and Sexual Selection." In *Sexual Selection and the Descent of Man*, pp. 136–179. Edited by B.H. Campbell. Chicago: Aldine.

Tulkin, S.R. 1972. "An Analysis of the Concept of Cultural Deprivation." *Developmental Psychology* 6(January–May):326–339.

van den Berghe, P. 1979. *Human Family Systems: An Evolutionary View.* New York: Elsevier.

Wagatsuma, H. 1981. "Child Abandonment and Infanticide: A Japanese Case." In *Child Abuse and Neglect: Cross-Cultural Perspectives*, pp. 120–138. Edited by J.E. Korbin. Berkeley, University of California Press.

Weisner, T.S. 1981. "Cities, Stress, and Children: A Review of Some Cross-Cultural Questions." In *Handbook of Cross-Cultural Human Development*, pp. 783–808. Edited by R.H. Munroe, R.L. Munroe, and B.B. Whiting. New York: Garland.

Werner, E.E. 1979. *Cross-Cultural Child Development: A View from the Planet Earth.* San Francisco: Brooks-Cole.

Whiting, B.B. 1967. "The Problem of the Packaged Variable," In *The Developing Individual in a Changing World*, Vol. 1: *Historical and Cultural Roots*, pp. 303–309. Edited by K.R. Riegel and J.A. Meacham. Chicago: Aldine.

Whittaker, J., J. Garbarino, and associates. 1983. *Social Support Networks in the Human Services.* New York: Aldine.

Wolff, P.H. 1977. "Biological Variations and Cultural Diversity: An Exploratory Study." In *Culture and Infancy: Variations in the Human Experience,* pp. 357–381. Edited by P.H. Leiderman, S.R. Tulkin, and A. Rosenfeld. New York: Academic Press.

Wright, J.D., and S.R. Wright. 1976. "Social Class and Parental Values for Children: A Partial Replications and Extension of Kohn's Thesis." *American Sociological Review* 41(August):527–537.

Wu, D.Y.H. 1981. "Child Abuse in Taiwan." In *Child Abuse and Neglect: Cross-Cultural Perspectives,* pp. 139–165. Edited by J. Korbin. Berkeley: University of California Press.

3
Child Rearing in Black Families: Child-Abusing Discipline?

Ruby F. Lassiter

W hat do we know about the extent to which black children are victims of child abuse? Official statistics and agency reports on child abuse frequently show that black children (and children of other racial minorities) are overrepresented in case reports (Hampton, Daniel, and Newberger 1983). A recent article in a leading magazine (*Ebony* 1985), however, suggests that the statistics may be distorted due to income, education, and cultural factors that make racial minorities more vulnerable to be singled out and labeled as deviants by those in the reporting process. This position is supported by many empirical studies (Gil 1971; Newberger et al. 1977; Turbett and O'Toole 1980; Gelles 1985; Hampton and Newberger 1985). But even if the overall statistics are distorted, there is clear evidence that child abuse among blacks is an issue for concern (Lindholm and Willey 1983; Showers and Bandman 1986). For example, in 1984 the Division of Child Protection at the Children's Hospital National Medical Center, Washington, D.C., saw 1,400 cases of child abuse. Eight cases involved children's death; 96 percent of the victims were black (*Ebony* 1985).

Black children suffer disproportionately from virtually every form of stress affecting full and healthy development. Too many black children live in conditions of poverty that deprive them of necessary medical care, adequate housing, food, and clothing. Yet none of these stressors is more threatening to the healthy development of black children and to the stability of their families than intrafamilial child abuse.

What causes a family, the unit designated to protect children, to abuse its children? More important, what can we do to prevent abuse? The first crucial step is awareness of the problem. Unfortunately, it is often difficult for members of a community or group to acknowledge or recognize the problem. Since child abuse occurs among all racial and economic groups, this reluctance among blacks is probably rooted to some extent in family values and abiding reverence for children. In addition, there are different definitions of child abuse. In some instances, parental behavior that is defined as good discipline by some observers can be defined as child-abusing discipline by others.

This chapter focuses on child-abusing discipline in black families, conceptualized here as a form of child abuse that arises out of the parenting act of child discipline. In this respect, it is not the expression of senseless violence. Rather, an indicator of inadequate parenting, which may occur even in an otherwise warm, loving, and secure family.

How does one reconcile a warm, loving, secure family with child abuse? How and why do we make a distinction between child-abusing discipline and the general concept of child abuse? These are difficult questions but important because more than 50 percent of all reported cases of child abuse in black families (as well as among other groups) may be related to the family's child-disciplining practices.

Child Discipline:
The Concept and the Controversy

For most parents the concept of child discipline carries a positive connotation, but at the same time it can be troubling. One reason for this ambiguity is the multidimensional aspect of discipline.

Discipline is generally accepted as desirable. In addition, disciplining is a process through which discipline is acquired. In this sense, child disciplining is conceptualized as a set of parenting actions or responses set into motion to meet the child's need (Harrison 1981). The disciplining actions can correct behavior or provide teaching and training in ways the parent believes will produce a disciplined child. In this sense, *disciplined* translates to statements like "the child is well behaved" or is a "good child." The process of discipline in this context is positive.

Family values provide a foundation upon which the child comes to view social roles, social responsibilities, and social relations. A child is exposed to family values as part of the socialization process. Teaching right from wrong, for example, is basically a process of instilling values that a family, community, or culture deems acceptable. Child discipline is an important element in this process. We can see an example in this poignant glimpse from the life of Bryant Gumbel, the black co-host of the NBC Today Show:

> Bryant Gumbel's father died just a few months before Bryant entered broadcasting. But he has never forgotten the example his father set.
> "He [my father] was turned down at various schools in the South because he was Black," relates Gumbel. "So he simply went off and got accepted to Georgetown University Law Center. He had two kids at the time, but he didn't let that hold him back. He worked two jobs to support us, went to school full time, and graduated." The elder Gumbel went on

to become a judge and to instill in his children his personal rule: "Whatever you do, be the best at it."

Today, Bryant Gumbel's goals are not set by critics, not by the ratings, and not by salary or public acclaim. "It's his father he wants to please," says the Today Show writer Paul Brubaker. "So Bryant works for more than perfection. It's almost perfection squared. He's proving himself to someone who can never be satisfied—because his father's no longer here." (Kalter 1986, p. 32)

This insight into Gumbel's drive for success demonstrates that the transmission of guiding values is clearly one of the most solid and long-lasting aspects of child disciplining.

Although some form of child disciplining is usually viewed as necessary in responsible parenting, how to discipline the child is one of the most controversial issues in child rearing. There continues to be a lively debate among family experts concerning the appropriateness of physical punishment. Some experts believe that spanking is never appropriate. Others feel that spanking is an appropriate parental response under certain conditions.

In addition to the controversy among experts, other factors must be considered in assessing what is and is not appropriate disciplining. Important variables include the child's age, mental capacity, and the severity and frequency of the child's discipline-precipitating behavior. Culture is another important factor; each group has its own way of training its young to become adults who will fit into society. For this reason, various cultures and subcultures have slightly different standards for appropriate disciplinary practices. Barnes (1977) provides the following example of how child discipline is viewed in another culture.

The sentiment of motherhood is so highly developed among the so-called savage and the semi-civilized peoples that they cannot chastise or bear to see a child punished. The Eskimos, for example, do not feel that white people deserve to have children since they are so heartless as to strike them, not to mention the parent who often gets angry or yells while administering the cursing, slapping or hitting of a child.

Actually, children are rarely punished in Eskimo culture and almost the only type of punishment known (and one common to all Eskimos) consists of plunging a crying infant into cold water.

This parental behavior is socially acceptable among the Eskimo; it would be considered child abuse in many other cultures.

Child Abuse versus Child-Abusing Discipline

In many ways, child-abusing discipline cannot be distinguished from general child abuse, but a significant distinction can be seen in working definitions of the terms.

Defining general child abuse is not easy. Medical professionals have traditionally defined it as a clinical condition in children who have been deliberately injured by physical assault (Kempe et al. 1962). Armed with this definition, they have typically defined and diagnosed child abuse conditions where clear evidence of injury exists indicating that the injury was the result of an intentional act of commission by the child's caretaker(s) (Newberger, Newberger, and Hampton 1983).

Although the definition speaks to child abuse as acts of commission, recent definitions include parental acts of omission (Newberger, Newberger, and Hampton 1983). The 1974 Federal Child Abuse Prevention and Treatment Act (Public Law 93-247) expanded the definition to include "physical or mental injury, sexual abuse, negligent treatment, or maltreatment of a child under the age of eighteen by a person who is responsible for the child's welfare under circumstances which indicate that the child's health or welfare is harmed or threatened thereby" (U.S. Congress, 1974).

Surveys of professionals reveal patterns of agreement and disagreement over what actions constitute child abuse. The complexity of the problem makes an attempt at achieving a single definition somewhat like the story of six blind men describing an elephant, in which each man described the whole elephant according to the small area he had touched. The medical profession emphasizes physical trauma to the child; the legal profession is concerned with establishing guilt for the perpetrator; the sociologist discusses general child abuse as a symptom of the disintegrating family and a disintegrating society; and the social worker observes that child abuse involves a hurt child.

Taken separately, each view provides a restricted perception of the problem. In combination, however, these views provide a basis for understanding based on the perspectives of several professions that come in contact with either victims or perpetrators. For purposes of this chapter, general child abuse will be defined as the intentional maltreatment of a child resulting from self-serving, brutal acts committed by a parent (or other caretaker) expressing violence toward the child victim. By contrast, child-abusing discipline is defined as any form of child discipline that results in or risks maltreatment of a child, whatever the considerations (such as culture, age of child, or precipitating circumstances).

Because both general child abuse and child-abusing discipline involve the maltreatment of a child, the distinction may seem merely academic. With the exception of sexual abuse, both may produce similar injuries to the child, and both may have the same consequences to the child and to the family, such as threats to the child's immediate comfort and future physical and emotional development, or even to his or her life. Abusing parents can lose their rights of parenthood when the child is removed from the home temporarily or permanently.

It is clear that we are interested in the parent's motivation for committing an act. In general, child abuse, because of the abusing parent's perverse fascination with terror and violence, is self-serving and motivated by violence for its own sake. On the other hand, an act of discipline may reflect violence, but the act is not meant to express violence; it is meant to express parental love and caring. It is a tragic irony when acts of parental caring have similar consequences to acts generally viewed as abusive.

Description of Child-Abusing Discipline

Even if it is not clear how parents should discipline children, it is obvious that discipline should not endanger the child. When does discipline become child endangering? This example is taken from a daily paper:

> A Jacksonville man, whose conviction of second-degree murder in the beating of his girlfriend's three-year-old daughter was reversed, pleaded guilty Monday to a less charge of manslaughter. . . . In 1976 Nazworth was found guilty of second-degree murder in the death of Sandra Kay Walker and sentenced to life in prison. The girl was the daughter of Frances Kay Jenkins, a go-go dancer with whom Nazworth lived. Nazworth was arrested June 16, 1976, at Memorial Hospital after he carried the dead child there. An autopsy showed that the girl died of a brain hemorrhage and a ruptured stomach.
>
> Nazworth's half-brother, John Stinson O'Neal, testified at a bond hearing that Nazworth hit the child a few times with his belt as punishment and made her stand in the corner. The child's mother was at work at the time. (Kerr 1985, p. 4)

This example characterizes the most extreme example of child-abusing discipline; fortunately, it represents the exception, which is probably why it was detected. No one knows how many black children suffer less extreme but nonetheless distressing forms of child-abusing discipline.

The often unrecognized risks of shaking a child were described in the following news item:

> A 7-month old girl, dazed and vomiting, was brought to the hospital where she suffered an epileptic seizure. Her blood pressure was high, there was bleeding at the back of her eyes; an x-ray scan showed a large blood clot on the right side of her brain. Emergency room doctors suspected abuse. Yet the child's body bore no bumps or bruises. When the diagnosis was finally provided—it was whip-lash shake syndrome, or WSS, the often serious or fatal result of severely shaking an infant or young child.
>
> Despite surgery and intensive care, the child suffered permanent damage; she is blind, mute, and has severe paralysis of both arms, legs,

and has convulsions. . . . Unfortunately many doctors don't recognize WSS. . . . The suspicion is that WSS is a source of other serious injuries from shaking such as brain damage, mental retardation, learning disabilities and vision problems. (*Wilson Daily Times* 1980)

Perceptions of Discipline in Black Families

Virtually all black families understand that discipline is one of the most significant variables affecting their lives. They know that the best-disciplined family members escape the crippling problems of teenaged pregnancy, dropping out of school, drug and alcohol addiction, crime, unemployment, and welfare dependency. Frazier (1948) recognized the significance of discipline in the early 1940s when he said about the destructive socioeconomic problems in black families: "If some black families were able to escape disorganization [in society], it was because they were able to instill a strong sense of discipline in their members."

In the general sense that discipline is an effective technique in socializing the child, Billingsley (1968) addressed the subject by pointing out that socialization of children remains the most exclusive and significant domain of black families. It is within the intimate circle of family that the child develops personality, intelligence, aspirations, and, indeed, moral character.

The strong belief in the effectiveness and clear rewards of discipline, combined with the equally strong belief that a lack of discipline and parental authority can destroy a child, explains readily why blacks equate acts of discipline with acts of parental love and a strong family life. By contrast, a lack of discipline in the home is equated with a weak family life and uncaring parents. It is clear, then, that because acts of discipline are perceived as expressions of parental love and caring, discipline itself is not the problem. The problem is the family's reliance on and lack of awareness of high-risk, child-abusing methods used to achieve the perceived rewards and blessings of well-disciplined children.

Causes of Child-Abusing Disciplinary Practice

Why do black parents rely on high-risk child-abusing discipline? Why are they unaware of the risk? How does one reconcile black family perceptions of child discipline as expressions of parental love and caring with evidence of inadequate parenting? The answers to these questions are complex and disturbing. As in cases of general child abuse, child-abusing discipline can occur in any family, but specific socioeconomic and historical factors make black families more vulnerable. The stress often associated with general child abuse is just one of many factors.

Stress. Evidence shows that being black in a hostile society increases vulnerability to stress (Peters and Massey 1983; Hampton, Daniel, and Newberger 1983). A large number of poor black families suffer the cumulative effects of poverty, inadequate housing, unemployment, and low self-esteem. The following news item illustrates how unemployment, alcohol, and drugs were cited as factors in one case of child-abusing discipline:

> "No way," Dr. Robert Segal of the Medical Examiner's office responded when asked if the injuries [multiple bruises and a lacerated liver] which led to the death of a three year old girl could have been caused by reasons given by the stepfather. In a statement given to police following his arrest, Clarence Williams, 27, . . . of North Philadelphia, said his stepdaughter, Andrea Nicholson, slipped in the bathtub and hit her face on a faucet and again later when she fell out of bed.
>
> . . . Williams admitted spanking the youngster three times because she refused to brush her teeth.
>
> Attorney Ronald White said his client Williams had worked off and on for the past eight years because problems with drugs and alcohol make it difficult for him to hold a job. (Young 1980)

Another stress factor specific to nonpoor black families concerns the frustrations and harassments they encounter in a pervasively racist society. Consider the black working mother who is harassed by a racist employer. There is a high risk that when her child needs to be disciplined, she may displace her aggression onto the child, creating the potential for excessive and endangering discipline. The following case illustrates this point:

> A D.C. policewoman has been convicted of cruelty to children and assault with a dangerous weapon for allegedly holding the arm of her 6 year old son over the flame on the kitchen stove of their apartment after the youth ate a piece of cake without permission. . . .
>
> Paige contended that she merely wanted to "frighten" her son and was "trying to teach her child right from wrong," according to her attorney, when the boy pulled away from her and burned his arm on the stove. . . . A Superior Court grand jury found that Paige "did torture, cruelly beat, abuse, and otherwise willfully maltreat" her son and charged that she used the flame as a weapon. Paige's attorney had asked that the charges be dropped, saying that Paige had a right to choose the means of disciplining her child. . . . Her attorney maintained that there was no evidence that she "acted willfully" or "with evil intent or with bad purpose to maltreat the child." Paige's conduct he said "may appear to be poor judgment but is not criminal." (Bruske 1985, p. 5)

Although it is true that the policewoman's acts of discipline demonstrated poor judgment, one cannot overlook the stresses of functioning in a hostile society, which may have been a contributing factors (Peters and Massey 1983). In addition, the excessiveness of the punishment suggests another factor that is both specific and unique to black families. I have identified this factor as "the legacy."

The Legacy. *The legacy* refers to pervasive patterns of harsh, child-endangering discipline that developed during the black family's experiences in a hostile society. It affects the lives of many black families, even when both poor and nonpoor families manage to escape or to cope successfully with the stresses of poverty and racism. What Billingsley (1968) described as the double challenge of black parenting provides an oversimplified explanation of the legacy: the black family must teach its young members to be human, and it must teach the meaning of being black in a white racist society (p. 28). Billingsley's point and the legacy can be understood best in the light of what we know about child rearing as a generational phenomenon.

The generational nature of child rearing explains why parents tend to raise their children as they were raised themselves. The legacy of harsh discipline in black families is somewhat like the intergenerational transmission of child abuse. In general, child-abusing parents were mistreated as children and never experienced the positive parenting that would prepare them to love and nurture their children. In turn, these deprived and abused individuals perpetuate the cycle of violence with their children. The legacy of child-abusing discipline, however, does not mean that black parents do not love and nurture their children. Black families have demonstrated remarkable strengths in meeting their children's needs.

The important aspects of the legacy cannot be understood fully without a perspective on the slavery period, which produced it, and the black family's rural southern experiences, which perpetuated it. These long-past experiences can explain the generational nature of child-endangering discipline in black families.

The Slave Experience. During slavery the prevailing mentality demanded the total subjugation and dehumanization of the black slave. There were few limits to the terrorism and brutality imposed by whites to remind blacks that their total responsibility was to serve whites, who considered themselves superior.

Many slaveholders had no conception of marriage and family bonds of love and protection among slaves and viewed the black male-female relationship simply as a means of producing economically profitable children. The responsibility of the family was to perpetuate the slave system by training the children to be "good" (meaning compliant) slaves. The model for this type of discipline, which was necessary to maintain this state of docility and obedience, was furnished by the white slave owner: swift, harsh, and violent punishment, whatever the infraction. The punishment included severe beatings, loss of limbs, or even violent death. Blacks suffered in relative silence, for there was no higher authority to which they could appeal.

These were the conditions under which harsh discipline developed as a survival strategy in the black family. In order to teach children how to avoid violent punishment at the hands of the white slaveholder, the family used a less severe but still harsh form of discipline. This period also produced what might be seen as unrealistic expectations on the part of parents for their children. When a slave was escaping, the very young child could not be permitted to cry or to walk slowly when tired; because the life of the child and the lives of others were at stake, the child had to be silent and walk fast.

Although there were free blacks, they were few in number and inconsequential in shaping more positive child-rearing practices in black families. In fact, although the life-style of free blacks differed from that of slaves in many respects, child rearing in these families was also controlled to some extent by white racist thinking. The perpetuation of slavery was based upon indisputable white control of blacks, including free blacks. Therefore whites could ignore laws protecting free blacks and carry on a campaign of terror and vilification against them (Franklin 1947).

Black Experiences in the Rural South, 1865–1940. Although black families are now about 90 percent urbanized, life in the rural South represents the bridge between slavery and the contemporary urban experience.

The continuing impact of racism on black family life has perpetuated the legacy. White control of blacks, formerly maintained through legal slavery, was maintained through legal discrimination until the mid-twentieth century. Whites controlled every institution necessary for black family functioning, and they continued to terrorize defenseless and dependent black families.

These factors did not promote a safe and secure family life for blacks that would permit or encourage positive parenting. As long as survival depended upon docility, taught best through swift, harsh discipline, the legacy was perpetuated. Thus black families used harsh discipline, in both deeds and words, to teach children the dangers of being black in a racist society and to show that the best defense against the danger was to be well disciplined in ways that did not challenge white authority. Parents impressed upon the child the importance of not being uppity. The child was constantly cut down, ignored, or answered with ridicule and criticism rather than encouragement, understanding, and praise. Often parents' negative words were reinforced with harsh punishment.

The "whupping" is a prominent example (a whupping is much more severe than a whipping). Even the young child recognized and responded to threats of a whupping. Halpern (1973) relates an example of a seven-month-old black infant who screamed in fear, making it difficult for a white doctor to draw a blood sample. When the mother threatened the child with a whupping, the screaming stopped immediately, and the doctor had no more trouble. The concept of fear and punishment had already become a powerful force in the child's life at his early age.

One must wonder why the mother used the threat of punishment to control the child. Would she not have achieved the same effect by calming and reassuring the child and holding him close? Two explanations are possible: that the love and security-oriented response did not occur to the mother or that she felt that the situation demanded the threat and, if necessary, the use of harsh punishment. The mother's reliance on the latter suggests another aspect of the legacy. Much of the repressive, punitive behavior black parents employ in dealing with their children is not a result of any conscious thought or careful consideration on their part. The mother did not say to herself, "My child's survival depends on harsh discipline." The legacy, however, had led the black family to believe that a compliant attitude toward whites is necessary for survival and that it is the parents' duty to teach the child to accept the role.

Many contemporary black families are not cognizant of the legacy or the history that produced it, but they accept and follow the harsh, child-endangering disciplinary practices transmitted to them by their parents. Their lack of educational opportunities has limited exposure to alternative parenting models. Even if a higher proportion of black families had learned about alternative disciplinary theories, some theories would have been difficult to implement within the social and economic context in which many black families exist.

Despite harsh discipline, black children respond with feelings of love and respect for a number of reasons. First, the warmth and love they enjoy in the early months of life foster reciprocal positive feelings for the surrounding family. Second the extended family system, so important to black children, offers the comfort and security of belonging to a large and loving family. And, third, when black children compare their disciplinary experiences with those of their peers, they find similar patterns; harsh physical punishment is accepted within their reference group.

Recommendations

Unless immediate and firm steps are taken to interrupt the patterns of harsh discipline in black families, far too many black children will continue to be at risk. The existing child protective services come into play only after someone recognizes that a child has been abused, but the very nature of the problem—the legacy, the often unrecognized act, the immeasurable consequences to the child and the family—declares that prevention is the most effective way to protect endangered children.

Intervention in the Black Community

The black community represents the primary levels of intervention for interrupting the legacy of child-abusing discipline. The initial crucial—but difficult—task for the community is to recognize the problem and accept the primary responsibility for formulating solutions. Then several community self-help strategies will become apparent.

The legacy of harsh discipline in black families indicates the pressing need for education in parenting. The content should be structured to provide parents with a general understanding in such areas as realistic expectations for a child based on his or her age and developmental level; alternative methods of child discipline to replace the overreliance on high-risk methods; and children's psychological and emotional need for consistency. This education could be offered through literature, workshops, adult education classes, and training programs, which might be sponsored by such traditional self-help community organizations as churches, fraternities and sororities, and civic groups.

The 1984 National Black Family Summit, which included the heads of the National Association for the Advancement of Colored People, the National Urban League, and other national black organizations, is a heroic example of a black community self-help program at the national level (*Crisis* 1984). The major concern of the summit was to develop and mobilize strategies and resources to support black families. The recommendations of the summit's task force on patterns of child rearing and socialization in black families could be adopted easily for local community-based parent-education programs.

To address the problem of stress as related to child-abusing discipline, community-based workshops and programs on stress reduction are needed.

As a final recommendation, the risk factors related to the alarming increase in black teen parents indicates that perhaps the black community should support parenting-education classes in high schools and even at the junior high levels.

Implications for Family Service Worker

What can family service workers do to prevent child-abusing discipline in black families? Surely their primary concern is to protect the child in whatever way may be necessary. At times they may have to remove the child from the family, but preventing the problem by working with the parents is certainly the effective alternative to removal.

Because of the subtle but important distinctions between general child abuse and child-abusing discipline in black families, workers must understand the distinctions and be trained to offer responsive, culture-sensitive services. They must be clear about their purpose. Is it to care for and help the child or to punish the parent? Because the parents' responsiveness to services will depend on their perceptions of a worker's genuine concern, as well as the worker's demonstrated ability to help them, the guiding values must be acceptance and a nonjudgmental attitude. These values are even more difficult to attain when the abusing family is black and the worker is white; mutual distrust may arise if the white worker is in a black home for the first time or if the black family has had only negative experiences with hostile white workers.

Because recognizing the potential for child-abusing discipline is a critical factor in prevention, the worker needs to mobilize skills in observation, active listening, and problem assessment. The following clues will alert the skilled worker:

1. Does the parent insist on complete docility and obedience in the child?
2. Does the parent demonstrate fear or excessive sternness (in voice or behavior) toward the child who expresses curiosity about the worker, perhaps by touching the worker's hand or purse?
3. Can you observe child discipline (punishment) that is clearly disproportionate to the child's offending behavior?
4. Does the parent demonstrate unrealistic expectations for the child, such as expecting a young child to sit still for long periods of time while the parent and the worker are talking?
5. Can you observe inconsistencies in discipline or in other areas—for example, is one room very clean while the rest of the house is filthy?
6. Does the parent complain about the child in such terms as "she is mean," "he has the devil in him"? Are there threats to the child's safety, such as "I'm going to beat the devil out of him?"
7. Does the parent explain harsh disciplinary practices by saying, "This is the way I was raised"?
8. Does the child express excessive fear of punishment?
9. Does the parent display verbal abuse, such as referring to the child as a "bastard," "whore," or "no good"?
10. Does the angry parent keep a distance between herself and the child, as if she is afraid to trust having the child near her?

A worker who fails to pick up on these clues, especially verbal threats to the child, may tend to reinforce the parent's misconception that his or her actions are appropriate. It is important for the caring worker to talk openly about the parent's inappropriate attitudes and behaviors not in terms of general child abuse but in terms of their potential for child-abusing discipline. Finally, the worker should reassure the parents that although anger is an appropriate emotion, it must be directed at the child's offending behavior and not the child.

Such reassurance requires that the worker be skilled in logical discussion. The difficulty is that abusing parents may not be amenable to "talking therapy." In this situation, an important goal for the worker is to increase the parent's verbal communication skills. Until the parent achieves these skills, the worker's nonverbal skills are very important. The worker will also find activity-related techniques helpful. Talking with the nonverbal client is made easier, for example, when the worker and the parent are participating together in such activities as arts and crafts, shelling peas, hanging clothes, folding diapers, or watching a child at play.

Role playing is another helpful technique for providing the nonverbal parent with a chance to "act pit" whatever he or she is trying to communicate to the worker (Welles 1981).

Once the worker is sure about his or her helping purpose, has a clear understanding of the problem and what needs to be done, and has the proper skills, he or she will be more effective, efficient, and responsive in dealing with the problem. The goals are clear: the worker supports and encourages parental growth in replacing child-endangering disciplinary patterns with appropriate parenting skills.

References

American Humane Association. 1986. *Highlights of Official Child Abuse and Neglect Reporting Annual Report 1984*. Denver: American Humane Association.

Barnes, Willie. 1977. "Child-Rearing Patterns in the Black Family and the Endangering of Violent Behavioral Tendencies." Paper presented at the Third Annual National Conference on Black Families, Louisville, Ky.

Billingsley, Andrew. 1968. *Black Families in White America*. Englewood Cliffs, N.J.: Prentice-Hall.

Bruske, Ed. 1985. "D.C. Policewoman Convicted of Cruelty to 6 Year Old Son." *Washington Post*, March 15.

Comer, James. 1985. "Black Violence and Public Policy." In *American Violence and Social Policy*. Edited by Lynn Curtis. New Haven: Yale University Press.

Crisis. 1984. "The Black Family Summit: Facing the Challenge." *Crisis* 91(6):28–31.

Daniel, Jessica H., Robert L. Hampton, and Eli H. Newberger. 1983. "Child Abuse and Accidents in Black Families: A Case Controlled Comparison." *American Journal of Orthopsychiatry* 53:645–653.

Ebony. 1985. "What to do about Child Abuse." Ebony 40(7):158–164.

Franklin, John Hope. 1947. *From Slavery to Freedom.* New York: Alfred A. Knopf.

Frazier, E. Franklin. 1948. *The Negro Family in the United States.* Chicago: University of Chicago Press.

Gelles, Richard J. 1985. "Family Violence." *Annual Review of Sociology* 11:347–367.

Gil, David. 1971. "A Socio-Cultural Perspective on Physical Child Abuse." *Child Welfare* 50:392–402.

Halpern, Florence. 1973. *Survival: Black/White.* Fairview Park, N.Y.: Pergamon Press.

Hampton, Robert L. 1986. "Family Violence and Homicide in the Black Community: Are They Linked?" In Department of Health and Human Services, *Report of the Secretary's Task Force on Black and Minority Health,* vol. 5: *Homicide, Suicide and Unintentional Injuries,* pp. 69– Washington, D.C.: Government Printing Office.

Hampton, Robert L., Jessica H. Daniel, and Eli H. Newberger. 1983. "Pediatric Social Illnesses and Black Families." *Western Journal of Black Studies* 7:190–197.

Hampton, Robert L., and Eli H. Newberger. 1985. "Child Abuse Incidence and Reporting by Hospitals: Significance of Severity, Class, and Race." *American Journal of Public Health* 75:56–60.

Harrison, Debra Sears. 1981. "The Meaning and Methods of Disciplining in a Sample of Black Parents." In *Proceedings of Conference on Empirical Research in Black Psychology,* pp. 111–124. Edited by Algea O. Harrison. New York: Ford Foundation.

Hawkins, Darnell. 1986. "Longitudinal-Situational Approaches to Understanding Black-on-Black Homicide. In Department of Health and Human Services, *Report of the Secretary's Task Force on Black and Minority Health,* vol. 5: *Homicide, Suicide, and Unintentional Injuries,* pp. 97–114. Washington, D.C.: Government Printing Office.

Kalter, Joanmarie. 1986. "Personal Glimpses." *Readers Digest* (June), p. 32.

Kempe, C.H., F.N. Silverman, B.F. Steele, W. Dragmueller, and H.K. Silver. 1962. "The Battered Child Syndrome." *Journal of the American Medical Association* 181:17–24.

Kerr, Jessie-Lynn. 1985. "Charge Cut in Death Case." *Florida Times-Union* (Jacksonville), March 14.

Lindholm, Kathryn J., and Richard Willey. 1983. "Child Abuse and Ethnicity: Patterns of Similarities and Differences." Spanish Speaking Mental Health Research Center, UCLA Occasional Paper Number 19.

Newberger, Eli, Robert Reed, Jessica Daniel, James Hyde, and Milton Kotelchuck. 1977. "Pediatric Social Illness: Toward an Etiologic Classification." *Pediatrics* 60:178–185.

Newberger, Eli H., Carolyn M. Newberger, and Robert L. Hampton. 1983. "Child Abuse: The Current Theory Base and Future Research Needs." *Journal of the American Academy of Child Psychiatry* 22, no. 3:262–268.

Peters, Marie, and Grace Massey. 1983. "Mundane Extreme Environment Stress in Family Theories: The Case of Black Families in White America." *Marriage and Family Review* 1, 2:197–213.

Showers, Jacy, and Rosalyn Bandman. 1986. "Scarring for Life: Abuse with Electric Cords." *Child Abuse and Neglect* 10:25–31.

Straus, Murray, Richard J. Gelles, and Suzanne Steinmetz. 1980. *Behind Closed Doors*. Garden City, N.Y.: Doubleday.

Steele, Brandt. 1975. "Working with Abusive Parents: A Psychiatrist's Point of View." *Children Today* 4:3–5.

Turbett, J.P., and Richard O'Toole. 1980. "Physicians' Recognition of Child Abuse." Paper presented at the Annual Meeting of the American Sociological Association, New York.

U.S. Congress. 1974. Child Abuse Prevention and Treatment Act of 1974. Public Law 93–247, January 31.

Welles, Susan J. 1981. "A Model of Therapy with Abusive and Neglectful Families." *Social Work* 27, no. 2:113–119.

Wilson (North Carolina) *Daily Times*. 1980. "Shaking an Infant or Young Child Can Do Permanent Damage." April 5.

Young, Patricia. 1980. "Child 3, Dies after Spanking over Not Brushing Teeth." *San Jose* (Calif.) *Mercury*. December 30.

4

Child Abuse and Accidents in Black Families: A Controlled Comparative Study

Jessica H. Daniel
Robert L. Hampton
Eli H. Newberger

C hild abuse and neglect, accidents, poisonings, and failure to thrive are prominent among the "social illnesses" of pediatrics. They derive from many causes in the child, the family, and the environment. Their clinical classification, however, suggests overly simplified models of etiology (Newberger et al. 1977). For a clinician, for example, a diagnosis of "child abuse" requires the suspicion and verification of parental responsibility for the injuries of the victim. We have previously noted the susceptibility of poor and socially marginal families to receiving this diagnosis (Newberger and Daniel 1976) and to the risks of a preventive approach that emphasizes screening (Daniel et al. 1978). The public clinical settings in which most of these diagnoses are made and the highly value-laden nature of the clinical judgments involved in the formation that a given child is "abused" appear to account for the special tendency of these families to be *reported* as families who abuse their children. This reporting exposes children to the public child welfare system, which, as the Carnegie Council on Children underlined (Keniston 1977), may have only the crudest implements of protective service available (for example, placing the child in a foster home).

Accidents, by contrast, are suggested, in the conceptual model implicit in the name, to occur at random. They are numerically prevalent and account for the lion's share of childhood morbidity and mortality in the United States. Because the name implies chance etiology, however, the causes of the traumatic events, in child, family, and environment, are most often ignored in practice and in the formulation of social policy. Practitioners who care for the children of more affluent families, where there is a

Reprinted with permission from the *American Journal of Orthopsychiatry* 5, no. 4. Copyright 1985 by the American Orthopsychiatric Association, Inc.

small social distance between clinician and family, seem less likely to accuse the parents by suggesting in their clinical diagnoses that the injuries they treat derive from some parental responsibility or fault. They are paid, for the most part, on a fee-for-service basis; an economic incentive favors the choice of the least offensive diagnosis for how the child received an injury. The ethics of practice in regard to the sharing of confidential personal data seem also to differ for the affluent in contrast to the poor. Even when child abuse is suspected, it appears less likely to be reported.

Discussions with physicians and empirical research suggest that social and economic characteristics of families play an important role in determining which children are labeled as "abused." Turbett and O'Toole (1980) found that child abuse recognition among physicians is affected by severity of injury and by parents' socioeconomic status and ethnicity. When children were described as having a major injury, black children were nearly twice as likely to be recognized as victims of abuse as were white children. With respect to reporting child abuse, black children were one-third more susceptible than white children suffering from identical major injuries. Lower-class white children suffering from major injuries were more likely to be classified as abused than were upper-class white children.

The National Black Child Development Institute has drawn attention to the unique health risks that accrue to black children (*The Status of Black Children* 1980):

> Black children are much more likely to suffer from poor health than the majority of their American peers. While poverty, unsafe housing, and poor nutrition expose many black children to harmful and hazardous conditions, their plight is compounded by a systematic inaccessibility to competent health care. Together, these factors help to make many black children a population substantially at risk with no resources for assistance.
>
> The statistics detailing the effects of deteriorating environments are particularly grim. Black infants are almost twice as likely as white infants to die before their first birthday. Even afterwards, a black child has a 30% greater probability of dying by his/her fourteenth birthday than does a white child (p. 34).

Black children have a higher death rate as a result of accidental injuries than whites. Also, black children appear to receive less medical attention for their injuries than do white children (Manheimer, Dewey, and Mellinger 1966).

The data on family violence, of which child abuse can be seen as a subset, are inconsistent, and their interpretations can be misleading

(Straus, Gelles, and Steinmetz 1980). In an effort to define the extent and nature of family violence among black Americans, Cazanave and Straus (1979) analyzed a subsample of a 1976 survey of violence in 2,143 black families and 427 white families. While black husbands tended to be more violent toward their wives, self-reported acts of physical violence toward their children showed little difference between blacks and whites. No conclusions could be drawn with respect to the differential levels of violence in black and white families.

In the National Study of the Incidence and Severity of Child Abuse (Burgdorf 1980), ethnicity and family income did not emerge as major factors in the reporting or nonreporting of identified cases of child maltreatment. Among high income groups (that is, families with annual incomes of $15,000 or more), incidence rates for all forms of maltreatment were approximately the same for white and nonwhite children. For white children, incidence rates for all forms of maltreatment were much higher in the low income groups than in the higher income groups. For nonwhite children, a similarly strong association between poverty and incidence of maltreatment was found, but only with regard to child neglect. Child abuse incidence rates were low and essentially constant across income groups for nonwhite children.

These findings of ethnically variant patterns of family violence suggest a need for a deeper analysis of risk factors within racial groups rather than the traditional between-group comparisons. This chapter presents a comparison of risk indicators for accidents and abuse among the black families that participated in a larger study of pediatric social illnesses.

The Family Development Study

The Family Development Study is a prospective case-control study of pediatric social illnesses: abuse, neglect, failure to thrive, accidents, and ingestions. These illnesses appear to derive primarily from the child's physical and social interaction with the nurturing environment. They are distinguishable from illnesses of a more primary biomedical etiology. The goals of the study are to determine which ecological factors place a child at risk for each of the specific social pediatric illnesses and to identify commonalities and differences in risk indicators across the diagnostic categories.

Two successive samples of "cases" and matched "controls" were identified. The first sample (Phase I), reported previously (Newberger et al. 1977), yielded data that suggested interrelationships among the social illnesses. This report derives from a second wave of observations (Phase II), which built on the main conceptual leads of the earlier study a more focused and rigorous approach to analysis.

With a view to building a structural element that would regularly oblige us to consider the special visibility and vulnerability of minority families, especially in regard to increasing the utility of our research products for clinical practice and social policy, we entered into a contractual agreement with the Boston Community Research Review Committee to meet with us at regular intervals and to monitor continuously our draft instruments and data gathering.

Subjects

All families with children four years of age or younger who were hospitalized at Children's Hospital Medical Center (CHMC) with a diagnosis of child abuse, child neglect, accident, ingestion, or failure to thrive (FTT) were eligible for inclusion in the study. Families of children who did not bear a pediatric social illness diagnosis but who were hospitalized for medical or surgical illnesses of acute onset, such as pneumonia or meningitis, were eligible for selection as controls. Children suffering from chronic or terminal illnesses were excluded from the control population. Families seen in the outpatient department or emergency room were not eligible for study.

For each case, children were matched on a one-to-one basis with a control according to the following criteria: race, socioeconomic status (that is, same social class on the Hollingshead Two-Factor Social Index), and age plus or minus two months). No violations from these matching criteria were permitted.

All classifications for the purposes of this study are based upon final hospital diagnosis. The diagnosis of child abuse was made by the hospital's Trauma X Team. This multidisciplinary team, composed of a psychologist, a psychiatrist, pediatricians, a social worker, nurses, and a lawyer, had primary responsibility for consulting on all child abuse cases in the hospital (Newberger et al. 1973). All cases of child abuse were reported to the state's child protective services as mandated by state law.

The sample was ascertained from July 1975 to April 1977. Prior to making contact with a mother to ask permission to interview, the physician responsible for the child's hospital care and the social worker, if one was assigned, were asked for their permission to interview the mother. Only then was contact made with the mother. After explaining the goals and nature of the study but before beginning the interview, the mother's written informed consent was obtained. All families' participation was voluntary and without remuneration.

As summarized in table 4-1, 209 cases and 209 controls were interviewed. Eight cases of failure to thrive (FTT) were also reported to the state's department of welfare as being seriously abused or neglected.

Table 4–1
Number of Potential Cases Interviewed

Category	Interviewed	Missed	Percentage Interviewed
Trauma X	48	17	73.8
FTT	41	20	67.2
Accidents	97	40	70.8
Ingestions	23	15	60.5
Total	209	91	68.8
Controls	209	—	100.0

These children are included in both the Trauma X and FTT categories. Just under 70 percent of all eligible families were interviewed. Post-hoc testing reveals no major differences between missed and interviewed families, either across or within any specific attribute of race, sex, social class, urban residence, or duration of hospital stay (a sign of medical severity).

Data

Data on each child and family were obtained from four sources: maternal interview, paternal interview, the child's medical records, and a Vineland Social Maturity index based on information derived from the maternal interview. The principal instrument was a standardized, precoded maternal interview. It included a wide range of questions about family structure, housing, employment, finances, availability of relatives and friends, mobility, and psychological stresses, as well as questions about the respondent's history, focusing on the demographic characteristics of the family of origin, events and care in childhood, and prior and current experiences in caring for the child. The mother was asked questions about her child's temperament (based on Carey's interview adaptation of the Thomas, Chess and Birch Infant Scales) and health, as well as her knowledge of developmental norms for children. Finally, questions regarding the frequency and methods used to punish and praise the child were asked. The same interview was administered to the father or any other regular male caretaker. Both parents were asked questions about themselves and their spouse. From the medical records, physical characteristics were ascertained, that is, height, weight, hematocrit, head circumferences, and duration of hospitalization.

All interviews were conducted by specially trained, sensitive interviewers. Each interview lasted approximately one hour. All were conducted in the hospital, either during the child's hospitalization or upon the child's first visit to a follow-up clinic. All data were checked by a supervisor immediately following the interviews to ensure that they were appropriately coded and recorded.

Given the emphasis on environmental realities during the interview, it was felt that the project had an obligation to offer assistance to ameliorate the identified problems. To this end a family advocacy program was developed and was available to all participants. Designated initially to help families obtain such essential supports as adequate housing, child care, legal services, and adult health care, the program evolved into an organized service available to all hospital patients. Personnel with no formal professional education were trained and supervised in helping families deal with contemporary life stresses and in gaining access to essential services (Morse et al. 1977).

Demographic Characteristics

No differences in race were found across the case categories. By race the sample was 73 percent white, 22 percent black, and 5 percent Hispanic; these proportions did not vary markedly from category to category. No sex differences across the case categories were found. The majority of the sample was male; this is consistent with the generally observed higher morbidity for males at these ages.

On age, however, cases differed. The children bearing abuse or FTT diagnoses were significantly younger than those with accidents and ingestions: 85 percent of both child abuse and FTT thrive victims were under 2 years of age; 55 percent were under 1 year of age. Those with accidents were almost evenly distributed in all the age groups. Children with ingestions tended to be older; none were below 1 year of age.

Families differed with respect to welfare dependency. A high percentage of abused children (four out of five) were members of families on welfare. The families of abuse victims were, as a group, very poor. The families of victims of accidents and ingestions were more evenly distributed across all five of the Hollingshead social classes. Excluding all of the child abuse cases from the FTT sample brings its social class distribution into line with the accidents and poisonings. The prevalence of poverty in the families of abuse victims is one of the striking demographic findings of this study.

Results

The subsample consisted of ninety-four black families. There were fifteen cases of child abuse, nine of failure to thrive, seventeen with accidents, and six with ingestions. Each of these was matched with a control. The following analysis addresses the differences across the accident, abuse, and control categories in the black subsample.

Case Control Differences

Black child abuse cases differed from their controls in several ways, including a higher level of social isolation, more geographic mobility, maternal childhood history of corporal punishment extending through adolescence, and a generally more stressful present living situation.

The mothers of the black child abuse cases tended to describe their childhood as having been less happy and cold in tone. These mothers were struck more frequently and spanked more severely than were the mothers in the matched control group. Mothers of the child abuse victims reported having been spanked on parts of the body other than the hand and bottom through adolescence. But they had more prior experience with children, and they were happy during their pregnancies. The pressures on these mothers seemed extreme. They suffered more losses due to recent deaths in their families, more recent changes in their life situations, and, overall, more negative family stress. It is not surprising that they described their living situation as being less happy than did the controls.

Fathers of black child abuse cases, like case mothers, were spanked more frequently than the controls, and their childhood punishments were more severe. These fathers reported that they liked infants less than did the fathers of the matched controls (note that black child abuse cases had a mean age of 14 months).

The victims of accidents were older (mean age of 23.3 months) and relatively more healthy as a group in comparison to their controls. While these families were highly mobile, they appeared to have greater access to shopping and to recreation than did the comparison group. They expressed greater satisfaction with social service agencies. The fathers in the families of accident victims had moved less frequently during their childhood. They left their parents' homes relatively shortly before the birth of their first child. The mothers of accident victims, however, appeared to be more depressed as a group than did the control mothers.

Fewer factors differentiated black families bearing the diagnosis of accidents. Although they appeared as a group to require fewer social services, they seemed more capable of establishing relationships with service providers. The fathers had experienced fewer changes in childhood and had been on their own relatively fewer years before assuming the responsibilities of parenthood.

Accident-Abuse Differences

As noted in table 4–2, 86.6 percent of the Trauma X families and 64.7 percent of the accident families were in the lowest social class. To control for confounding on this variable, the cases were matched on social class. The significant variables summarized in table 4–3 suggest that, among black families, victims of child abuse and accidents differ in several ways. The children bearing the diagnosis of abuse scored lower on the Vineland

Table 4–2
Demographic Characteristics of Sample
(Matching Variables)

Category	Under 2	Male	Low SES[a]	N
Trauma X, white	82.7%	44.8%	72.4%	33
Trauma X, black	86.6	65.9	86.6	15
FTT, white	83.3	60.0	30.0	32
FTT, black	100.0	66.6	66.7	9
Accidents, white	56.5	60.5	18.4	80
Accidents, black	64.7	64.7	64.7	17
Ingestions, white	62.5	43.7	31.2	17
Ingestions, black	33.3	66.6	50.0	6

[a]Hollingshead Scale, Category 5.

Table 4–3
Family Variables Distinguishing Black Victims
of Child Abuse and Childhood Accidents

Child factors
  Vineland Social Maturity Quotient* (−)
  Child perceived as easy to care for* (−)
  Communication score* (−)

Mother-child interaction
  Mother felt guilty when she punished child* (−)
  Mother-child contact in the first few weeks* (−)
  Frequency of spanking*

Family factors
  Mother unable to "get going" each day* (+)
  Mother felt no one was interested in her problems* (+)
  Mother described situation as happy** (−)
  Father made rural-urban move* (+)
  Recent death in the family** (+)
  Recent family stress* (+)

Note: Parenthetical sign indicates direction of difference.
* $p < .05$.
** $p < .001$.

Social Maturity Index. Their mothers' occupational status, as a group, was lower. Maternal reports of the number of times per week they spanked their child indicated no differences between the two case subsamples. Mothers of accident victims reported that they were more likely to feel guilty if they punished the child than did mothers of abuse victims. They were, as a group, also more likely to describe their relationship with their infant during the first few weeks as pleasant.

The parental social environment and support network differed between the two groups. Our data strongly suggest an important degree of social isolation and of maternal depression for black mothers of child abuse victims. Although the mothers' marital status did not differentiate at a statistically significant level in the study, it is noteworthy that the abuse sample contained more single parents. Relatively more of these mothers had moved to the greater Boston area from rural areas, which may have separated them from their familial support systems. The fathers, on the other hand, tended to be from urban areas.

The mothers of child abuse victims described their living situations as unhappy. They expressed as a group the sad feeling that no one was interested in their problems, and they described themselves as being unable to "get going" each day. An unexpected finding was that these differences existed in such a magnitude. Although there was no significant difference in the number of times per week the mothers reported seeing relatives, there appeared to be a substantial qualitative difference in the extent to which they felt nurtured by their contacts with kin.

Stress appeared to bear onerously on families with children diagnosed as abused. Recent losses of loved ones exerted a strong impact, and the cumulative stress levels for families of abuse victims were extremely high.

Discussion

In the present study, black families who abuse their children appear to suffer from poverty, social isolation, and stressful relationships with and among kin. Maternal depression and poor mobility were noted more frequently in black families whose children's injuries were seen as having been accidental, yet they had many strengths in comparison to the families whose children were diagnosed as abused. The accident-abuse comparison suggests that although a family's ability to protect a child from an environmental hazard may be enhanced by the association of a mother's sense of well-being and connection to kin and community, the crushing burdens associated with child abuse seem qualitatively and quantitatively to erode the family's parental competency. For the black families in this study, the contexts of child abuse appear to be those of severe economic adversity, no one to turn to for help, a death in the family, a history of having suffered serious personal violence, and a child who may be delayed in social and cognitive development. Any parent would be severely affected by such circumstances, and, indeed, the parents of victims of child abuse in this study could easily be seen as victims themselves.

The implications of these data for prevention and for practice seem clear, but, in the light of present trends in social policy, they would not seem to be able to translate into action quickly. As a matter of priority, to strengthen these most vulnerable families, we feel that society must provide, at least, and in this order: (1) financial support; (2) a line of contact with a professionally trained or supervised individual who can give help in times of personal distress; (3) diagnostic consultation; and (4) therapeutic intervention to promote the development and health of the children. Now is, perhaps, the least propitious time in recent years, however, to urge these supports for the prevention of child abuse in black families that seem to bear a disproportionate brunt of a stagnant economy and the general withdrawal of fiscal support, social services, and medical services for the poor. Moreover, the racial prejudice implicit in present social policies, which blame the victim for his or her life circumstances, visits additional cruelty and violence upon the black family and its children. When such auxiliary supports to social work counseling as child development services are not available for the treatment of child abuse, the only choice may be to separate child from parent and to place the child in a foster home. This final protective "service" is well documented to affect black families disproportionately. For them, too frequently the last resort becomes the first resort when society's resources—in the workplace; in the housing market; and in the education, health, and social service systems—are in short supply.

Thus, child abuse in the black family is conceptualized best as a symptom rather than as a disease. To address the origins of the symptom in individual families, for both children and parents, requires a thoughtful professional response. Nevertheless, the professional community cannot ignore the social action imperatives to work on the problem of child abuse. Responsibility for child abuse in the black family resides as much in the society as in the relationships among family members.

References

Allen, W. 1978. "The Search for Applicable Theories of Black Family Life." *Journal of Marriage and the Family* 40:117–128.

Burgdorf, K. 1980. "Recognition and Reporting of Child Maltreatment: Findings from the National Study of the Incidence and Severity of Child Abuse and Neglect." Washington, D.C.: National Center on Child Abuse and Neglect.

Cazenave, N., and M. Straus. 1979. "Race, Class, Network Embeddedness and Family Violence: A Search for Potent Support Systems." *Journal of Comparative Family Studies* 10:281–300.

Daniel, J., et al. 1978. "Child Abuse Screening: Implications of the Limited Predictive Power of Child Abuse Discriminants in a Controlled Family Study of Pediatric Social Illness." *International Journal of Child Abuse and Neglect* 2:247–259.

Fontana, V. 1973. *The Maltreated Child: The Maltreatment Syndrome in Children.* Springfield, Ill.: Charles C. Thomas.

Gelles, R. 1980. "Violence in the Family: a Review of Research in the Seventies." *Journal of Marriage and the Family* 42:873–885.

Gil, D. 1970. *Violence against Children: Physical Child Abuse in the United States.* Cambridge: Harvard University Press.

Keniston, K. 1977. *All Our Children: The American Family under Pressure.* New York: Harcourt Brace Jovanovich.

Manheimer, D., J. Dewey, and G. Mellinger. 1966. "50,000 Years of Accidental Injury" *Public Health Report* 81:519–532.

Marx, T., E. Newberger, and K. White. 1981. "When an Injury Is a Symptom." Paper presented to the National Conference for Family Violence Researchers, University of New Hampshire.

Morse, A., et al. 1977. "Environmental Correlates of Pediatric Social Illness: Preventive Implications of an Advocacy Approach." *American Journal of Public Health* 67, no. 7:612–615.

Newberger, E., et al. 1973. "Reducing the Literal and Human Cost of Child Abuse: Impact of a New Hospital Management System." *Pediatrics* 51, no. 5:840–848.

Newberger E., and J. Daniel. 1976. "Knowledge and Epidemiology of Child Abuse: A Critical Review of Concepts." *Pediatric Annals* 5, no. 3:140–145.

Newberger, E., et al. 1977. "Pediatric Social Illness: Toward an Etiologic Classification." *Pediatrics* 60:179–185.

"One Child Dies Daily from Abuse: Parent Probably Was Abuser." 1975. *Pediatric News* 9, no. 3.

Staples, R., and A. Mirande. 1980. "Racial and Cultural Variations among American Families: A Decennial Review of the Literature on Minority Families." *Journal of Marriage and the Family* 42:887–903.

The Status of Black Children 1980. Report from the National Black Child Development Institutes, Washington, D.C.

Straus, M., R. Gelles, and S. Steinmetz. 1980. *Behind Closed Doors: Violence in the American Family.* Garden City, N.Y.: Doubleday.

Turbett, P., and R. O'Toole. 1980. "Physicians' Recognition of Child Abuse." Paper presented to the American Sociological Association, New York.

U.S. Department of Health and Human Services. 1980. *Vital Statistics of the United States.* Washington, D.C.: Government Printing Office.

U.S. Senate. Committee on Labor and Public Welfare. Subcommittee on Children and Youth. 1973. *Hearings on S. 1191,* Child Abuse Prevention Act. 93d Cong., 1st sess.

5
Child Sexual Abuse: A Black Perspective

Robert L. Pierce
Lois H. Pierce

T his chapter will address an area of family abuse that has only recently penetrated public consciousness: childhood sexual abuse. From all accounts (Finkelhor 1979; Sgroi 1982; Mrazek and Kempe 1981), the issue is not new, yet certain aspects and dimensions of this problem deserve further analysis. One aspect of child sexual abuse that has been almost totally ignored in both the empirical and practice literature on the subject deals with the issue of race. Pierce and Pierce (1984) and Wyatt (1985) have observed the need to consider more seriously the aspect of race in research and practice with sexually abused children and their families. Since the family is the key context in which child sexual abuse is being considered, the issue of incest in black families becomes the focal point of our discussion. Certainly questions will be raised about the need for an analysis of this nature. However, we are firmly convinced that based on the following two points, a beginning dialogue on the topic is in order:

1. On a macrolevel, concern for the survival of black families (Norton 1985) demands that the professional community examine all aspects of black family life (including those that are socially repulsive) in order to reverse the present trends.

2. Generalizability of research conclusions—the application of practice strategies across populations as well as the development of prevention programs—can be seriously questioned if the issue of race or ethnicity is excluded from consideration.

More specifically the questions raised in this chapter are: to what extent does the literature on incest, and more broadly child sexual abuse, address the issue of race in terms of definitions, prevalence, approaches to understanding, and treatment? and what can be gleaned from the findings that show potentials for positively affecting practice and research?

To answer these questions, two sources were used: yearly publications (those available) of *Highlights of Official Child Neglect and Abuse Reporting* and approximately 140 pieces of literature that included journal articles and books on child sexual abuse and/or incest.

We want to believe that the family, as a major socializing agent for society, is the center of peace, love, and tranquility. Yet the darker side of family life conflicts with this perception because it reveals a picture of families that is everything but peaceful and content. In fact, in many instances we have come to learn that family life is actually the training ground for violence (Steinmetz and Straus 1974). Many parents and other trusted adults who care for children are known to beat, sexually exploit, poison, neglect, and abandon approximately 1 million children annually (U.S. Department of Health and Human Services, 1981). Moreover, we are beginning to identify and recognize home environments where adults, some in marital unions or other intimate relationships, often engage in brutal physical combat that sometimes results in either one partner is being severely injured (usually the woman) or murdered. Consequently, we have come to know that for some, particularly children, family life can be hell.

Within the last decade, the sexual victimization of children, especially incestuous sex at home, has become a topic of major concern for lay citizens and professionals representing widely divergent fields of practice and research. The topic is emerging as a national concern as federal, state, and local legislators ponder the "rapid proliferation of these incidents" (U.S. House 1977).

As Sgroi (1982) notes, the offender is almost always someone, usually a male, within the child's own family or someone else who has access to the child and is involved in his or her daily activities. Nonrelated offenders known to exploit children sexually are school teachers, nurses, day care staff, judges, priests, coaches, and Scout leaders, just to name a few.

Definition

To most people, the term *child sexual abuse* refers to intercourse between an adult and child. Researchers, clinicians, and theorists who write about this subject, however, have identified a much broader range of sexual behaviors subsumed within this term. Sgroi (1982) compiled a list of fourteen actions that supposedly represent the spectrum of sexually abusive behaviors. She begins the list with what appear to be the more benign acts like nudity or disrobing in front of children. These are followed by the more specific or direct acts (fondling, masturbation, digital penetration of the vagina or anus), which leave little doubt about the sexual intent of the perpetrator. As Mrazek and Kempe (1981) observed, although adult-child sexual encounters have existed throughout history, whether such beliefs and practices are defined as abuse is dependent upon "societal values of a particular period" (p. 5). In ancient Greece and Rome, sexual practices between children and adults were quite open and acceptable to the community. Consequently adults, men for the most part, used children in a variety of ways to satisfy their sexual needs. Today any behavior between an adult and child that is even remotely sexual in nature is considered immoral, criminal, and pathological. Mrazek and Kempe believe that the definition of behaviors that characterize a sexually abusive situation for a child should not be manipulated or changed to suit the perpetrator's socioeconomic level, race, or religion. Thus, unlike the cultural variance that is often attributed to physical child abuse (Parke and Collmer 1975), the following definitions are intended to cut across all cultural groups.

This chapter addresses race and its relationship to intrafamilial adult-child sexual encounters or incest (although we use the broader literature on child sexual abuse to supplement and fill voids in the literature on incest where this relationship has only recently begun to emerge). Defining intrafamilial adult-child sexual encounters is no less difficult or perplexing than are the same acts committed by individuals outside the family. In fact, there is reason to believe that defining the issue as it occurs within families may be much more difficult to pinpoint and certainly to record. The private nature of family life, plus the limitless prerogatives extended to parenthood, and the unwillingness of many victims to disclose information about their experiences, least of all to anyone outside the family, make this issue an extremely illusive subject to pursue. Yet definitions of incest, unlike physical child abuse, where outcome and intent are key definitional issues to consider (Parke and Collmer 1975), rest on two different considerations: the relationship between the involved adult and child and the behaviors that emerge through this interaction.

Porter's (1984) review of the legal definition of incest points out that it applies to "acts of sexual intercourse between a man and a woman" who is his "daughter, sister or half-sister, mother or grandmother or granddaughter" or "a woman over sixteen years of age with a man who is her father, brother or half-brother, son or grandfather" (p. 3). Also covered under this definition are illegitimate children, but adopted and stepchildren are not. Acts not involving intercourse between an adult and child in any of these relationship categories would constitute other offenses. DeYoung's (1982) definition also focuses on the relationship between the victim and the offender. In her study, incest is defined as "sexual intercourse, attempted sexual intercourse, or sexual contact of either heterosexual or a homosexual nature between people too closely related to legally marry" (p. 3). Mrazek and Kempe (1981), in noting that incest laws vary across cultures, observed that within some cultures, incest laws focus on only relationships between close blood relatives. In contrast, Sgroi's (1982) definition of incest extends beyond close relatives to include "surrogate family members or a stepparent or extended family member" (common-law spouse or foster parents) (p. 10). Attempting to arrive at a more inclusive definition of child sexual abuse, the Child Abuse and Neglect Treatment Act of 1974 defines relatedness as anyone responsible for the child's welfare. Clearly there is confusion surrounding how broad or narrow the net should be cast to identify potential offenders.

Definitions of incest that focus on behaviors of the offenders reveal similar confusion. The central question here seems to focus on the judgment of outside investigators. Some outside source (police, doctor, nurse, social worker, teacher) must hear the victim's story, and where appropriate, medical examinations must be performed prior to labeling an event incestuous. The continuum of behaviors ranges from acts that are the least intrusive and intended to stimulate the perpetrator to those that are more intrusive and involve various forms of intercourse. Williams and Money (1980) imply that the perpetrator's behaviors need not always be obvious or open. To illustrate a more benign or less intrusive form of incest, Williams and Money talk about the "mother who has an orgasm from suckling, while her infant at the breast has an erection" (p. 412). Mayer (1983) and Pierce (1984) consider the use of pornographic materials as a stimulating agent (for both offender and victim) to entice youth into having a sexual liaison. Finkelhor (1979) and Giaretto (1981) have identified sexual propositioning as another form of benign behavior that should be included in definitions of incest.

Given this range of sexually abusive behaviors, Sgori's list is certainly enlightening, particularly in terms of demonstrating that the sexually abusive acts tend to progress through phases—the least to the most intrusive. Thus it is understandable why investigators attempt to use specific rather than vague descriptions of behaviors when defining the concept. Perhaps because adult sexuality can be part of so many behavioral interactions with children, the burden of proof lies with the intervener to determine what is a nonsexual interaction. In spite of this word of caution, Meiselman (1978) noted, and rightfully so, that research definitions of incest should extend beyond mere genital contact since sexual interactions with very young children often involve other forms of sexual and nonsexual behaviors. Thus, Mayer's (1983) and Summit and Kryso's (1981) conceptualization of the entire spectrum of parent-child sexuality is overwhelming, particularly for the clinician or the investigator who must labor with discrete components of this multifaceted phenomenon.

Perhaps a useful way to summarize the discussion on defining incest or sexual abuse is to pay particular attention to the following.

A strictly legal or medical definition of incest is typically too narrow to be of use to clinicians.

A definition of incest for reporting purposes may pose severe methodological questions for the investigator who tries to sort through the various behavioral components of this phenomenon.

Clinical definitions of incest and, more broadly, child sexual abuse should focus on identifying what occurred, noting the age and development of those involved, understanding the nature and scope of the relationship between the people involved, and noting the attitudes and involvements of other family members, including the cultural context in which the incident occurred (Mrazek and Kempe, 1981).

Prevalence

Because of the private nature of family life, tremendous family loyalties, and the problems that abound with the current reporting system, there is no way to determine how frequently children are sexually misused by their parents or other relatives within the general population. Moreover, the emphasis on sexually abused children is recent; early attempts to examine prevalence tended to be more general in their definition of child maltreatment. They emphasized physical child abuse and neglect and ignored the sexually abused child.

In 1970, Gil conducted a national survey that determined that 2.53 million to 4.07 million adults personally knew families who were involved in abusive incidents with children during the year preceding the study. Gil also initiated a substudy in which he tried to explore the "many possible contributing causal contexts that may precipitate incidents of physical abuse of children" (p. 126). His conclusions come as no surprise. Of the fourteen causal environments he identified, three, which represented over one-fourth of the cases, were directly related to child sexual abuse. One was an incident precipitated by either a frustrated perpetrator whose sexual advances to a child were rejected or was actually part of a "perverse sexual interaction," another the "sadistic gratification of the perpetrator" (p. 128), and the third what Gil called the "typical constellation," which occurs when the mother or mother substitute is away from the home and the child is left in the care of a boyfriend or male caretaker.

All of these environments have been identified as crucial settings that place children at risk for sexual abuse (Sgroi 1982).

Gil's findings on the problem of physical child abuse also held the potential of clarifying for some basic issues about sexually abused children and their families. But at that time the topic was dismissed as being too delicate and thus not deserving of further investigation. Thus early attempts to investigate child sexual abuse began much slower than those focusing on physical child abuse.

Nevertheless, there were several early attempts to determine the extent of incest in the general population. Weinberg (1955) estimated that within the total U.S. population, children were being sexually victimized at a rate of 1.1 per million population. In a retrospective study, Landis (1956) surveyed 1,800 middle-class college students and learned that various forms of childhood or adolescent sexual abuse had occurred in one-third of the sample cohort (35 percent of the females and 30 percent of the males). Of the 360 females who experienced incest, only about half disclosed the abuse to parents, and only one-tenth of the experiences were ever reported to the authorities. Male victims who participated in the study were even more secretive. Only one in six reported the incident to a parent. The American Humane Association (1978) projected that each year at least 4,000 cases of sexual abuse would be discovered in every large city—20,000 annually across the country.

Almost a decade later, Herman and Hirschman (1981) concluded that close to a million Americans may have been involved in an incestuous relationship. Forward and Buck (1982) concluded that the national incidence of sexual victimization of children exceeded reports of physical child abuse. Finkelhor (1979) estimated that one male to every two females was sexually victimized in childhood. Adams-Tucker and Adams (1984) pointed out that of the 60 million children under 18 years of age, one in four to one in three girls are sexually victimized by the time they reach their eighteenth birthday. Rogers and Terry (1984) focused on boys and estimated that "one-fourth of all victims of sexual assault or molestation are boys" (p. 91).

The establishment of the national reporting and data collection system through the American Humane Association (1978) was an attempt to begin compiling accurate statistics on all reports of abuse received by authorities across the country. Summarized and disseminated each year by the American Humane Association, these data provide a range of information on child maltreatment, including rates of increases or decreases for any given year since 1976 and detailed demographic data on involved children and their families. The association's report for 1984 revealed that "overall reporting levels have increased 158 percent between 1976 and 1984" (p. 2). The association's estimate for all forms of abuse in

1984 was 1,726,649, with the rate of reporting estimated at 27.3 children per 1,000 U.S. population. Data the association has collected in its efforts to document the frequency of reported incidents of sexual abuse indicate that the overall rate has increased significantly since 1976. In particular, the increase of sexually maltreated children in 1985 "translates into an increase of about 35 percent from 1984" (p. 16). This is a sharp contrast compared to the findings reported by the Child Welfare League of America (1986) for the same period. According to its data, reports of sexual abuse of children jumped by 59 percent between 1983 and 1984. The data also show that generally child abuse and neglect reports increased by 16 percent between 1983 and 1984 and that one out of every seven of these cases involved a sexually abused child.

A valid question at this point is who to believe. Are the data generated through survey research or the data derived through mandated reports more accurate in reporting the prevalence of child sexual abuse? DeYoung (1982) identifies four reasons for the confusion surrounding the estimates. First, researchers often use different or no definitions at all when examining child sexual victimization. Second, they tend to employ methodologies and research designs that are "subjective in nature and may not render results which can be accurately generalized" (p. 2). Third, research samples are likely to vary, and the subjects may not represent the typical victim or offender. Fourth, the researcher's own biases about the topic or the sample being studied may cloud or infiltrate the study design and conclusion. As Sgroi (1982) points out, working with child sexual abuse situations is new and disturbing, and often difficult to resolve. In order to defend themselves against becoming emotionally drained and burned out, clinicians become blasé about their work and the people needing their help. Under conditions like these, it is easier for clinicians, especially white clinicians, to assume that the abusive families they observe irrespective of race or ethnicity are representative of all abusive families.

In the past, a color-blind attitude in the broad field of research and clinical practice was highly valued. Cooper (1973) noted, however, "that such an attitude is not totally possible, realistic or useful" (p. 129), and Pinderhughes (1982) observed that "effective intervention with families requires knowledge of ethnic factors as they influence family functioning both internally and externally" (p. 109). More attention to the relationship between race and child sexual abuse in general and incest in particular will increase the understanding of this delicate issue and improve the quality of services provided to children and their families.

For the most part, examining the prevalence of incest, or more generally child sexual abuse, within a specific subgroup has apparently not been viewed as a fruitful avenue to pursue. Data are relatively sparse when it comes to providing specific clues to resolving dilemmas about race or ethnicity that may arise in research or practice with various racial groups. Although the actual act of sexually victimizing a child is no different from one group to the next, there may be variables associated with the intervention, treatment, or research process that will vary across groups.

The earliest work we reviewed for this analysis was written in 1937. In general the materials touched on a host of topics addressing such issues as the etiology of sexual abuse (Bender and Blau 1937; Weinberg 1955; DeFrancis 1969; Browning and Boatman 1977; Sgroi 1982; Finkelhor 1984), intervention issues (Terrell 1977; Sgroi 1982; Coute and Shore 1982), treatment considerations (Eist and Mandel 1968; Giaretto 1977; Courtois 1979; Sgroi 1982), psychodynamics of offenders, victims, and nonoffending parent (Cormier, Kennedy, and Sangowicz 1972; Peters 1976; Herman and Hirschman 1981; Goodwin and Simms 1979; Finkelhor 1984) and effects (Peters 1976; James and Meyerding 1977; Meiselman 1978; Yorukoglu and Kemph 1966).

Overall the extent to which the subject of race was either directly or indirectly addressed is almost negligible. This is not to say that the authors of these materials did not have the opportunity to do so. In fact, in many cases, quite the opposite was true. Bender and Blau (1937) dealt with the issue of race subtly and almost stereotypically. The sample consisted of sixteen prepubescent children admitted to a psychiatric hospital after it was discovered that they had had sexual relations with an adult. Of the sample of eleven girls and five boys, two of the girls were identified as "colored." They characterized one black girl, 9 years old, as being "preoccupied with sex to an unusual degree" (p. 504), with a "restlessness and irritability [that] could be related very definitely to increased sex tension" (p. 505). They described the other black girl, a year older, as "showing no evidence of anxiety, guilt or shame" about her precocious sexual drives and open solicitation of men and boys. About a white girl, whose sexual experiences appear to be similar to those of the black girls, the authors noted that she related her sexual experiences "freely and shamelessly, and showed no evidence of unusual sex behavior or sex tension" (p. 503), yet they described her as a "girl with superior intelligence" and "endowed with an affectionate personality" (p. 504). The authors' descriptions of other cases showed a similar imbalance, typically a cynical, almost hopeless outlook and prognosis for the black patients and generally a more positive labeling and prognosis for the white patients.

Clearly we must consider the historical context in which this work was done. On the other hand, if we look at the data from a minority perspective, a different light is cast on the understanding and approach to the problem. In Weinberg's classic work (1955), the fact that his sample included twenty-two black families seemed of little consequence beyond the author's overall conclusions about incestuous behavior. Yet the study revealed some interesting findings about these incestuous families that call for further exploration. For example, the author noted that fewer cases involving blacks, as compared to whites, were reported, although blacks had a higher ratio of reports when compared to the general population. Also of interest in this study was the author's observation that black incestuous fathers were on the average younger (40.6 years old) than majority (white) fathers (43.5 years old). The other areas where blacks were mentioned concerned family size. Black incestuous families, according to the author, contained the smallest number of children (3.9 versus 4.9 for whites) and the smallest family (3.31 versus 3.52 for white families). In other critical areas (how the incest was detected, disposition, economic level, education, personality dynamics, or perpetrators), the author's summary was color-blind.

Meiselman's (1978) work is another example of an author citing the fact the blacks were included in the study but failing to make comparisons among subjects. Other writings tend to follow the same or similar patterns: Benward and Densen-Gerber (1975), Caruso (1975), Peters (1976), Burgess, Holmstrom, and McCausland (1977), Falland (1977), Rosenfeld (1979), and Scherzer and Lala (1980). Other investigations, like Kercher and McShane (1984), had an opportunity to look at the issue of race but failed to capitalize on the information.

A few studies, however, have looked at the question of how race and child sexual abuse relate. Pierce and Pierce (1984) explored the connection between race and child sexual abuse by comparing the records of 56 black children to 149 white children. They noted that "although several well-known studies of sexual abuse have included racial minorities in their studies, none have looked at these groups individually" (p. 9). They reached a number of significant conclusions, among them that sexually abused black children were significantly younger (8.7 years compared to 11.1) than their white counterparts and that black males comprised 14 percent of the total black sample versus 11 percent for white males.

Approaches to Understanding

All parents at some point in their parenting experience have erotic feelings toward their children (Mrazek and Kempe 1981). Explaining why some parents elect to go beyond these feelings and engage their children in sexual liaisons remains for the most part a highly complex puzzle. In many families, the incest barrier or taboo is meaningless. In talking about the breakdown of the barrier, Lustig and coworkers (1966) note that five conditions exist within incestuous families when this occurs. First, in nonincestuous families, the dominant institutionalized familial interactions are orchestrated along sexual and generational lines in order to achieve culturally defined goals for its members—as individuals and as a family. Incestuous families, by contrast, rely on noninstitutionalized roles and relationships where generational differentiation is destroyed (role reversal between mother and daughter). Consequently the first component of the familial breakdown occurs: the daughter emerges as a key individual in the household replacing the mother. Second, the incestuous or dysfunctional family's relation to and interaction with the larger community or society is fragile and superficial, thus isolating the family and its members from full participation in its endeavors. In part, the isolation from community and friends is contributed to by the incestuous offender's need to keep hidden his or her exploits with the sexually abused child(ren).

Cut off from public scrutiny, individuals within this isolated group look to each other almost exclusively to express and seek "gratification for their instinctual wishes" (Lustig et al. 1966, p. 38). The third component of the breakdown involves the father's willingness to initiate the sexual liaison with his daughter and the degree of her willingness to participate in the arrangement by exchanging sexual roles with her mother. Additionally, the fear of outside discovery makes it necessary for the father to concentrate his activities and gratification within rather than outside the house. The fourth component considers the notion of familial equilibrium, which is based on shared fear of disintegration. The public facade of a stable and competent family is maintained at all cost. Not surprisingly, all family members participate in the transaction, although some family members may not know (some suspect but do not act on their suspicions) about the incest. The final component of the breakdown is the presumed sanction given to the sexual liaison by the mother. Lustig and coworkers conclude by suggesting that all members vicariously benefit (certainly not in a real sense) from this dysfunctional arrangement: the parents' pregenital needs are met, the daughter gains revenge against the mother for not protecting her, the threat of familial disintegration is reduced for all members, and the larger community perceives a family that appears to be contributing positively to the life of the community.

Weinberg (1955), on the other hand, traced backgrounds and modes of development of his sample of incestuous fathers in order to arrive at two types. First is the impulse-ridden, disorganized person who had been raised in a disorganized family or shifted from family to family, making it difficult (or impossible) to learn the constraints of sexual behavior that operate within families. These men, whose behavior resembles Lustig's components of incest, were reared in highly impulsive families where sexual gratification from the daughter was an imposed form of behavior. A slight difference between Weinberg's offenders and Lustig's data did emerge, however. Weinberg noted in his typology that when other women, outside the family, were accessible to the offender, the offender disregarded his daughter. Weinberg's second group of offenders, the endogamic incest aggressors, emerged from ingrown families that were considered "emotional hothouses" (p. xv). In these families the incestuous behavior came about through an "ingrown sexual desire for the female family member" (p. xv). Unlike the impulse-ridden offenders, who were promiscuous and violence prone, the endogamic offender was intensely controlling and possessive of his daughter's attention and affection. Typologies of other groups of incestuous experiences Weinberg identified include those that are mainly situational and transient. The outset of these relationships can be attributed to weak self-constraints on the part of the offender. The lack of sexual privacy in the house presented situational opportunities (for example, sleeping in the same room, observing females dress or undress) that the offender seized upon. Weinberg, however, noted that these situational experiences tend not to be binding and are more transient in nature.

Taking a slightly different approach, Finkelhor's (1984) research showed that the risk factor for girls doubled her vulnerability to sexual victimization if a stepfather was in the home. A "stepfather and the stepfather's male friends were five times as likely to sexually victimize a daughter than was a natural father" (p. 25). He suggested two reasons to explain this high yet inconsistent correlation. First, the stepparent has no blood ties to the daughter; therefore, learned familial constraints are not present. The second consideration deals with mothers who through their dating bring sexually opportunistic men into the house, thus placing the daughter at risk of being sexually victimized. Another perspective, which emerged as a result of the feminist movement, asserts that incest or sexual abuse is brought on by the power differences between men and women (Herman and Hirschman 1981). As these authors note, incest is "one of the most unequal relationships imaginable," and it represents a "paradigm of female sexual victimization" (p. 4). Sgroi (1982) earlier had used this idea, suggesting that the dynamics of sexual abuse involve the notions of power, authority, and subordination, where the offender's position over the child is used as leverage in determining what occurs between the offender and victim, how it occurs, where, when, and why it occurs, whether the act is disclosed or kept secret, and in determining what happens when and if disclosure is made.

An all-encompassing perspective is offered by Tierney and Corwin (1983), whose system's model addressed socioecological factors (geographical and social isolation), family structure (family composition, levels of affections, power distribution), and individual considerations (maladaptive personalities, emotional dependency, marital dissatisfaction, and sexual estrangement from spouse).

Finally, according to some theorists, incestuous behavior is the result of major mental deficiencies. Other investigators, however, are quick to note that only a small portion of offenders exhibit such psychosis (Finkelhor 1984; Sgroi 1982).

Considering all of these positions, a useful conceptualization of why incest occurs will obviously depend upon a host of factors. Finkelhor, however, suggests that combining existing perspectives and integrating or borrowing theories from other fields will add to our knowledge base about a highly complex issue.

Treatment

Considering the evidence, which suggests that the prevalence of child maltreatment (particularly child sexual abuse) differs among blacks versus other racial and ethnic groups, and the following comment by Sgroi (1982), several concerns about treating black sexually abusive situations emerge.

> Most cases of child sexual abuse are managed badly. Those who are responsible for case managers tend to have limited knowledge of the problem and an inadequate understanding of the issues involved. They tend to work for agencies that are reluctant to be responsible for child-sexual-abuse cases and unwilling to make the commitment to train staff properly and to develop appropriate responses (p. 81).

Conceptualizing treatment strategies and options for black sexually abused children and their families is no easy task. The need to engage individuals and families of color in treatment relationships that are more solidly grounded in the clients' rather than clinician's base of reality is vital to positive treatment outcomes. Utilizing a treatment perspective in abusive situations that is racially or ethnically sensitive to the clients does not negotiate, minimize, or shift responsibility for the sexual abuse away from significant family members. Rather, the perspective merely provides the clinician with an additional set of tools that provides greater insight into the preconditions and dynamics of abuse. As Pinderhughes (1982) notes, therapists must understand two realities—those of black families and their adaptive behaviors and those of the therapist's own attitudes toward blacks—if therapy is to proceed unconfused. One of the realities confronting black families seeking services (usually involuntarily) from child welfare agencies for their abusive behavior is that the workers and supervisors are typically white females. When Vinokur-Kaplan and Hartman (1986) examined staffing patterns in a representative sample of child welfare agencies across the country, they found that of the 307 supervisors sampled, 78 percent were white and 15 percent were black, and of the 955 child welfare workers, 80 percent were white and only 13 percent were black. This black-white issue in therapy is particularly sensitive in the light of the fact that child welfare staff are typically undertrained to do the sensitive tasks they are called upon to perform and yet they represent the agency that has been mandated by law to intervene on behalf of sexually abused children. When these supervisors and workers were asked to indicate how much of their work time was devoted to staff development and training activities, the most frequent response category recorded was "not much time" (p. 333). Yet over 25 percent of the workers indicated that blacks comprised 51 percent of their caseloads. Based on these data, it would be safe to conclude that many clinicians within the child welfare system (mandated to receive reports of abuse and neglect), and perhaps the private sector also, who supposedly treat black sexually abused children and their families, utilize a stereotypical perspective of these families based on their personal perception of reality as opposed to the reality of black people. In short, the system of child welfare services, public and private, is failing black children and their families (Chestang 1978; Billingsley and Giovannoni 1972).

Another dimension of the client-worker (and indirectly the agency) relationship deals with the question of how treatment outcomes are affected by the race or ethnicity of either therapist or client. According to the literature, this focus is not a new concern (Brown 1950; Barrett and Perlmutter 1972; Banks 1972; Proctor and Davis 1983) within the helping professions, but it is an important one. As Proctor and Davis (1983) noted, "Consideration of the attitudes of professional helpers is related to the effectiveness of their work with clients" (p. 87). Yet within the broader field of family abuse, and the more specific topic of child sexual abuse, the literature is relatively silent about the issue of race in conceptualizing treatment issues and strategies. The dilemma is similar to the issues involving the child welfare system: the majority of staff who design and implement treatment programs are white, as are the majority of individuals conducting research and publishing in the field of child sexual victimization, who project that perspective as the direction or path to follow. White or "Anglo researchers tend to investigate ethnic minorities, especially blacks, without an appropriate set of guiding principles and without an appropriate framework for their methodology" (Bush et al. 1983, p. 118). Consequently white investigators have consistently ignored rich opportunities to add yet another perspective to this multifaceted problem.

For example, after reviewing five important studies in the field, Herman and Hirschman (1981) noted that blacks and other minorities—"those groups that are stereotypically suspected of deviant sexual activities— were conspicuous by their absence from these studies" (p. 12).

The clinician's or worker's investment in the issue does not appear to be much greater than that of the researcher. In most cases, though, researchers can ignore the issue of racial diversity by not including blacks in their sample. At least in the public sector, child welfare workers cannot avoid racial differences so directly. Workers can, however, indirectly ignore or minimize services to minority clients, which in the long run may be more damaging to these clients than refusing to acknowledge their existence. There are negative consequences whichever direction a worker pursues.

Another dimension of the dilemma is that typically treatment strategies designed to engage black families have focused on black women and their children and excluded black men (Hines and Boyd-Franklin 1982). For example, although the vast majority of black families reported for child maltreatment are headed by black women (American Humane Association Highlights 1984), black men predominate as perpetrators of childhood sexual abuse. Therefore treatment approaches that focus entirely on black women and exclude black men are lacking in substance and meaning for the victim, the victim's mother, and the offender. This exclusion is particularly important since the inappropriate use of power and domination by the perpetrator are key aspects requiring attention in the therapeutic process for victims (Sgroi 1982). Yet treatment consideration of black men who sexually abuse children is seldom, if ever, mentioned in the literature. Certainly care and consideration must be given to those dyads where the male perpetrator of the sexual abuse is not a central part of the family system. Yet where possible, and where the benefits outweigh disregarding this man, every effort should be made to include him in the therapy process. Finally, because black males seem to pose a special threat to society (particularly to white female clinicians), there is a need to become better acquainted with his role in American society. As Staples (1982) notes, black men tend to be "the most feared and the least understood and studied of all sex-race types" (p. 1). The far-reaching implications of this observation are critical to the practice arenas responding to the needs of sexually abused black children and their families.

Focusing more attention on the black male in the treatment process does not exclude the important role of black women. "One distinguishing feature of black families is that they continue to be more likely than other families to include young children" (Glick 1981, p. 107). Thus, irrespective of how parenthood evolved, the task for many black women is well defined, and these roles need to be sensitively dealt with by white clinicians in planning and implementing treatment interventions.

Summary

Those who are developing and implementing more meaningful and successful treatment outcomes should consider the following:

1. It is important for the therapist to be aware of the differences between his or her values and those of the ethnic or racial families being served (Spiegal 1982).
2. If clinicians and investigators have dealt successfully with their own issues about engaging racially different families, "they will be better able to distinguish when race is their own issue or one for the family" (Hines and Boyd-Franklin 1982, p. 103).
3. The first step for clinicians is to become familiar with the family's culture and the various roles played by different individuals within the family system.
4. The key to successful intervention and treatment is the ability to communicate respect.
5. Treatment should be directed toward helping individuals capitalize on their strengths as they attempt to regain stability and adjust to societal shifts and movements.
6. Regardless of the problem area, treatment must be flexible and reinforcing rather than rigid and dehumanizing.
7. "Assertiveness can help family members counteract reactions of powerlessness that get internalized in family interactions" (Pinderhughes 1982, p. 117).

References

Adams-Tucker, C., and P. Adams. 1984. "Treatment of Sexually Abused Children." In *Victims of Sexual Aggression: Treatment of Children, Women and Men*, pp. 57–74. Edited by I. Stuart and J. Greer. New York: Van Nostrand Reinhold.

American Association for Protecting Children. 1985. *Highlights of Official Child Neglect and Abuse Reporting 1983*. Denver: American Humane Association.

———. 1986. *Highlights of Official Child Neglect and Abuse Reporting 1984*. Denver: American Humane Association.

American Humane Association. 1978. *National Analysis of Official Child Neglect and Abuse Reporting 1976*. Denver: American Humane Association in association with the Center for Social Research and Development, Denver Research Institute.

_____. 1981. *National Study on Child Neglect and Abuse Reporting.* Denver: American Humane Association.

_____. 1983. *Annual Report, 1981 Highlights of Official Child Neglect and Abuse Reporting.* Denver: American Humane Association.

_____. 1984a. *Trends in Child-abuse and Neglect: A National Perspective.* Denver: American Humane Association.

_____. 1984b. *Highlights of Official Child Neglect and Abuse Reporting 1982.* Denver: American Humane Association, Child Protection Division.

Banks, W. 1972. "The Black Client and Helping Professionals." In *Black Psychology*, pp. 205–212. Edited by R.L. Jones. New York: Harper & Row.

Barrett, F., and F. Perlmutter. 1972. "Black Clients and White Workers: A Report from the Field." *Child Welfare* 51:19–24.

Bender, L. and A. Blau. 1937. "The Reaction of Children to Sexual Relationships with Adults." *American Journal of Orthopsychiatry* 8(October):500–518.

Benward, J., and J. Densen-Gerber. 1975. "Incest as a Causative Factor in Antisocial Behavior: An Exploratory Study." *Contemporary Drug Problems* 4:323–40.

Billingsley, A., and J. Giovannoni. 1972. *Children of the Storm: Black Children and American Child Welfare.* New York: Harcourt Brace Jovanovich.

Brown, L. 1950. "Race as a Factor in Establishing a Casework Relationship." *Social Casework* 13:91–97.

Browning, D., and B. Boatman. 1977. "Children at Risk." *American Journal of Psychiatry* 134:69–72.

Burgess, A., L. Holmstrom, and M. McCausland. 1977. "Child Sexual Assault by Family Member." *Victimology: An International Journal* 2:236–250.

Bush, J., D. Norton, C. Sanders, and B. Solomon. 1983. "An Integrative Approach for the Inclusion of Content on Blacks in Social Work Education." In *Mental Health and People of Color: Curriculum Development and Change.* Edited by J. Chunn II, P. Dunston, and F. Ross-Sheriff. Washington, D.C.: Howard University Press.

Caruso, P. 1975. "Pelvic Inflammatory Disease: Rare Sequel of Battered Child Syndrome." *New York State Journal of Medicine* 75:2405–2406.

Chestang, L. 1978. *The Delivery of Child Welfare Services to Minority Group Children and Their Families.* DHEW Publication DHDS 78-30158. Washington, D.C.: Government Printing Office.

Child Welfare League of America. 1986. *Too Young to Run: The Status of Child Abuse in America.* New York: Child Welfare League.

Cooper, S. 1973. "A Look at the Effect of Racism on Clinical Work." In *Dynamics of Racism in Social Work Practice*, pp. 127–140. Edited by J. Goodman. New York: National Association of Social Workers.

Cormier, B., M. Kennedy, and J. Sangowicz. 1972. "Psychodynamics of Father-Daughter Incest." *Canadian Psychiatric Association* 7:203–217.

Courtois, C. 1979. "Victims of Rape and Incest." *Counseling Psychologist* 8:38–40.

Coute, J., and D. Shore, eds. 1982. *Social Work and Sexual Abuse.* New York: Haworth Press.

DeFrancis, V. 1969. *Protecting the Child Victim of Sex Crimes Committed by Adults.* Denver: American Humane Association.

DeYoung, M. 1982. *The Sexual Victimization of Children.* Jefferson, N.C.: McFarland.

Devore, W., and E. Schlesinger. 1981. *Ethnic-Sensitive Social Work Practice.* St. Louis: Mosby.

Eist, H., and A. Mandel. 1968. "Family Treatment of Ongoing Incest Behavior." *Family Process* 7:216–232.

Falland, D. 1977. "Gonorrhea in Preadolescent Children: An Inquiry into Sources of Infection and Mode of Transmission." *Pediatrics* 60:153–156.

Finkelhor, D. 1979. *Sexually Victimized Children.* New York: Free Press.

————. 1984. *Sexually Victimized Children.* New York: Free Press.

Finkelhor, D., and G. Hotaling. 1984. "Sexual Abuse in the National Incidence Study of Child Abuse and Neglect: An Appraisal." *Child Abuse and Neglect* 8:12–33.

Forward, S., and C. Buck. 1982. *Betrayal of Innocence: Incest and Its Devastation.* New York: St. Martin's Press.

Giaretto, H. 1977. "Humanistic Treatment of Father-Daughter Incest." *Child Abuse and Neglect* 1:411–426.

————. 1981. "A Comprehensive Child Sexual Abuse Treatment Program." In *Sexually Abused Children and Their Families.* Edited by P. Mrazek and C. Kempe. Oxford: Pergamon.

Gil, D. 1973. *Violence against Children.* Cambridge: Harvard University Press.

Gitterman, A., and A. Schaeffer. 1973. "The White Professional and the Black Client." In *Dynamics of Racism in Social Work Practice,* pp. 152–170. Edited by J. Goodman. New York: National Association of Social Workers.

Glick, P. 1981. "A Demographic Picture of Black Families." In *Black Families,* pp. 106–126. Edited by H. McAdoo. Beverly Hills: Sage Publications.

Goodwin, J., and M. Simms. 1969. "Hysterical Seizure: A Sequel to Incest." *American Journal of Orthopsychiatry* 49:698–703.

Herman, J. 1981. *Father-Daughter Incest.* Cambridge: Harvard University Press.

Herman, J., and L. Hirshman. 1981. "Families at Risk for Father-Daughter Incest." *American Journal of Psychiatry* 138(7):967–970.

Hines, P., and N. Boyd-Franklin. 1982. "Black Families." In *Ethnicity and Family Therapy,* pp. 84–108. Edited by M. Goldrick, J. Pearce, and J. Giordnao. New York: Guilford Press.

James, J., and J. Meyerding. 1977. "Early Sexual Experiences and Prostitution." *American Journal of Psychiatry* 134:1381–1385.

Kercher, G., and M. McShane. 1984. "The Prevalence and Child Sexual Abuse Victimization in an Adult Sample of Texas Residents." *Child Abuse and Neglect* 8:495–501.

Kitano, H. 1985. *Race Relations.* Englewood Cliffs, N.J.: Prentice-Hall.

Landis, J. 1956. "Experiences of 500 Children with Adult Sexual Deviants." *Psychiatric Quarterly,* supplement 30:91–109.

Lauderdale, M., A. Valivnas, and R. Anderson. 1980. "Race, Ethnicity, and Child Maltreatment: An Empirical Analysis." *Child Abuse and Neglect* 7:163–169.

Lustig, N., J. Dresser, S. Spelling, and T. Murray. 1966. "Incest: a Family Group Survival Pattern." *Archives of General Psychiatry* 14:31–40.

Mayer, A. 1983. *Incest: A Treatment Manual for Therapy with Victims, Spouses, and Offenders.* Holmes Beach, Fla.: Learning Publications.

Meiselman, K. 1978. *Incest: A Psychological Study of Causes and Effects with Treatment Recommendation.* San Francisco: Jossey-Bass Publishers.

Mrazek, P., and H. Kempe. 1981. *Sexually Abused Children and Their Families.* New York: Pergamon.

Norton, E. 1985. "Restoring the Traditional Black Family." *New York Times Magazine,* June 2, pp. 43, 79, 93, 96, 98.

Parke, R., and C. Collmer. 1975. "Child Abuse: An Interdisciplinary Analysis." In *Child Development Research.* Vol. 5. Edited by M. Hetherington. Chicago: University of Chicago Press.

Peters, S. 1976. "Children Who Are Victims of Sexual Assault and the Psychology of Offenders." *American Journal of Psychotherapy* 30:398–421.

Pierce, R. 1984. "Child Pornography: A Hidden Dimension of Child Abuse." *Child Abuse and Neglect* 8:483–493.

Pierce, R., and L. Pierce. 1984. "Race as a Factor in the Sexual Abuse of Children." *Social Work Research and Abstracts* 20:9–14.

Pinderhughes, E. 1982. "Afro-American Families and the Victim System." In *Ethnicity and Family Therapy,* pp. 108–122. Edited by M. Goldrick, J. Pearce, and J. Giordano. New York: Guilford Press.

Porter, R., ed. 1984. *Child Sexual Abuse within the Family.* New York: Tavistock Publications.

Proctor, E., and L. Davis. 1983. "Minority Content in Social Work Education: A Question of Objectives." *Journal of Education for Social Work* 19:85–93.

Rogers, C., and T. Terry. 1984. "Clinical Intervention with Boy Victims of Sexual Abuse." In *Victims of Sexual Aggression: Treatment of Children, Women, and Men.* Edited by I. Stuart and S. Greer. New York: Van Nostrand Reinhold.

Rosenfeld, A. 1979. "Incidence of a History of Incest among 18 Psychiatric Patients." *American Journal of Psychiatry* 136:791–795.

Scherzer, L., and P. LaLa. 1980. "Sexual Offenses Committed against Children." *Clinical Pediatrics* 19:679–685.

Sgroi, S. 1982. *Handbook of Clinical Intervention in Child Sexual Abuse.* Lexington, Mass.: Lexington Books.

Spiegal, J. 1982. "An Ecological Model of Ethnic Families." In *Ethnicity and Family Therapy,* pp. 31–51. Edited by M. Goldrick, J. Pearce, and J. Giordano. New York: Guilford Press.

Staples, R. 1982. *Black Masculinity: The Black Male's Role in American Society.* San Francisco: Black Scholar Press.

Steinmetz, S., and M. Straus, eds. 1974. *Violence in the Family.* New York: Dodd, Mead.

Summit, R., and J. Kryso. 1981. "Sexual Abuse of Children: A Clinical Spectrum." In *Administration of Children and Youth, National Center on Child Abuse.* U.S. DHHS Publication OHDS 73–30161. Washington, D.C.: Government Printing Office.

Terrell, M. 1977. Identifying the Sexually Abused Child in a Medical Setting." *Health and Social Work* 2:112–130.

Tierney, K., and D. Corwin. 1983. "Exploring Intrafamilial Child Sexual Abuse: A Systems Approach." In *The Dark Side of Families: Current Family Violence Research.* Edited by D. Finkelhor, R. Gelles, G. Hotaling, and M. Straus. Beverly Hills: Sage.

U.S. Congress. House of Representatives. Hearing before the Subcommittee on Children and Youth. 1973. 93d Cong., 1st sess.

———. Hearing Before the Subcommittee on Crime. 1977. 95th Cong., 1st sess.

U.S. Department of Health and Human Services. 1979a. *National Analysis of Official Child Neglect and Abuse Reporting 1977.* DHHS Publication OHDS 80-30232. Washington, D.C.: Government Printing Office.

———. 1979b. *National Analysis of Official Child Neglect and Abuse Reporting 1979.* DHHS Publication OHDS 81-30232. Washington, D.C.: Government Printing Office.

———. 1980. *National Analysis of Official Child Neglect and Abuse Reporting 1978.* DHHS Publication OHDS 8030271. Washington, D.C.: Government Printing Office.

———. 1981. *National Study of the Incidence and Severity of Child Abuse and Neglect: Study Findings.* Publication (OHDS) 81-03026. Washington, D.C.: Government Printing Office.

Vinokur-Kaplan, D., and A. Hartman. 1986. "A National Profile of Child Welfare Workers and Supervisors." *Child Welfare* 65:323–336.

Weinberg, K. 1955. *Incest Behavior.* New York: Citadel.

Williams, G., and J. Money, eds. 1980. Introduction to *Traumatic Abuse and Neglect at Home.* Baltimore: Johns Hopkins University Press.

Wyatt, G. 1985. "The Sexual Abuse of Afro-American and White American Women in Childhood." *Child Abuse and Neglect* 9:507–519.

Yorukoglu, A., and J. Kemph. 1966. "Children Not So Severely Damaged by Incest with Parents." *Journal of the American Academy of Child Psychiatry.* 51:111–124.

II
Interspousal Violence

6

African-American Women in Violent Relationships: An Exploration of Cultural Differences

Jo-Ellen Asbury

S hortly before completing this chapter, I attended the nineteenth annual convention of the Association of Black Psychologists, where comments made by a number of researchers and scholars, notably Na'im Akbar and Wade Nobles, reminded me of my original reason for undertaking this work. In essence, they proposed that in order to affect positively the lives of African-American people, one must operate from an appropriate theoretical perspective based on their background and experiences. This chapter, part of that larger agenda, examines the experiences of African-American women in violent relationships from an Afrocentric perspective.

Approaches to the Study of African-American Families

Literature on African-American families leaves the surveyor confused at best about the nature and dynamics of these families. Some researchers portray the African-American family as a "tangle of pathology" (Moynihan 1965), an abnormal, female-dominated environment offering little stability and structure. Others portray it as a supportive, nurturing unit, a refuge from the harsh realities of a discriminating society (Barnes 1980; Nobles 1974; Stack 1974). These diverse perceptions apparently result from different approaches to the subject, which Dodson (1981), Johnson (1981), and Staples (1974) have identified.

Early in the history of this field, states Staples (1974), certain African-American scholars, the poverty acculturationists, attempted to highlight

Special thanks to Sharon Singleton for reading earlier drafts and catching typographical errors and for typing (and retyping) the reference list. Thanks also to Yvonne Williams for listening at each stage of the project, even to random thoughts.

the similarities between African-American and European-American families. As a result of this original position, or perhaps because of their view of themselves as liberals, a number of European-American researchers approached the study of African-American families with the assumption that it was appropriate to use European-American norms in studying these families. When African-American families were assessed by European-American standards, however, the researchers concluded all too frequently that African-American families were different and therefore deviant. The Moynihan (1965) study is an example of this "pathological" (Staples 1974), "culturally deviant," or "ethnocentric" (Dodson 1981) perspective. Among the more negative conclusions drawn by Moynihan (1965) and others is the idea that African-American families are female-dominated environments lacking in structure and stability. Moynihan laments the need for male role models for young African-American males and strongly urges military service as a means of correcting this deficiency.[1]

In response to studies like Moynihan's, other researchers approached the study of African-American families from a reactive (Staples 1974) perspective. Studies from this perspective (Willie and Greenblatt 1978) show that the African-American family has been portrayed as matrifocal because (to give one explanation) this egalitarian arrangement appears deviant from a Euro-American perspective (Nobles 1974). Staples even questions whether such standards are appropriate or realistic for European-American families.

A more appropriate approach to research on African-American families has been labeled "cultural variant" (Johnson 1981), "cultural relativity" (Dodson 1981), "black nationalist" (Staples 1974), or "Afrocentric" (Nobles 1974). This view assumes that African-American families are a function of a unique culture (Nobles 1974; Staples 1978) and should be studied within the context of that culture. In fact, Khatib et al. (1979) suggest that this is the only valid approach to the study of all aspects of African-American behavior. Within the Afrocentric perspective, one is forced to question the validity of mainstream spouse abuse literature regarding the experiences of African-American women.

Mainstream Spouse Abuse Literature

The literature on battered women shows that the experiences of non–European-American women have not been represented adequately. Current literature typically addresses the issue of ethnicity in one of three ways: by failing to mention the race of the women included (Flynn 1977; Roy 1982), by acknowledging that only European-American women are included (Bowker 1984; Steinmetz 1977), or by including some women of other ethnic groups but not in proportions comparable to their numbers in the national population (Hofeller 1982; Walker 1984). Two notable exceptions are essays that are not part of the mainstream behavioral science literature. White's (1985) work is used best as a self-help guide for African-American women, and Scarf's (1983) essay describes the experiences of Jewish women in violent relationships.

Any woman, regardless of color, needs shelter and counseling when she finds herself in an abusive relationship. That counseling is not likely to be effective if it is blind to color and the cultural experiences that go with it. As Thomas and Sillen (1972) write:

> "Color-blindness" is no virtue if it means denial of differences in the experience, culture, and psychology of black Americans or other Americans. . . . To ignore the formative influence of substantial differences in history and social existence is a monumental error. (P. 58)

Researchers have yet to investigate whether there are any issues unique to African-American women in violent relationships and, if so, what they are and how we can address them best. The purpose here is to explore those cultural differences and to identify some preliminary questions for investigation.

Straus (1977) defines battering according to the Wife Beating Index, comprised of the four most severe acts from the Physical Violence Index of the Conflict Resolution Scale: kicking, biting, or punching; beating up; threatening with a knife or a gun; and use of a knife or gun. The index excludes throwing objects, pushing, shoving, grabbing, or slapping. Most researchers, however, consider a broader range of acts to be abusive. Martin considers as battering any "deliberate, severe and repeated physical injury . . . with the minimal injury being severe bruising" (1976; quoted in Moore 1979, p. 8).

Moore (1979) suggests that physical battering is only one way in which a woman can be abused and points out that psychological abuse may also be part of a violent relationship. It has been suggested in a number of cases that the psychological abuse is even more damaging because psychological debilitation keeps women in these violent relationships (Walker 1979a, 1979b, 1983, 1984).

As Staples (1982) and Straus (1977) state, violence is very much part of the American way of life. The United States began through violent struggle and maintains itself through violence. The degree of violence so frequently displayed and even glamorized in the media shows general acceptance of violence as a legitimate means of accomplishing a goal. Social psychologists have long noted the effect of observing violence upon the subsequent use of violence by both children and adults (Bandura 1973; Bandura, Ross, and Ross 1963; Donnerstein and Berkowitz 1981). Therefore it is hardly surprising that violence as a vehicle for conflict resolution has permeated family interactions (Straus 1977).

In addition to this societal sanction, family violence is encouraged by the belief that outsiders should not intervene in family conflicts, probably a result of the general attitude that wives and children are a husband's property (Davidson 1977; Martin 1983). Shotland and Straw (1976) found that 65 percent of their subjects were willing to intervene when they thought a woman was being attacked by a stranger, but only 19 percent attempted to intervene when they thought the man and the woman were married. This view that family interactions are of no concern to outsiders, regardless of the nature of those interactions, exemplifies clearly how the use of violence in the family has been legitimized (Straus 1977).

Wives also engage in physical violence toward their husbands. Some researchers suggest that these acts occur as often as husbands abuse wives (Steinmetz 1977; Straus 1977), but others report that husbands abuse wives more frequently (Walker 1979b). As with statistics on wife abuse, however, one must consider whether many incidents of husband abuse go unreported. Steinmetz suggests that husband abuse goes unreported even more frequently than wife abuse because of societal expectations that males dominate women physically. Flynn (1977) and Straus (1977) suggest that when wives do engage in violence against their husbands, the acts are more frequent and more serious. Flynn indicates, for example, that wives are more likely than husbands to use weapons. In general, however, husbands seem to inflict more physical damage on their wives than wives on husbands (Steinmetz 1977).

The environment in which the husband was raised seems to be an important contributor to wife abuse (Roy 1982; Straus 1977; Walker 1979a, 1979b, 1983, 1984). Roy found that 81 percent of the batterers had been brought up in homes where the parents used violence toward each other, toward the children, or toward both. Studies have shown that the sex role socialization of both the batterer and the victim is also an important aspect of the home environment (Walker 1979a, 1984). Typically both partners have been raised with traditional views. As a result, many of these individuals believe that husbands have the right to dominate their families, even if this domination includes the use of violence. Some even believe that the use of violence is manly.

We must be cautious in interpreting any data that claim to indicate the frequency with which women are abused. Because of the shame and the stigma involved, many of these incidents go unreported. Further, some women may be unsure what degree of violence is "normal" and what is not (Straus 1977; Walker 1979a). Accounting for these limitations in the available data, experts estimate that such violence occurs in 50 to 60 percent of all families (Flynn 1977; Steinmetz 1977; Straus 1977; Walker 1979b).

Although most sources indicate that wife abuse is equally likely across all demographic indicators (Flynn 1977; Walker 1979b), others suggest that women in certain groups are battered more frequently (Bowker, 1984; Straus, Gelles, and Steinmetz 1980). Straus et al. report that wife abuse is 400 percent more likely among African-Americans than in any other racial group. Bowker (1984) also suggests that wife abuse is more likely among African-Americans and the poor but offers no evidence for this claim. When researchers control for social class, however, wife abuse seems to be less common among middle-income African-Americans than among middle-income European-Americans (Cazenave and Straus 1979). One possible explanation for these conflicting findings is that many of the studies that found ethnic and social class differences failed to account for differential reporting across these groups. Middle- and upper-class women (who are more likely to be European-American) have greater financial resources at their disposal. Therefore they are more able to afford private physicians and to obtain safe shelter away from the home. In such cases, public officials and social agencies are less likely to become aware of the incidents.

Among women who are involved in battering relationships, some general traits and characteristics can be identified. One should not conclude, however, that only individuals who conform to a specific profile are involved in violent relationships. Roy (1982), who conducted an analysis of 4,000 victims of wife abuse in the New York City area, found that the majority of the women (66.2 percent) were married to their abusers. Most had children between the ages of 1 and 12, though nearly 30 percent had children outside this range. Seventy-five percent of the abusers in Roy's study held blue-collar jobs, which accounted for nearly 45 percent of the family financial resources. On the average, the victim's employment accounted for 30 percent of the family's resources. Contrary to popular myth, Roy found that abusers were not atypical social deviants; only 10 percent had any past criminal record, and most of these were for past wife abuse convictions.

Within families where women are abused, Roy's data indicate that the majority of women describe violence as occurring "often"; another 30 percent describe the violence as "occasional." Although Roy does not quantify these labels, her four-point scale is anchored by "very often" (two to seven times per week) and "less often" (less than once a month). Hofeller (1982) examined the frequency of violent episodes during the most and least violent periods of the relationship. During the least violent period, the largest percentage of women reported that the violence occurred about once a month (22 percent). During the most violent period, the largest percentage of women reported that the violence occurred once a week (16 percent) or unpredictably (16 percent).

Walker (1979a, 1979b, 1983, 1984) suggests that a cyclic pattern can be identified in battering relationships. Her "cycle of violence" theory includes three phases: tension building, in which tension escalates gradually, making the woman increasingly uncomfortable in anticipation of the impending abuse; acute battering, in which the wife is the victim of severe physical and verbal abuse; and loving contrition, in which the man apologizes for his behavior, professes his love, and promises that it will never happen again. Sixty-five percent of the women Walker (1984) interviewed reported a tension-building phase before the battering incidents described, and 58 percent described a loving-contrition phase after the incidents. These figures suggest some general support for the external validity of the model.

When violence does occur, Roy reports that the abuse is more often physical (60.8 percent). Other common forms of violence are verbal abuse (19.0 percent), physical abuse with a weapon (18.0 percent), and sexual abuse (2.2 percent). Roy reports that the most frequent injuries are bruises (49.8 percent) and black eyes (17.8 percent).

In descending order of importance, Roy lists the following factors as catalysts to specific violent episodes: arguments over money; jealousy, questioning the wife's fidelity; sexual problems; alcohol; disputes over the children, in which the husband seems to resent the responsibility; husband's unemployment; wife's desire for outside employment; pregnancy; and wife's use of alcohol or drugs.

Researchers have been able to identify a number of factors that keep women in these abusive relationships. These factors may be categorized as external and internal or psychological. External factors include the concrete aspects of the woman's situation that she did not bring about. They represent her observable reality. Women may remain because they are economically dependent upon their abuser, especially if there are children; many batterers oppose their wives' working outside the home. The lack of sufficient social support from family, friends, and social institutions may also contribute to keeping women in violent relationships. In many cases, the husband has isolated the wife intentionally from family and friends so that those options are no longer open to her (Martin 1983; Walker 1979a).

In addition to these external realities, internal or psychological paralysis may keep women in violent relationships. Many women remain out of fear that if they leave, their mates may find them and retaliate. Studies indicate that such concern is justified in the light of the number of abusers who pursue their wives after they leave. Many abused women also believe that the violence is temporary. Further, an abused woman is likely to retain some positive feelings for her abuser and to feel that he needs her help in reforming. Some women may believe that all marriages are violent; therefore they believe that their own experiences are not unusual. All of these beliefs (Walker 1979a) contribute to the relationship and help justify the woman's remaining.

Seligman's theory of learned helplessness has also been helpful in explaining why women remain (Walker 1977a, 1984). These women may have come to believe that they cannot survive without their mates' financial and emotional support.

From this review of the spouse abuse literature, it appears that three general types of issues emerge regarding the concerns of battered women. One issue is the factors that influence why the violence occurs and the nature of that violence. Researchers have been able to develop general profiles of violent relationships and of specific violent incidents. A second issue is the factors that influence whether the woman obtains the help she needs. Third is the question of changing the woman's situation, either by removing her and terminating the relationship or by modifying her abuser's behavior (primarily) and her own behavior so that she will no longer accept abuse (secondarily).

Spouse Abuse Literature with an Afrocentric Perspective

Within these three categories, we must highlight some aspects of the special experiences of African-American women. In the light of these experiences, it is impossible to address the needs of African-American women on the basis of the knowledge available from mainstream spouse abuse literature.

Contributors to Violence and the Nature of Violence

Research shows that 81 percent of batterers came from violent homes (Roy 1982). Further, both batterers and victims are often the products of traditional sex role socialization. Although present spouse abuse research has not included African-Americans in sufficient numbers to assess the cross-cultural validity of that figure, researchers have investigated the nature of sex role socialization in African-American families.

Lewis (1975) proposes that the male-female duality that dominates the sex role socialization in European-American families is not typical in African-American families. In keeping with their African roots, Lewis suggests that unity and synthesis of these roles is more typical: "The black child, to be sure, distinguishes between males and females, but unlike the white child he is not inculcated with standards which polarize behavioral expectations according to sex" (Lewis 1975, p. 228).

Findings reported by Allen (1981) serve to exemplify this flexibility and fluidity. Allen interviewed African-American and European-American mothers and fathers and their adolescent sons. Although African-American parents paralleled their racial counterparts in some traditional behaviors, African-American mothers rated their husbands as more involved in child care than European-American mothers rated theirs. Cole (1979), however, reports relative traditionalism in child rearing among African-American men and women. Whether these differences translate into differences in violent relationships cannot be determined with the data currently available.

Roy's trend analysis suggests that economic difficulty is the factor that most often triggers violent episodes. Focusing on the African-American experience suggests that this factor may be even more problematic for African-American families (see table 6-1). Hare (1979) outlines the ways in which African-American males are the victims of psycho-socio-economic suppression relative to African-American women and European-American women and men. Hare reviews national data sets showing that African-American males consistently earn less than European-American males. In addition, although African-American males earn more than females of their race (implying mates or potential mates), the difference is less than among European-Americans. As Hare (1979) and Hampton (1980) indicate, racial discrimination has prevented African-American males in many cases from fulfilling the traditional male role of head of household and provider. Thus, to the extent that African-American males internalize mainstream standards for appropriate masculine roles (the focus of some debate), they are confronted with the conflict between what they are and what they have been led to believe they should be.

Merton (1949) identifies two important elements of social and cultural structures: (1) culturally defined goals, purposes, and interests and (2) structure, which defines, regulates, and controls acceptable modes of attaining those goals. Merton proposes that when the institutional means for attaining those cultural goals are not available (anomie), an individual must find alternative means of adapting. Of the five ways in which Merton (1949) suggests that individuals adapt to cultural goals and to institutional means for achieving them, four represent deviations from the normative structure for goal attainment:

1. Innovation: Finding alternative means of achieving the same cultural goals.

Table 6-1
Analysis of European-American Catalysts of Violent Episodes from an Afrocentric Perspective

Catalysts of Specific Violent Episodes, in Descending Order of Importance[a]	*Analysis from an Afrocentric Perspective*
1. Arguments over money	Likely to be an even greater determinant, given the lower SES of most African-Americans
2. Questioning the wife's fidelity	No way to assess, but if Merton's (1948) methods of adaptation are valid, the male may be especially patriarchal in this area, one of his few spheres of influence
3. Sexual problems	No way to assess. No reason at this time to assume any differences
4. Alcohol use	Staples (1982) suggests that this is an important factor in African-American communities
5. Arguments over children	Would assume to be less of a determining factor, given the flexibility of family roles and tradition of celebrating children in African-American communities
6. Husband's unemployment	As with arguments over money, likely to be an even greater determination of abuse among African-Americans
7. Wife's work	No way to assess but would assume to be a less important determining factor because African-American women have long been employed outside the home.
8. Pregnancy	No way to assess. Traditional importance of children may make less problematic, but economic stressors may make it more so
9. Wife's use of alcohol	Would assume, as with alcohol use, the stress of the lower Socioeconomic status, combined with racial discrimination, would make this equally problematic

[a]From Roy 1982.

2. Ritualism: Diminishing aspirations to a point at which the individual can attain the goals.

3. Retreatism: Complete withdrawal from cultural goals and aspirations.

4. Rebellion: Seeking to replace cultural goals with a new social structure.

Cazenave (1981) and Taylor (1981) have applied Merton's modes of adaptation to behaviors of African-American males. Both scholars suggest that when African-American males are unable to achieve cultural goals of masculinity through traditional means, innovation is common. These innovative strategies may include hypersexuality, concern with expressive styles of speech, dress, and appearance, and toughness or violence.

Both authors also suggest that some degree of retreatism and rebellion occur through drug and alcohol use.

Staples (1982) suggests that the explanation of violence among African-American males as a means of attaining masculinity is somewhat limited, but he does not succeed in discounting the idea totally. He points out that in general, African-Americans are overrepresented in violent crime statistics, probably as a function of the stressful conditions under which they live; the most obvious of these stressors are relatively low socioeconomic status and large family size. Staples also suggests that children growing up in African-American communities may be exposed to violence at earlier ages than children of other cultures and may come to accept violence as a natural part of their lives. Staples identifies this acceptance of physical violence as a contributing factor to marital violence. He does not deny, however, that the African-American male's inability to maintain a superior male position (given the social structure) may also contribute.

This state of anomie among African-American males represents one aspect of the African-American experience that has not been considered in mainstream spouse abuse literature. Such consideration is important not only because it represents a potential causal factor that has yet to be investigated but also because it may play a part in the African-American woman's response to being battered.

Alcohol and/or drug use by each of the partners is identified as a catalyst for violent episodes. Although the impact of substance use on family violence among African-Americans needs empirical investigation, preliminary evidence suggests that it may be a serious contributor.

As another contributing factor, Roy also lists arguments over children and pregnancy. Again, because this question has yet to be addressed specifically, only speculation is possible. On the basis of research by Lewis (1975), who has implied flexibility in family roles, and by others, who have attested to the African-American tradition of valuing children, one might believe that this issue would not be as important in trying to predict violent episodes among African-Americans. When one also considers the additional economic stress they represent, however, children (especially those still unborn) may increase the likelihood of violence among African-Americans.

Because African-American women have traditionally been part of the paid labor force, one would not expect the wife's employment to be a major predictor of family violence. If the woman's mate has internalized European-American standards of masculinity, however, he may resent her working. In those cases, it would be an important predictor.

Finally, Roy suggests that questions about the wife's fidelity and sexual problems may be important contributors. On the basis of the available information, it is difficult to assess the importance of these variables relative to violence among African-Americans.

Walker's cycle of violence theory (1979a, 1984) outlines the pattern of abuse; Roy's data describe the nature of the abuse. Although the validity of these findings relative to African-Americans has yet to be determined, the mechanism is in place. Initially there seems no evidence to suggest that any major differences would emerge, but this null assumption should not deter further investigation.

Obtaining Help

For a battered woman to be helped, help must be available; she must know that it is available and how to gain access to it; and she must decide to use it. In the case of African-American women, some special factors must be considered relative to each of these considerations.

Just as other public services are in short supply in African-American communities, there may be inadequate numbers of domestic violence shelters in those communities. Thus the tendency of African-American women to seek shelter outside their own neighborhoods must also be addressed.[2]

Asbury (1985) conducted a preliminary study of shelter use. In keeping with basic laws of probability, she assumed that the percentage of African-Americans among shelter clients would parallel the percentage of African-Americans in the population of that city, county, or state. Using data from domestic violence shelters across Ohio, the study concluded that comparisons of the state, county, or city level were not especially informative, as inconsistent patterns emerged in the analyses. Post hoc investigations suggest that the analyses at those levels may not have been specific enough; comparisons of different shelters within the same city revealed quite different proportions of African-American and non–African-American clients. As the percentages in table 6–2 suggest, the effect of neighborhood or community cannot be overlooked.

Table 6–2
African-American Clients at Domestic Violence Shelters in Cities with Two Shelters

City	Percent Black in City Population	Shelter A	Shelter B
City 1	33.82%	4.00%	37.00%
City 2	43.80	47.00	61.00
City 3	22.30	22.00	24.00

Source: Asbury 1985.

One resource that typically has been available to African-American women, perhaps to a greater extent than to women of other cultures, is the extended family. As Flynn (1977) and Bowker (1984) suggest, battered women, regardless of culture, are likely to seek support and guidance from family and friends. This predilection is likely to be even stronger among African-American women, given the longstanding tradition of extended families and social support in African-American communities. Hill (1972), Nobles (1974), and Stack (1974) are only a few of the many scholars and researchers who have written about this support system. McAdoo (1980) and Manns (1981) have shown that it exists not only among the lower classes but among middle-class African-Americans as well. This option may not be advantageous, however, because most family members and friends lack the professional training necessary to handle such crises. Certainly they lack the objectivity that someone outside the family network is likely to possess.

Beyond questions of whether appropriate help is available, the women must choose to take advantage of the help. The African-American woman's special experience results in different considerations in making that choice. Again, Durkheim's concept of anomie is useful (Parsons 1960). Hemmons (1980) assesses the feelings of anomie in African-American and European-American nonbattered women and finds a slightly higher feeling of anomie among the African-American women. Though small, this difference suggests a greater feeling of social isolation among African-American women, which may influence their decision to seek out domestic violence shelters. Because they are African-Americans in a society dominated by European-Americans, they may feel that they will not be understood or even welcomed at shelters outside their immediate community.

An African-American woman's decision to seek help may also be influenced by her feelings about her abuser. Although studies have shown that battered women of all ethnic backgrounds may be reluctant to reveal their abuse out of concern for their abusers (Walker 1979a), this may be an even greater consideration among African-American women. Cazenave (1981) and Hare (1979) have suggested that African-American males are in a more vulnerable position than other males relative to the dominant culture. Being aware of this suppression, as Hare describes it, may make African-American women reluctant to expose them to more ridicule.

An African-American woman may also be more reluctant to bring attention to her situation if she has internalized common stereotypes about African-American women. In the media and in popular literature, these women are portrayed as everything from sexual temptresses to ugly mammies, from the sturdy bridges who hold together the race (and therefore the community) to emasculating matriarchs who are responsible for the instability of the family (and therefore the community) because they drive away their men with their domination. Of particular interest to the present discussion is the image of African-American women as a source of strength and independence. To gain this impression, one has only to survey the titles of some recent publications about African-American women, such as *Sturdy Black Bridges* (Bell, Parker, and Guy-Sheftall 1979) and . . . *But Some of Us Are Brave* (Hull, Scott, and Smith 1982).

An African-American woman's decision to seek help may also depend on whether she has internalized some of these stereotypes. While many African-American women have had to exhibit strength and independence for their own survival, this image may be problematic for those women who find themselves in violent relationships (White 1980). When an abused woman believes that strength and independence are expected of her, she may be more reluctant to call attention to her situation, feeling that she should be able to handle it on her own; she may deny the seriousness of her situation. Thus she may remain immobile, hampered by her belief in inner resources she may not possess.

Confronted continually with European-American standards of beauty and femininity, an African-American woman might well conclude that she is unattractive. This possibility, combined with recent estimates that there are four African-American women for every African-American male (Braitwaite 1981), may make her less likely to risk endangering the relationship by exposing the batterer.

Changing the Situation

Finally, we must consider unique aspects of the African-American experience in attempts to change the battered woman's situation. Most of the mainstream literature on this question focuses on ways of inducing the woman to end the relationship. Certainly this is often the only alternative. The African-American woman, however, has typically been led to believe that it is her responsibility to maintain the family, regardless of the costs to herself; thus she may be likely to remain and do nothing (White 1985). She may also be more interested than women of other ethnic groups in working with a professional toward modifying her abuser's behavior. These differences must be considered in designing a therapeutic approach in working with African-American women.

Other factors, however, suggest that it may be less difficult for an African-American woman to walk away from an abusive relationship. Though typically they occupy the lowest-paying positions, African-American women have historically participated in the paid labor force in greater proportions than European-American women. Combined with the image of strength and independence, this concrete indicator of her ability to support herself and her children may facilitate her leaving. Obviously this hypothesis contradicts the notion that the image of strength and independence is debilitating and raises yet another question for future study. Does the internalization of these images immobilize the African-American woman or empower her? Because it is likely that both possibilities occur, what are the differentiating variables or conditions? Counseling African-American women without this knowledge is not likely to be appropriate or effective.

Summary and Conclusions

A number of questions have emerged relative to the experiences of African-American women in violent relationships. Research is needed to address more completely the factors that are believed to contribute to wife abuse among African-Americans, specifically the relationship (if any) between sex role socialization and violence and the validity of the specific catalysts reviewed. One particularly interesting question is whether African-American males truly subscribe to European-American standards of masculinity.

Initially we must determine whether African-American women have reasonable access to shelters and whether they are more or less likely to use shelters outside their own communities. Other factors may also influence the decision to seek help, including the impact of common images of African-American women; these factors must be assessed. Finally, we must examine the extent to which African-American women turn to family and friends in the event of a violent episode and assess the adequacy of these resources.

For African-American women, leaving the relationship may be more difficult than for other women, though it is certainly a difficult decision for all women. Given the "scarcity" of African-American men, women may be less willing to consider this option. Any counseling with African-American women must consider these added constraints. Again, the common images of these women may have an impact that needs to be considered.

It is difficult to rank these questions according to importance for a specific research agenda. Different cases and situations dictate different strategies. In general, however, it would seem that issues regarding the availability and adequacy of help for African-American women would be most essential. Once the immediacy of a woman's situation has been addressed, the next step is to examine questions about changing the situation and to learn enough about the contributing factors to have a long-term impact upon violence in African-American families.

Notes

1. Although this European-American perspective focuses upon the "pathologies" of African-American families, it actually suggests that African-American women occupy a more favorable position than European-American women regarding physical abuse. How can a woman be abused if there is no male head of household or if she is in control? This perspective certainly does not imply that the matriarchial view of the African-American family has any validity, but it is amusing to note that an intended negative results in a positive.

2. This question is essential because most published studies of battered women tend to be based upon shelter clients. If African-American women are not represented adequately in these data, meaningful information about their experiences will never be disseminated.

References

Allen, Walter R. 1981. "Moms, Dads and Boys: Race and Sex Differences in the Socialization of Male Children." In L.E. Gary, ed., *Black Men*, pp. 99–114. Beverly Hills: Sage.

Asbury, Jo-Ellen. 1985 "Black Women in Violent Relationships: A Preliminary Analysis of Shelter Utilization." Paper presented at Great Lakes Colleges Association Eleventh Annual Women's Studies Conference, Dayton, Ohio.

Bandura, Albert. 1973. *Aggression: A Social Learning Analysis*. Englewood Cliffs, N.J.: Prentice-Hall.

Bandura, A., D. Ross, and S. Ross. 1963. "Imitation of Film-Mediated Aggressive Models." *Journal of Abnormal and Social Psychology* 66:3–11.

Barnes, Edward J. 1980. "The Black Community as the Source of Positive Self-Concept for Black Children: A Theoretical Perspective." In *Black Psychology*, pp. 106–130. 2d ed. Edited by Reginald L. Jones. New York: Harper & Row.

Beale, F. 1978. "Double Jeopardy: To Be Black and Female." In *The Black Family: Essays and Studies*, pp. 118–123. Edited by Robert Staples. Belmont, Calif.: Wadsworth.

Bell, R.P., B.J. Parker, and B. Guy-Sheftall. 1979. *Sturdy Black Bridges*. Garden City, N.Y.: Anchor Books.

Bowker, Lee H. 1984. "Coping with Wife Abuse: Personal and Social Networks." In *Battered Women and Their Families*, pp. 168–191. Edited by Albert R. Roberts. New York: Springer.

Braitwaite, R.L. 1981. "Interpersonal Relations between Black Males and Black Females." In *Black Men*, pp. 83–97. Edited by Lawrence E. Gary. Beverly Hills: Sage.

Cazenave, Noel A. 1981. "Black Men in America: The Quest for 'Manhood'." In *Black Families*, pp. 176–185. Edited by Harriette P. McAdoo. Beverly Hills: Sage.

Cazenave, Noel, and Murray A. Straus. 1979. "Race Class, and Network Embeddedness and Family Violence." *Journal of Comparative Family Studies* 10:281–300.

Cole, O.J. 1979. "Scale Constriction in the Assessment of Sex-Role Stereotypes among Minorities." In *Research Directions of Black Psychologists,* pp. 57–73. Edited by A. Wade Boykin et al. Beverly Hills: Sage.

Davidson, T. 1977. "Wifebeating: A Recurring Phenomenon throughout History." In *Battered Women,* pp. 2–23. Edited by Maria Roy. New York: Van Nostrand Reinhold.

Dodson, Jualynne. 1981. "Conceptualization of Black Families." In *Black Families,* pp. 23–36. Edited by Harriette P. McAdoo. Beverly Hills: Sage.

Donnerstein, E., and L. Berkowitz. 1981. "Victim Reactions in Aggressive Erotic Films as a Factor in Violence against Women." *Journal of Personality and Social Psychology* 47:710–724.

Flynn, J.P. 1977. "Recent Findings Related to Wife Abuse." *Social Casework* 58, no. 1:13–20.

Hampton, Robert L. 1980. "Institutional Decimation, Marital Exchange, and Disruption in Black Families." *Western Journal of Black Studies* 4(2):132–139.

Hare, N. 1979. "The Relative Psycho-Socio-Economic Suppression of the Black Male." In *Reflections on Black Psychology,* pp. 359–381. Edited by William D. Smith et al. Washington, D.C.: University Press.

Hemmons, Willa Mae. 1980. "The Women's Liberation Movement: Understanding Black Women's Attitudes." In *The Black Woman,* pp. 285–289. Edited by La Frances Rodgers-Rose. Beverly Hills: Sage.

Hill, Robert. 1972. *The Strengths of Black Families.* New York: Emerson-Hall.

Hofeller, Kathleen H. 1982. *Social, Psychological and Situational Factors in Wife Abuse.* Palo Alto: R and E Research.

Hull, Gloria T., P.B. Scott, and B. Smith. 1982. *All the Women Are White, All the Blacks Are Men, But Some of Us Are Brave.* Old Westbury, N.Y.: Feminist Press.

Johnson, Leanor B. 1981. "Perspectives on Black Family Empirical Research: 1965–1978." In *Black Families,* pp. 87–102. Edited by Harriette P. McAdoo. Beverly Hills: Sage.

Khatib, S.M., D.P. McGee, N. Akbar, and W. Nobles. 1979. "Voodoo or I.Q.: An Introduction to African Psychology." In *Reflections on Black Psychology,* pp. 61–78. Edited by William D. Smith et al. Washington, D.C.: University Press of America.

Lewis, Diane K. 1975. "The Black Family: Socialization and Sex Roles." *Phylon* 36, no. 3:221–237.

McAdoo, Harriette P. 1980. "Black Mothers and the Extended Family Support Network." In *The Black Woman,* pp. 125–144. Edited by La Frances Rodgers-Rose. Beverly Hills: Sage.

Manns, Wilhelmina. 1981. "Support Systems of Significant Others in Black Families." In *Black Families,* pp. 238–251. Edited by Harriette P. McAdoo. Beverly Hills: Sage.

Martin, Del. 1983. *Battered Wives.* New York: Pocket Books.

Mathis, Arthur. 1978. "Contrasting Approaches to the Study of Black Families." *Journal of Marriage and the Family* 40:667–676.

Merton, Robert K. 1949. *Social Theory and Social Structure.* Glencoe, Ill.: Free Press.

Moore, D.M. 1979. "Editor's Introduction." In *Battered Women.* Edited by D.M. Moore. Beverly Hills: Sage Publications.

Moynihan, Daniel P. 1965. "The Tangle of Pathology." In *The Black Family: Essays and Studies*, pp. 3–13. Edited by Robert Staples. Belmont, Calif.: Wadsworth.

Nobles, Wade W. 1974. "Africanity: Its Role in Black Families." *Black Scholar* 9:10–17.

Parsons, Talcott. 1960. "Durkheim's Contributions to the Theory of Integration of Social Systems." In *Emile Durkheim, 1858–1917*, pp. 118–153. Edited by K.H. Wolff. Columbus: Ohio State University Press.

Prescott, S., and C. Letko. 1977. "Battered Women: A Social Psychological Perspective." In *Battered Women*, pp. 72–95. Edited by Maria Roy. New York: Van Nostrand.

Roy, Maria. 1982. "Four Thousand Partners in Violence: A Trend Analysis." In *The Abusive Partner*, pp. 17–35. Edited by Maria Roy. New York: Van Nostrand.

Scarf, M. 1983. "Marriages Made in Heaven? Battered Jewish Wives." In *On Being a Jewish Feminist*, pp. 51–67. Edited by Susannah Heschel. New York: Schocken.

Shotland, R.L., and M.K. Straw. 1976. "Bystander Response to an Assault: When a Man Attacks a Woman." *Journal of Personality and Social Psychology* 34, no. 5:990–999.

Stack, Carol B. 1974. *All Our Kin*. New York: Harper & Row.

Staples, Robert. 1974. "The Black Family Revisited: A Review and a Preview." *Journal of Social and Behavioral Sciences* 20:65–78.

———. 1982. *Black Masculinity*. San Francisco: Black Scholar Press.

Steinmetz, Suzanne K. 1977. "Wifebeating, Husbandbeating—A Comparison of the Use of Physical Violence between Spouses to Resolve Marital Fights." In *Battered Women*, pp. 63–72. Edited by Maria Roy. New York: Van Nostrand.

Straus, Murray A. 1977. "Wifebeating: How Common and Why?" *Victimology* 2, nos. 3–4:443–458.

Straus, Murray A., Richard J. Gelles, and Suzanne K. Steinmetz. 1980. *Behind Closed Doors: Violence in the American Family*. New York: Anchor.

Taylor, R.L. 1981. "Psychological Modes of Adaptation." In *Black Men*, pp. 141–158. Edited by Lawrence E. Gary. Beverly Hills: Sage.

Thomas, Alexander, and Samuel Sillen. 1972. *Racism and Psychiatry*. Secaucus, N.J.: Citadel.

Walker, Lenore E. 1979a. "How Battering Happens and How to Stop It." In *Battered Women*, pp. 59–78. Edited by D.M. Moores. Beverly Hills: Sage.

———. 1979b. *The Battered Woman*. New York: Harper & Row.

———. 1983. "Victimology and the Psychological Perspectives of Battered Women." *Victimology* 8, nos. 1–2:82–104.

———. 1984. *The Battered Woman Syndrome*. New York: Springer.

Wallwork, Ernest E. 1972. *Durkheim: Morality and Milieu*. Cambridge: Harvard University Press.

White, Evelyn C. 1985 *Chain, Chain, Change*. Seattle: Seal Press.

White, Joseph L. 1980. "Toward a Black Psychology." In *Black Psychology*, pp. 5–12. 2d ed. Edited by Reginald L. Jones. New York: Harper & Row.

Willie, Charles V., and Susan L. Greenblatt, 1978. "Four 'Classic' Studies of Power Relationships in Black Families: A Review and Look to the Future." *Journal of Marriage and the Family* 40:691–684.

7

See How They Run: Battered Women in Shelters in the Old Dominion

Maurice C. Taylor
Pamela V. Hammond

R esearchers have focused for some time on the link between familial relationships and homicide, but until recent years similar attention was not given to other aspects of family violence, such as spouse abuse. McCaghy (1985) suggests that only recently has spouse abuse become the focus of research and official action. Much of this research has concerned the battered woman or the laws affecting spousal relationships. Research on the former has often concentrated on the self-esteem of the abused woman and treatment modalities to improve her self-concept.

One of the most significant expressions of increased public and professional attention to the plight of battered women is the emergence of community shelters as temporary havens from intrafamilial violence, but research on the women who enter these shelters is quite limited. This chapter reports on a study that focused on the characteristics of women who have sought the services of community shelters in Virginia, with the purpose of developing a profile of sheltered women in that state.

Such a profile should not be construed as representative of all abused women in the Old Dominion. The characteristics of women who remain in abusive homes may differ significantly from those who seek shelter or require hospitalization as a result of their beating. A profile of adult females in community shelters is important, nonetheless, for two reasons: it delineates the characteristics of one group of likely victims of family violence, and it reveals what happens to the residents when they enter the shelter and where they go when they leave. Thus, research that uses shelter data presents an opportunity to explore not only the characteristics of battered women but also important organizational features of community shelters.

Inside Shelters for Battered Women

Other than their sex, little is known about the residents of community shelters, for two reasons. First, early European and U.S. laws tacitly (and in some instances openly) endorsed the right of men to punish their wives and children physically. At best, any legal restrictions on corporal punishment within families have focused on tempering excessive levels of violence rather than preventing men from abusing women and children. McCaghy (1985) writes: "Whatever the intent of nineteenth-century lawmakers and enforcers . . . one cannot deny that until recently legal reaction to wife beating was weak. Assuming that the victims found the courage to report offenses, police were reluctant to make arrests, district attorneys were reluctant to prosecute, and judges were reluctant to do more than issue warnings or impose trivial sentences" (p. 182).

The perception that battered women should be regarded as a social problem is scarcely more than a decade old. According to Walker (1978), the first shelter for battered women was begun in England as late as 1971. The concept of sheltering battered women did not take hold in the United States until 1975. Between 1975 and 1978 more than 170 community shelters for abused women opened in the United States (Tierney 1982). As a result, not enough time has passed for data on shelters to be collected and disseminated regularly.

Second, information on residents of these shelters is scarce because shelter personnel are often selective and secretive in releasing information about their operations. The covert nature of sheltering is reportedly necessary to protect the women and children from vengeful males. The address of the shelter may not be public knowledge. The business of the shelter—granting interviews, paying bills, soliciting funds and volunteers—is often conducted from an office located away from the shelter. Even the battered women themselves may not know the exact address of the shelter; when they request assistance, they may be steered first to the office and transported later to the shelter site. Like secular convents, community shelters tend to be cloistered societies of females and their children.

In addition, information such as the residents' demographic characteristics, marital status, and fertility is not generally released. This reluctance to give information about the women stems not only from the cloistered nature of community shelters but also from the transitory nature of sheltering. Because shelters are temporary havens, information on residents would be obsolete by the time it is released.

Yet it is important to review the characteristics of the residents of shelters because such information may reveal as much about the shelters as about those whom they serve. Kitsuse and Cicourel (1963) were among the first to argue that data collected by agencies serve better as indicators of organizational processes than as indexes of the actual behavior of an agency's clients. In addition, although there is considerable descriptive information on the services provided by shelters (Tierney 1982; U.S. Attorney General 1984) and abundant information on the personality (Wetzel and Ross 1983), self-esteem (Drake 1982), and treatment (Finley 1981; Lichtenstein 1981) of battered women, little empirical information is available on battered women who choose shelter to escape abuse. Clearly not every abused woman seeks shelter; some solicit help from friends, family, police, or hospitals. Developing a profile is the first step in determining whether the choice of assistance varies according to social characteristics.

Data on the exit status of the residents ought to reveal what happens to women once they leave the temporary safety of the shelter. Studies suggest that incidents of family violence such as assault, wife abuse, incest, and child beating tend to recur. Newman (1979, p. 147) describes the repetitive nature of wife beating as a cycle of violence in which women tolerate beatings over a long period, leave home to escape violence on more than one occasion, and ultimately return home to endure additional violence. Exit data derived from the shelters' statistics can provide empirical insight into the percentage of women who return home to abusive mates.

The Attorney General's Task Force on Family Violence calls community shelters "an important resource for a diverse group of victims of family violence who must leave home to escape life-threatening abuse and have nowhere else to go" (U.S. Attorney General 1984, p. 51). These shelters are typically nonprofit organizations staffed largely by community volunteers. Shelters extend a variety of services to victims of family violence, including emergency housing, telephone hot lines, support groups, counseling, recreation, employment assistance, permanent housing assistance, and referrals to substance abuse programs. Although these services are purportedly available to abused spouses regardless of sex, the services are used for the most part by women.

These shelters typically have limited resources and are unable to assist all who might request services. The task force report claims, however, that "shelter policies and practices should accommodate the varied religious, cultural and ethnic backgrounds of residents" (U.S. Attorney General 1984, p. 51). In the light of the limited resources of community shelters and the socioeconomic diversity of battered women, a review of statistics regarding shelters can indicate whether and how the shelters are meeting the task force mandate.

Data and Method

Data for this research were gathered from the Monthly Program Summary Report of the Family Violence Prevention Program. These reports were generated by thirty community shelters for battered women throughout Virginia. The shelters collected monthly statistics on their residents and submitted the data to the state's Department of Social Services.

This study examines cases spanning the twelve-month period from July 1984 through June 1985, the year for which the most recent and most complete data on residents of community shelters are held by the Department of Social Services. In addition, this was the only twelve-month period for which complete records existed. Before 1983, statewide record keeping on residents of these shelters was incomplete.

The statistics generated by community shelters are collected in four categories: requests for service, shelter services provided, demographic information on new residents admitted to shelters, and status of family units leaving the shelter. All data on the Monthly Program Summary Report are represented by frequencies. Thus the monthly reports generated by the local shelters, as well as the combined report by the state, consist of enumerating cases according to the four categories.

From July 1984 through June 1985, 11,323 abused women and 665 abused men (11,988 cases) contacted community shelters in Virginia to seek relief from family violence. (In order to make comparisons in the tables more apparent, frequencies have been converted to percentages.) This study concentrates on sheltered women and children rather than men because the number of abused men is small and because residence privileges in community shelters are unlikely to be extended to men, although abused men may sometimes request services.

Shelter Data and Social Research

Numerous problems face researchers interested in examining data on battered women as collected by local shelters and ultimately compiled by a state agency. Many of these problems are inherent in using official records as the data base for social research. Several authors (Merton 1966; Douglas 1967; Nettler 1984) have already cautioned researchers about the limitations of such records. For example, official records generally underestimate the total amount of behavior under study because not every case is discovered by or reported to the appropriate officials. Specifically, we can expect that in any given year, the total number of battered women in Virginia is much larger than the number reported by local shelters because many women tolerate the abuse in silence. Others rely on non-shelter personnel—other family members, hospital personnel, or the police—to escape battering.

In addition, Nettler (1984, p. 42) warns that official records are often subject to "reactive measures"—extraneous factors that cause an apparent change in the behavior under study. One of the most common reactive measures is the record-keeping or coding practices of officials. The problem is compounded when, as in this study, more than one official and more than one agency are responsible for recording the data.

The impact of record keeping on the reliability of these data becomes readily apparent to researchers interested in sheltered women. Because shelters are often coordinated by volunteers, the incidents of abuse, the number of residents identified, and any other recorded characteristics depend on volunteers' attention to detail. Specifically, although the shelters' residents include women and children, the actual number of residents in this study is considerably fewer than the combined number of women and children identified by shelter officials. We attribute this inconsistency to a lack of attention to this detail by the many, often transient, volunteers across the Old Dominion who were responsible for collecting this information and submitting it to the Department of Social Services.

One other important limitation of these data became evident as we attempted to develop our profile. Although four categories of information are collected routinely by shelters, no apparent effort is made to ensure that the information is comparable from category to category. The terminology changes by category and sometimes within the same category. In the requests for service category, for example, data are collected on abused women and abused men. In the next category, shelter services provided, records are kept on women, children, and family units. In the third category, demographic information, data are collected on new residents, adult residents, new children, and family units. The same demographic information, however, is not collected for each of these subcategories. New residents are identified by race, adult residents by fertility and age, new children by age, and family units by geographic location. The final category, status of family units leaving the shelter, does not identify any of the residents by demographic characteristics or by any of the terms found in the preceding categories. Instead frequencies are recorded for the stated destination of the women as they leave the shelter. The only common feature among these four categories of data is the month of the year.

We could do little to adjust for the problem of comparable terminology. Therefore, in order to present a profile that best reflects the data collected by the shelters, we have used the same terminology in all tables. The only other adjustment we made to these data was to collapse the monthly statistics into a seasonal format: spring (March, April, and May), summer (June, July, and August), fall (September, October, and November), and winter (December, January, and February).

Although we found numerous problems in the state's data on sheltered battered women, these problems do not prevent systematic analysis. Commenting on the weaknesses found in official data, Quinney (1965, p. 402) states, "The amount of error is probably not so great as to preclude analysis." In this instance, we felt that the available data were sufficient to develop a tentative profile of shelter residents in the state of Virginia.

Findings and Discussion

Studies generally reveal two important features about family violence. First, battering and abuse are likely to be seasonal. Steinmetz and Straus (1980) noted that frequency of family violence increases during the summer. Second, researchers have concluded that the battering of women is a cyclical and repetitive family affair (Walker 1978; Newman 1979). Walker (1978, p. 146) writes, "Preliminary data obtained on battered women indicate the existence of a cycle of battering behavior. Rather than constant or random occurrences of battering, there is a definite cycle that is repeated over time."

Admittance Status and Age

Most women were admitted to a shelter in spring or fall (table 7-1). A chi-square test ($p < .05$) on the seasonal variations in the number of women admitted to shelters reveals only a small likelihood that these differences were due to change. In every season, the majority of these women were newly admitted. Eighty-four percent of all sheltered women in the Old Dominion that year were admitted for the first time. Only 16 percent of those housed in community shelters had been battered and sheltered on at least one other occasion. In contrast to the newly admitted women, readmitted women were somewhat more likely to find shelter in summer or winter.

It would be tempting to interpret the differences between the newly admitted and the readmitted women as due solely to their decisions about when to run and what constitutes a safe haven. Evidence suggests, however, that readmitting previously battered women to community shelters may have some limitations. Walker (1978, pp. 160–162), for example, acknowledges that the children of battered women, particularly adolescents, present special problems for community shelters because the children often display patterns of violence similar to those at home. Accordingly, Walker writes, "Other children, especially adolescents, engage in various acting-out behaviors that make communal living in cramped quarters a horror" (1978, p. 161). Thus, because their children are older and may pose additional problems for the women and the younger children already housed in the shelter, women who have been admitted previously to a local shelter may be encouraged to see other havens. Finally, a chi-square test ($p < .05$) on the seasonal variations among readmitted women reveals no statistical significance.

In summary, these data are consistent with other research pointing to a seasonal pattern in family violence. The data in table 7–1 also offer cautious support for the idea that family violence is repetitive because at least 16 percent of the women had previously sought shelter. We believe, however, that these data measure the shelters' response to battered women more accurately than the incidence of battered women in Virginia.

Table 7–2 shows the seasons of admission and the ages of the women admitted to shelters in Virginia. The age categories are those used by the

Table 7–1
Percentages of Sheltered Women, by Admittance Status and Season

		Admittance Status	
Season	N	New	Readmit
Spring	433	87.2	12.7
Summer	354	80.2	19.7
Fall	442	84.3	15.6
Winter	388	83.2	16.7
Total	1,617	83.9	16.0

Table 7–2
Percentages of Sheltered Women, by Age and Season

		Age				
Season	N	Under 18	18–29	30–45	46–60	60 or Over
Spring	507	2.1	57.0	36.0	4.1	0.5
Summer	318	1.8	54.0	39.3	4.7	—
Fall	425	1.1	61.6	31.7	4.0	1.4
Winter	368	1.3	54.0	38.5	5.4	0.5
Total	1,618	1.6	56.9	36.1	4.5	0.6

shelters. These data illustrate that sheltered women ranged in age from under 18 to over 60, but the largest percentage were relatively young. In each season, more than half the sheltered women were between the ages of 18 and 29. With the exception of those admitted in the fall, slightly more than one-third of the women were between the ages of 30 and 45. Overall, almost 57 percent of the total number were between the ages of 18 and 29; 36 percent were between the ages of 30 and 45.

A close review of table 7-2 reveals that the women between the ages of 30 and 60 were more likely to be sheltered in summer and winter, and those between the ages of 18 and 29 were more likely to find shelter in the spring and the fall. These findings, although statistically small aberrations, are nonetheless consistent with the data on admittance status in table 7-1 if it is assumed that women who are readmitted to a shelter are older, as a group, than women admitted for the first time. Thus, tables 7-1 and 7-2 reveal that older women and women who were previously admitted to a shelter are more likely than younger newly admitted women to find shelter in the summer and the fall. Although this idea cannot be tested with these data, it does offer a plausible link to the data collected only in discrete categories by Virginia's Department of Social Services.

Race of Shelter Residents

As an example of the problems with data collected in discrete categories, the Department of Social Services makes little effort to compare categories of sheltered women by a common variable such as age, race, or sex. The data on the race of the sheltered were collected on all residents. The department made no effort to identify the race of the women. Thus, for this analysis, we were forced to assume that black women and white women are accompanied to community shelters by approximately similar numbers of children.

Table 7-3 presents data on the race of sheltered residents. In every season, white women and children made up two-thirds or more of the

Table 7-3
Percentages of Residents of Community Shelters, by Race and Season

Season	N	Race				
		Black	*White*	*Hispanic*	Indo-Chinese	*Other*
Spring	696	31.1	65.5	1.0	1.0	1.1
Summer	504	29.1	66.6	1.9	0.1	0.3
Fall	641	23.7	73.1	1.7	—	—
Winter	496	28.4	67.3	0.6	1.6	2.0
Total	2,337	28.1	68.2	1.3	0.9	1.2

residents of community shelters in Virginia; blacks made up somewhat more than one-quarter of the residents. The largest difference between black and white residents by season is found in the fall, when whites were over three times more likely than blacks to be residents of community shelters. This seasonal difference may be simply an aberration because there is little in previous research or in these data to suggest that season is a significant variable in the amount of interpersonal violence among blacks and among whites. We believe that the two most important findings in this comparison are that whites were more than twice as likely as blacks to be residents of Virginia's shelters and that Hispanics, Indo-Chinese, and other racial groups played a relatively insignificant role as residents of these shelters.

One might interpret the higher percentage of white residents as an indication that white women and children are the most likely victims of family violence in Virginia, but this interpretation would run contrary to the voluminous research documenting that blacks are victimized disproportionately by interpersonal violence. A thorough understanding of this finding requires a review of the percentage of blacks and whites in Virginia's population.

Blacks constitute 19 percent of Virginia's total population (U.S. Bureau of the Census 1986, p. 29). The fact that black women and children make up 28.1 percent of the shelters' residents but only 19 percent of Virginia's total population underscores other research findings that note the higher rate of victimization of blacks by interpersonal violence. In summary, these data indicate that although the majority of residents in Virginia's community shelters were white, a disproportionately large percentage of these residents were black.

Going Home

Battered women do not leave home readily. Ferraro and Johnson (1984, pp. 280–284) point out that many women rationalize their victimization by neutralization. Denial of options is one neutralization technique, which serves not only to heighten a woman's anxiety about leaving home but also encourages her, if she does manage to escape temporarily, to return to the abuser. According to Ferraro and Johnson, "The belief of battered women that they will not be able to make it on their own—a belief often fueled by years of abuse and oppression—is a major impediment to [acknowledgment] that one is a victim and taking action" (p. 284). Thus, when women run to shelters, the length of stay may vary depending on the extent to which they have rationalized the violence against them.

Table 7–4 reviews the length of stay in shelters, by season. Perhaps the most striking finding in this table is the variety in the length of time spent by women in the shelters. In each season, battered women and their

Table 7–4
Percentages of Family Units, by Length of Stay and Season

Season	N	Less Than 24 hours	24 hours to Less Than 3 Days	3 Days to Less Than 1 Week	1 Week to Less Than 2 Weeks	2 Weeks to Less Than 1 Month	More Than 1 Month
				Length of Stay in Shelter			
Spring	426	10.3	28.2	19.0	15.7	14.15	11.5
Summer	333	15.6	28.8	15.3	20.7	14.4	5.1
Fall	457	12.4	33.6	16.8	12.0	15.3	9.6
Winter	368	9.7	33.9	20.6	15.2	15.7	4.6
Total	1,584	11.9	31.4	17.9	15.5	15.0	8.0

children were likely to remain sheltered from less than twenty-four hours to about a month. Although the length of stay varied by season, a significant number of women in every season were likely to be sheltered for longer as well as shorter periods of time. These seasonal variations are important in that once a woman has decided to run, the more favorable weather of spring and fall serves to increase her options. Certainly remaining in the close quarters of a shelter is more tolerable in moderate weather than in the extreme weather of summer and winter.

In each season the most common length of stay was twenty-four to seventy-two hours (one to three days). Indeed, during the fall and winter, one-third of the women elected to remain for this period of time. Of the total number of family units in Virginia's shelters in the period under study, the greatest percentage (31.4) stayed from one to three days.

We suggest that twenty-four to seventy-two hours is a time for crisis management. During this period, a woman can escape the episodic violence, calm herself and her children, and decide on her next move. We do not mean to suggest, however, that most women will manage this crisis successfully or that a majority will not return home to begin another cycle of abuse.

This crisis management period allows a woman to regain a sense of personal safety while she considers what to do about the episode of violence. If women used their time in the shelter to plan permanent separation, the length of stay presumably would be longer because there would be many more factors to consider, such as job, school, residence, and family. Apparently women stay in shelters long enough to recover from a violent episode but not long enough to develop long-term solutions to the violence. As the data in table 7–5, suggest, most women return home after this period of crisis.

Table 7–5 shows the destinations of family units leaving shelters in the Old Dominion. Data were gathered to show whether a woman was

Table 7–5
Destinations of Family Units Leaving the Shelter, by Season

Season	N	HB	H-B	OA	LA	F/R	OS	OU
				Destination				
Spring	500	28.2%	14.2%	11.6%	4.2%	28.2%	5.2%	8.4%
Summer	333	30.6	10.8	15.9	7.2	24.0	4.5	6.9
Fall	436	26.8	9.4	18.5	7.3	24.3	6.1	7.3
Winter	381	23.0	14.4	20.2	4.4	28.8	3.4	5.5
Total	1,650	27.1	12.3	16.3	5.6	26.4	4.9	7.1

Note: See text for explanation of symbols.

returning to home and abuser (HB); returning home without abuser (H-B); staying on her own in the area (OA); leaving the area (LA); staying with friends or relatives (F/R); going to another shelter (OS); or going to some other or unknown location (OU). These data reveal that in every season, after a length of stay in a shelter, women were most likely to collect their children and return home or go to stay with friends or relatives. Women were most likely to return home to the abuser in the summer and least likely to return in the winter. On the other hand, friends and relatives proved to be a consistent source of support for women and children on the run. McAdoo (1982, p. 484) identified this network of friends and relatives who help black women and children absorb stress as kin-help exchange. The data in table 7–5 indicate that kin-help exchange may be operative whenever women exert a measure of independence from the abuser; they were more likely to stay on their own in the area near him than to leave the area altogether or go home without his presence.

In summary, the data in table 7–5 reveal that upon leaving community shelters, most women return home (27.1 percent) or stay with friends and relatives (26.4 percent). Aside from these destinations, women were somewhat less likely to stay by themselves either on their own but near their home (16.3 percent) or in their own home in the absence of the abuser (12.3 percent). A chi-square test ($p < .05$) on the overall choice of destinations indicates only a slight probability that these differences are due to chance.

With the exception of the relatively small percentage of women who left the area (5.6 percent), most of the women who run for shelter may in fact be running in circles because all of the other destinations are well within striking distance of the abuser. The abused woman's friends and relatives are, for the most part, his friends and relatives; staying with them, like staying in a shelter, is likely to be a temporary solution. As long as the woman is in the same area as her abuser, it is likely that they will have physical contact. Short of a legal restraining order, her home is still his home. Thus, these data support the findings of previous research, which documents a cyclical and repetitive pattern of family violence.

Conclusion

The intent of this research was to develop a profile of battered women housed in community shelters in the state of Virginia. On the basis of our review of data on residents of thirty shelters across the state, we suggest that the typical sheltered women in the Old Dominion is one who has chosen to run in moderate weather, is being sheltered for the first time, is 18 to 29 years old, and is white, although she can expect to share shelter space with a disproportionately large percentage of black women and children. After arriving at the shelter, she will remain there for one to three days, long enough to manage the crisis of her most recent abuse. Upon leaving the shelter, she will most likely return home to the abuser or stay with friends or relatives. This kin-help exchange, however, is likely to be temporary.

Further research is necessary to understand how battered women run. The data collected by the Virginia Department of Social Services did not permit us to compare residents by race and length of stay or by race and destination, data necessary to determine whether the shelter experience is similar for black and for white women. McAdoo's (1982) research suggests that the kin-help exchange may be more significant among black women than among white. Therefore we might expect more blacks than whites to stay with friends and relatives upon leaving the shelter. Finally, research on women who run to hospitals or police stations would be particularly informative. It may be that the profiles of such women will differ significantly by race and age from those who take refuge in shelters.

References

Douglas, Jack. 1967. *The Social Meaning of Suicide*. Princeton: Princeton University Press.

Drake, Virginia K. 1982. "Battered Women: A Health Care Problem in Disguise." *Image* 14(June):40–47.

Ferraro, Kathleen J., and John M. Johnson. 1984. "How Women Experience Battering: The Process of Victimization." In *Deviant Behavior*, pp. 277–297. 2d ed. Edited by Delos H. Kelly. New York: St. Martin's Press.

Finley, Britt. 1981. "Nursing Process with the Battered Woman." *Nurse Practitioner* (July–August):11–13.

Kitsuse, John, and Aaron Cicourel. 1963. "A Note on the Uses of Official Statistics." *Social Problems* 11(Fall):131–139.

Lichtenstein, Violet R. 1981. "The Battered Women: Guidelines for Effective Nursing Intervention." *Issues in Mental Health Nursing* 3, no. 3:237–250.

McAdoo, Harriette P. 1982. "Stress Absorbing Systems in Black Families." *Family Relations* 31(October):479–488.

McCaghy, Charles H. 1985. *Deviant Behavior.* 2d ed. New York: Macmillan.

Merton, Robert. 1966. "Social Problems and Sociological Theory." In *Contemporary Social Problems.* Edited by Robert Merton and Robert Nisbet. New York: Harcourt, Brace and World.

Nettler, Gwynn. 1984. *Explaining Crime.* 3d ed. New York: McGraw-Hill.

Newman, Graeme. 1979. *Understanding Violence.* New York. Harper & Row.

Quinney, Richard. 1965. "Suicide, Homicide and Economic Development." *Social Forces* 43(March):401–407.

Steinmetz, Suzanne K., and Murray A. Straus. 1980. "The Family as Cradle of Violence." In *Criminal Behavior: Readings in Criminology,* pp. 130–142. Edited by Delos H. Kelly. New York: St. Martin's Press.

Tierney, Kathleen. 1982. "The Battered Women's Movement and the Creation of the Wife Beating Problem." *Social Problems* 29(February):207–220.

U.S. Attorney General. 1984. *Task Force on Family Violence: Final Report.* Washington, D.C.: Government Printing Office.

U.S. Bureau of the Census. 1986. *Statistical Abstract of the United States.* Washington, D.C.: Government Printing Office.

Walker, Lenore E. 1978. "Treatment Alternatives for Battered Women." In *The Victimization of Women,* 3:143–174. Edited by Jane Roberts Chapman and Margaret Gates. Beverly Hills: Sage.

Wetzel, Laura, and Mary Anne Ross. 1983. "Psychological and Social Ramifications of Battering: Observations Leading to a Counseling Methodology for Victims of Domestic Violence." *Personnel Guidance Journal* (March):423–428.

8

Raising the Awareness of Wife Battering in Rural Black Areas of Central Virginia: A Community Outreach Approach

Melvin N. Wilson
Deborah D. Cobb
Regina T. Dolan

Although wife battering is only one form of violence that occurs in American society, it is one of the most lethal social problems of our time. It is estimated that up to 60 percent of all marriages are affected by violence (FBI Uniform Crime Reports 1977, 1982; Roy 1977). Twenty-five percent of all murders occur between relatives, and over half of these murders occur between spouses (FBI Uniform Crime Reports 1977, 1982; Roy 1977).

This chapter examines an outreach strategy developed by the Shelter for Help in Emergency to increase the sensitivity to wife battering and the visibility of the shelter's services for battered women in rural and black communities located in a five-county area surrounding Charlottesville, Virginia. The significance of this program is that many victims were isolated not only by domestic violence but also by the long-standing issues of separation, suspicion, and marginality surrounding rural communities and racial status.

This program was conceived and implemented with the view that wife battering is an act of oppression. Wilson (1984) describes oppression as that state or condition within an ordered society where one segment of the society is differentially and involuntarily limited in its access to all the available opportunities, resources, services, and benefits of that society. According to Goldenberg (1978), oppression is characterized as a process of restricting and channeling an individual's available options, devaluing that person's worth, and blaming the person for his or her predicament. Domestic violence as an act of oppression is manifested through denial of the problem by members of the community, which leads to a failure to provide adequate services for victims of abuse and to protect them and gives the abusers tacit permission to continue their violent assaults on family members.

Historical Development of the Rural and Minority Community Outreach Effort

The shelter, a safe house for battered wives and their families in Charlottesville, Virginia, was created as a community response to the problem of domestic violence. Before the outreach services were developed in the rural and black communities, the shelter was confronted with resistance by rural communities and institutions regarding the problem of domestic violence. In 1979, it was not uncommon to read statements like this in the editorial section of a rural community newspaper: "We feel that this costly boondoggle would be redundant [to already existing social services]" (*Nelson County Times,* July 13, 1979). This statement expressed the legislative opinion of most local governing bodies in the five-county area.

Although 25 percent of all police deaths occur when officers are answering domestic calls (Richmond-Abbott 1983), police have generally denied the existence of a domestic violence problem. Frederick (1979) states that many police officers are reluctant to intervene in violent family disputes because they believe that they are private matters. The sheriff of Albemarle County, Virginia, once stated, "A man comes home after a few drinks, slaps his wife—do you call that abuse?" (*Cavilier Daily,* September 1979). This attitude was encouraged by Albemarle County and Charlottesville police departmental policies. A training manual for the Charlottesville Police Department (1979), for example, asserted that in most cases of domestic violence, a crime has not occurred; therefore it is not the job of the police to intervene.

If a battered woman succeeded in obtaining help from the police, her next hurdle was to obtain court assistance. Her only legal remedy required her to file a warrant with a magistrate. Court dates were set six weeks in advance, which left ample time for the abuse to recur or the abuser to express contrition. Often the long court delay resulted in dropped warrants or failure to appear. Even when proceedings led to a conviction, sentences were often light or suspended.

When battered wives seek assistance from members of the clergy, the results have been less than satisfactory. Several researchers have suggested that the clerical response often encourages continual domestic violence by advising the victim to keep the family intact (Fortune and Hormann 1980; Pagelow 1981). Pagelow (1981) finds a strong positive correlation between asking clergy for help and remaining in the battering relationship. Fortune and Hormann (1980) assert that religious teaching can be especially victim blaming. As for the religious value of family life, Fortune and Hormann (1980) note that the clergy often ignore the immediate danger of an abuse victim in the family in order to protect the sanctity of the family.

Pagelow (1981) notes that social services tend to minimize wife battering by offering "misdirected help or not enough help." Frederick (1979) echoes this concern by asserting that when police refer a victim to a social service agency, the agency frequently refers the victim to another agency, a frustrating merry-go-round experience for the victim.

In addition to these general barriers, services and interventions in rural communities and institutions encounter increased resistance and mistrust because of their geographic isolation (Blough 1982; Ridley 1984). To the rural individuals and families who suffer the physical and emotional injuries of violence in the home, help seems inaccessible or nonexistent. Lack of transportation and telephone service leaves many women and children cowering in fear with no hope of intervention from neighbors or social agencies. Even when police are called, women are reluctant to press charges because of shame, lack of anonymity, and lack of financial resources other than their spouse. Without the cooperation and support of the rural governments and social agencies, it is nearly impossible to work out the special problems of helping rural families who suffer the devastating effects of domestic violence. It is possible, however, for rural institutions to be sensitized to these issues through a tailored approach designed to demonstrate the seriousness and immediacy of the problem.

Black rural communities suffer from an additional cause of isolation: racial status (Acosta 1980; Ridley 1984). Although shelter services were available, these communities stood apart from the service referral network that frequently took advantage of the shelter's services. It has long been recognized that the failure of many social and mental health intervention programs in the black community is due to the mistrust and skepticism of the black constituency and to the stereotypic attitude held by the middle-class social service and mental health personnel (Acosta 1980). In general, social service and mental health professionals implicitly and explicitly expect clients to be young, attractive, verbal, intelligent, and successful (Schonfield 1964), attitudes they communicate to black clients. In fact, Acosta (1980) found that minority clients typically terminated therapy because of their negative reactions to the therapist. The black client's values and expectations are shaped by cultural experiences and social realities, which often differ from those of the middle-class therapist. Therefore, in addition to rural residency, race is a significant factor in delivering services to victims of domestic violence. A successful treatment plan must bridge the differences between the rural and black constituency and professional interventions.

The Shelter's Rural and Minority Community Education Outreach Program

Since it opened in January 1979, the shelter has made emergency respite and relief services for abused women its highest priority. Once these emergency services were in place and battered women requested help in increasing numbers, the organization began to see the necessity of making outreach and prevention strategies a major organizational task.

This new awareness reflected a change in the shelter's perceived role in the community. It was no longer enough to provide services to victims; the shelter began to see itself as a catalyst for social change. In presenting its mission to the public, the shelter began not only to describe the problem and the services it offered but also to recommend tactics for nonviolent conflict and the equalization of power between men and women. It began to encourage the community to value the rights of individuals (the abused victims) over the rights of the institution (the family). The shelter had become not only the provider of emergency service but also the community advocate for the rights of battered women. Thus the low involvement of rural black women was an obvious problem.

In January 1982, a project was designed, funded, and implemented with two major goals. The first goal was to increase the visibility of the shelter program in the rural and black areas of several counties in central Virginia (Albemarle, Greene, Fluvanna, Nelson, and Louisa), thereby increasing access to services by these target populations. To achieve this goal, the planners proposed to distribute pamphlets and other materials; to contact and inform influential individuals in rural and black communities; to obtain support from local governments, churches, and other institutions; to use local media in an advertising campaign; and to hold regular office hours in rural areas. The second goal was to increase the sensitivity of rural communities and institutions to the problem of domestic violence, thereby strengthening strategies for prevention and intervention as well as stabilizing services. The methods proposed for achieving this goal were to design, develop, and implement a training package for service providers; to develop and use presentations for the general public; and to develop suitable prevention programs for use in public schools.

To correspond to these goals, two kinds of outreach procedures, known as sensitivity and visibility, were developed and implemented. Generally these activities included providing information about domestic violence, establishing the accessibility and availability of existing services of the shelter, and developing and implementing prevention and treatment strategies in rural black communities. Although sensitivity and visibility activities commonly involve exchanges of information, there is a significant distinction between the two types of activities. The patterns for implementing the two primary strategies were different because of the nature of community outreach programs and because of the shelter's previous experience with such programs.

The visibility activities, which included personal and informal contacts, public service announcements, and media advertisements, were transitory in nature. Because the shelter staff had previously developed an advertising campaign for the urban areas of the planning district, the programs focusing on visibility were implemented immediately. Information and materials on the shelter, including pamphlets and posters, were distributed at local stores, barber shops, beauty salons, and laundromats. Social service agencies, volunteer fire departments, churches, and police and sheriff's departments were contacted to inform individuals about the shelter and its services. The shelter also maintained monthly office hours in rural areas. Media coverage included brief community announcements, generally presented on local radio and television stations and newspaper and radio news briefs, which included interviews with shelter staff members and newsworthy events regarding the shelter. The local television station also presented interviews, and rural area newspapers printed feature stories about the shelter, along with more general articles about domestic violence.

By contrast, sensitivity activities, including the development and implementation of instructional presentations, were more substantial. Because programs and procedures had to be tailored to rural and black constituencies, these activities represented more time and investment on the part of the shelter. Initially they were presented as workshops and training sessions, which involved community leaders, local officials, and social service personnel. These group meetings were adopted to meet the needs of each specific group. Later workshops were developed for church and school groups. These presentations usually consisted of slide presentations or puppet shows, depending on the age of the audience. The discussion that followed these presentations reflected the audience's concern about domestic violence, as well as the general lack of knowledge about dealing with this problem. The children's puppet show program, which encourages children to use nonviolent procedures to resolve conflicts, was adopted for preschool and primary school audiences; a slide presentation was developed and implemented for older audiences, who represented a variety of demographic backgrounds.

One significant aspect of the outreach program was the selection and training of coordinators who, because of their personal styles and past experiences, possessed the ability to communicate informally and directly with a rural and black constituency. They were responsible for a continuous effort by other staff members and volunteers to accomplish the outreach goals and objectives. The coordinators and volunteers interacted with rural and black citizens, service workers, and country officials.

The indigenous orientation and the nonprofessional status of the out-reach coordinators were important in establishing a bridge between the shelter and the targeted communities. In this regard, the coordinators had unique assets that contributed not only to their own effectiveness and credibility but to all other aspects of the outreach effort. Because the coordinators empathized and (in the case of one coordinator) identified with battered women, they were able to articulate the harmful conse-quences of battering to the women, to their children, and even to the battering husbands. Moreover, the coordinators possessed one important difference from the battered women: they represented women who had intimate relationships that were not abusive. As such, they were impor-tant role models.

Outcome

Figure 8-1 shows a steady increase and a stable pattern of participation of clients from the Charlottesville–Albemarle County area where the shelter is located over the six-year history of the shelter. Participation from out-side that area increased after the outreach effort was implemented. The visibility of the shelter among rural black women and participation by those women increased. A chi-square analysis comparing the rate of admissions of rural black and other rural women between 1979 and 1984

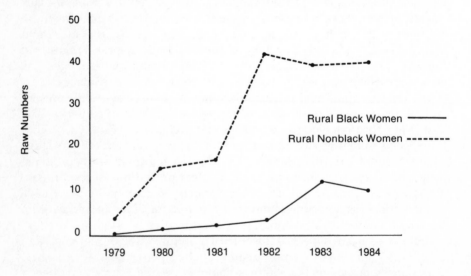

Figure 8-1. Admission Rate of Rural Black and Nonblack Women to Shelters, Charlottesville–Albemarle County Area

shows a significant increase (x^2 = 20.5, df = 8, $p <$ .05) after the implementation of the outreach program. Before the intervention, more shelter residents came from the Charlottesville–Albemarle community; after the intervention, this pattern changed.

An initial awareness survey was taken from each individual contact and from the participants in the training sessions. The survey requested information regarding knowledge of the shelter's services, awareness of domestic violence, and knowledge of any domestic dispute in the community. Among the 450 individual contacts made and the 150 presentations delivered during the first eighteen months of the outreach services, 70 percent of the respondents did not know about the existence of the shelter and its services. Most of those contacted, however—about 95 percent—knew someone who either had experienced or was experiencing domestic violence. These survey data, although rudimentary, indicated that most of the audience were not aware of the shelter. The training sessions and the community workshops notably increased the visibility of the shelter's services and sensitivity to domestic violence.

A wide variety of the rural people were surveyed or participated in a community workshop: business persons, ministers, teachers, sheriffs, police officers, volunteer firefighters, attorneys, judges, county officials, pharmacists, physicians, dentists, and ex-residents of the shelter. The anecdotal comments illuminate the attitudes of rural area citizens regarding violent domestic disputes. The comments show consistently that many respondents were aware of a friend or relative who was experiencing battering problems, lacked knowledge regarding the shelter's services and alternatives to abusive situations, and believed that the shelter pamphlet and/or community education program was extremely helpful.

In one county, on different occasions with different volunteers, several people described an abusive incident that shocked the community. A divorced woman was beaten brutally by her boyfriend, who seriously cut her inner thighs and threatened to cut out her vagina. Apparently the boyfriend was upset because his girlfriend's ex-husband visited his children. The narrators felt that the incident was an isolated occurrence, although each person could recall other violent domestic incidents. This incident provided the staff and volunteers with an unfortunate opportunity to demonstrate the seriousness of abuse as its community concern.

In a workshop for ministers, several ministers indicated that they had parishioners troubled with family violence. One minister had taken his daughter and a friend to the store one day, and while he sat in his car waiting for them, he witnessed the abuse of a young child, about a year old, by a young man in a car across the street. He did not know what to do; he considered whether he should go over to the car and say something, take the license number and report to the authorities, or stay in his car and mind his own business. He finally did nothing. The minister then stated that the presentation helped him to realize that as a concerned citizen, he had the right to report the episode to child protective services and allow them to follow up.

In a presentation at a meeting of school principals in one of the rural counties, the superintendent asked whether the presentation should be shown to adults rather than teenagers. The principal of the county high school responded with a description of a student who had used the shelter and benefited greatly. It is a common feeling that the issue of domestic violence should be discussed only with adult audiences. Younger people, however, especially those between the ages of 15 and 18, should be involved in the discussions because they are entering the developmental period where male-female relationships are becoming a focal point of life.

During presentations in another rural county high school, many young girls spoke freely about having a friend or relative who was a victim of abuse, and they asked specific questions about what they could do to help. Two common questions were, "How do I approach them?" and "How can I give them the information you have given me without putting them on the defensive?"

During a preview of the slide presentation, a local high school principal was concerned that his students would recognize the actors in the presentation. The presenter replied, "The point of the presentation is to bring the idea of domestic violence to the home. Too many people believe that it can't happen here or to them, and that is why the presentation is titled, 'It Can't Happen Here.'" The presenter pointed out that the workshop presentation was made not in a derogatory manner but so as to raise the community consciousness regarding the severity and prevalence of local domestic violence. About halfway through the preview, the principal commented again that the pictures in the presentation might be too much for high school students. His assistant replied, "Children see more violence than this on the TV screen or in the theater."

Not all contacts went smoothly. The county sheriffs' offices were bastions of strong resistance; of the seven most difficult contacts, five involved county sheriff's offices. At one training session with a rural county police department and sheriff's office, an officer reported advising a woman who had tried the legal route without success to beat her husband with a wooden stick if he abused her again. He said that the man had not abused her since. This was a difficult training session for the coordinator because the officers of the law, in her opinion, were advocating the use of violence by the women.

The anecdotal comments reflected several generally held but discrepant ideas regarding battering. Although the respondents were aware of violent domestic disputes experienced by an intimate, they were unaware of the prevalence of domestic problems in their communities. Respondents also believed that something ought to be done but did not know that shelters and other alternatives existed. Many persons supported the distribution of information on ways to respond to domestic violence but feared that their family, friends, and community would not listen. Most participants felt that the shelter's program should be presented widely in their communities and were willing to recommend the program to others. Those who felt negative toward the shelter's outreach program believed that the information was misleading and overstated, but these individuals made up a very small minority of those exposed to the outreach program.

Conclusion

Overall the outreach program continues to be highly successful in increasing the participation of black and rural women in shelter services. The success of the strategy can be understood in its conceptualization of the problem and in its intervention in wife battering. The problem of wife battering reflects not only society's ignorance of the prevalence of domestic violence and its insensitivity to battered women but also its lack of awareness of such longstanding issues as sexual equality, racial status, and rural isolation. The critical issues confronting the shelter arose from the interaction of several oppressive forces that limited the shelter services and alternatives to a population isolated by gender, race, and place of residence.

Society has long overlooked the needs of women in abusive relationships. Often when the lethality of an abusive relationship was recognized, local professional and clerical authorities blamed the abused woman for her own victimization. The substantive right to protection and physical safety gave way to the sanctity of the family.

Furthermore, isolation from mainstream America was—and is—a social reality for many black and rural communities. Problems were created by the dissonance between rural and urban, black and white values, expectations, and behaviors; by population dispersion and geographic distances in the rural areas; and by heightened visibility and lack of anonymity for individual community members. These obstacles intensified the isolation and prevented the involvement of abused women from rural and black communities.

Intervention in wife battering required the development of appropriate community responsibility in the treatment of battered women, the promotion of accessible and viable services to rural and black victims, and the establishment of prevention services. The shelter's outreach effort intervened on both the institutional and the individual levels of society.

Institutionally the shelter's intention was to change the inappropriate ways in which human service organizations, such as social service agencies, police departments, schools, and churches, responded to violent domestic disputes by encouraging the battered woman to return home, creating legal impediments in protecting the battered women, ignoring the problem, or failing to teach appropriate ways of behaving. The preventive element of the program sought to reduce the incidence of domestic disputes by promoting nonviolent behavior in intimate relationships.

On the individual level, the shelter's goal was to establish itself as an available safe home for battered women who were black and/or living in rural areas. The strategy for change reflected advocacy of women's rights, empowerment of battered victims, and the development of treatment alternatives, community education, and prevention services for rural and black areas.

The continuing success of this program demonstrates that a group- and area-specific design is important in combating domestic violence in rural black communities. The coordinators were pivotal to the success of the outreach effort in several ways. First, their approach to the communities reflected neighborliness, directness, informality, and familiarity, which comforted those unaccustomed to the austere professional facade of personnel in human service organizations (Fortune and Hormann 1980; Zax and Spector 1974; Reissman 1970). Second, their status as service providers made them positive role models for their constituents. Finally, because the coordinators were indigenous to rural areas, they were accepted as credible transmitters of information about alternatives to battering relationships. Overall the coordinators helped empower women who were suffering spouse abuse. Because the coordinators shared backgrounds and personal experiences with their constituencies, the success of shelter programs was increased.

More generally the shelter's outreach effort represents an important intervention in the destructive and oppressive effects of wife battering in rural and black communities. In this context, the shelter defined wife battering as a problem involving long-standing issues of isolation, suspicion, and marginality surrounding the status of gender, race, and rural residence. This community problem required a community-level intervention, which the shelter developed and implemented.

Epilogue

Since this evaluation period, the rural outreach activities have been expanded. The monthly outreach visits were replaced by biweekly visits to each of the rural areas, and individual contacts have tripled over the past year. The effectiveness of this effort continues to be evident in the increasing number of admissions from the rural black areas of the target region. The prevention program is particularly successful; approximately 3,500 young people have participated in the problem-solving puppet show or in discussion groups. This activity represents a 44 percent increase over the activity discussed in the evaluation.

References

Acosta, F.X. 1980. "Self-described Reasons for Premature Termination of Psychotherapy by Mexican American, Black American, and Anglo-American Patients." *Psychological Reports* 47:435–443.

Blough, R.G. 1982. "Rural People." In *Reaching the Underserved: Mental Health Needs of Neglected Populations*, pp. 75–94. Edited by L.R. Snowden. Beverly Hills: Sage Publications.

Federal Bureau of Investigation. 1977. *Crime in the United States: 1976*. Washington, D.C.: Government Printing Office.

———. 1982. *Crime in the United States: 1981*. Washington, D.C.: Government Printing Office.

Fortune, M., and D. Hormann. 1980. *Family Violence: A Workshop Manual for Rural Communities*. Seattle: Center for the Prevention of Sexual and Domestic Violence.

Frederick, R. 1979. *Domestic Violence: A Guide for Police Response*. Philadelphia: Pennsylvania Coalition against Violence.

Goldenberg, I.I. 1978. *Oppression and Social Intervention*. Chicago: Nelson Hall.

Pagelow, M.D. 1981. *Woman Battering: Victims and Their Experiences*. Beverly Hills: Sage Publications.

Reissman, F. 1970. "Strategies and Suggestions for Training Nonprofessionals." In *Community Psychology and Community Mental Health Introductory Reading*, pp. 197–209. Edited by P.E. Cook. San Francisco: Holden-Day.

Richmond-Abbott, M. 1983. *Masculine and Feminine: Sex Roles over the Life Cycle*. Reading, Mass.: Addison-Wesley.

Ridley, C.R. 1984. "Clinical Treatment of the Nondisclosing Black Client: A Therapeutic Paradox." *American Psychologist* 39, no. 11:1234–1244.

Roy, M. 1977. "Some Thoughts Regarding the Criminal Justice System and Wife-beating." In *Battered Women: A Psychosociological Study of Domestic Violence*, pp. 138–139. Edited by M. Roy. New York: Von Nostrand Reinhold.

Schonfeld, W. 1964. *Psychotherapy: The Purchase of Friendship*. Englewood Cliffs, N.J.: Prentice-Hall.

Wilson, M. 1984. "Notes on the Psychology of Oppression and Social Change." Lecture for Psychology 495, University of Virginia.

Zax, M., and G.A. Spector. 1974. *An Introduction to Community Psychology*. New York: John Wiley.

III
Homicides

9

Family Violence and Homicides in the Black Community: Are They Linked?

Robert L. Hampton

Although there has been an increase in the literature on domestic violence, only a few studies have examined racial and cultural differences (Garbarino and Ebata 1983; Lindholm and Willey 1983; Hampton, 1987). Few researchers have attempted to develop a more precise conceptual and empirical understanding of the nature, type, and severity of violence within black families. As a result, although there is widespread recognition of the fact that violence within black families is a serious problem, there has not been an attempt to study this issue within a larger context. This chapter examines previous research in this area as part of an effort to provide a framework for understanding violence within the black family and other forms of violence in the black community.

Child maltreatment, family violence, and homicide are arguably among the most serious social problems in the black community. The evident seriousness of these problems justifies the current high level of public and professional concern. As a result, the possible interrelationship among these phenomena is now under consideration.

Some researchers believe that child maltreatment, family violence, and homicide are specific and discrete dysfunctions. Others consider them as points on a continuum; in this view, some homicides could be classified as fatal child abuse or fatal family violence.

At the least, it would seem that child maltreatment, family violence, and homicide have many overlapping causes. At worst, there may be a causal path: maltreatment in the family of origin may lead to family violence in the family of procreation, which in some cases can result in homicide. Between these extremes we might argue for reciprocal causality (for example, interspousal violence leading to child maltreatment) or interaction effects (maltreatment in the family of orientation leading to family violence in the family of procreation when other factors are present).

It is possible that families affected by homicide may have been victims of other maltreatment as well. Not only the coincidence should be established but also the magnitude, meaning, direction, and significance of any apparent association. Is there a direct or indirect link joining child maltreatment, family violence, and homicide? If there is a direct or indirect relationship, which participants are most affected? Can adult family violence be predicted from knowledge about child maltreatment? Or is there some set of factors that act at the individual, group, community, or societal level to cause maltreatment, violence, and homicide? If so, what other factors influence these additional factors? These are only a few of the questions that need to be addressed.

Race and Child Maltreatment

General Issue

Although the true prevalence of child abuse is unknown nationally, reported cases of child abuse and neglect have increased 146 percent since 1976, when 416,033 child maltreatment cases were reported to the child protective service system (CPS). The number of reported cases in 1984, the last year for which data are available, was 1,726,699. This increase can be attributed to a number of factors, including definitional variability and surveillance artifact.

According to the 1980 census, black children accounted for about 15 percent of all children in the United States. From 1976 to 1980, the proportion of child abuse and neglect reports involving black children remained fairly constant at about 19 percent, but 1982 national reporting data show that black children were the reported victims in 22 percent of all child maltreatment reports (American Humane Association 1985).

Examinations of the relationship between race and family violence have yielded mixed results. In the first large-scale summary of national reports, Gil (1970) concluded that families reported for abuse were disproportionately drawn from the less educated, the poor, and ethnic minorities. Black children were overrepresented as victims of abuse. More recent compilations show a similar picture (Spearly and Lauderdale 1983; Jason et al. 1982).

Lauderdale and his colleagues (1980) computed annual rates of the occurrence of validated cases of abuse and neglect in Texas from 1975 to 1977 for whites, blacks, and Mexican-Americans. Without controlling for social class, blacks had the highest rates for all forms of maltreatment, followed by Mexican-Americans and then whites. In a follow-up study using the same data, Spearly and Lauderdale (1983) added to their earlier study by controlling for social class and community (county) characteristics. Once again their results indicated that blacks had higher rates of child maltreatment. The study also found that the greater proportion of high-risk families alone in a given area is not responsible for increased rates of maltreatment, but when combined with the presence of a highly urban environment, it may yield particularly high rates for blacks relative to the majority population.

The National Study of the Incidence and Severity of Child Abuse and Neglect (NIS), funded by the National Center for Child Abuse and Neglect (NCCAN) and completed in 1981, provides valuable information on racial differences in child maltreatment (NIS 1981). Based on a stratified random sample of twenty-six counties in ten states, this study collected information on child maltreatment cases from both CPS agencies and non-CPS agencies (hospitals, schools, law enforcement agencies, and others). Of particular relevance here is the fact that non-CPS professionals were asked to identify whether they had reported each known case to a CPS agency. This question allowed researchers to ascertain characteristics of cases known to professionals but not reported and to compare reported cases with unreported cases.

The NIS estimated that 10.5 children per thousand are maltreated each year in the United States. This estimate reflects not only physical abuse but other forms of maltreatment as well. In terms of ethnic group, incidence estimates are essentially the same for black and white children (11.6 and 10.5 per 1,000, respectively). The study also reported that contrary to the conventional wisdom, there were no observed reporting biases due to race (NIS 1981). Subsequent analyses of these data have challenged both of these findings.

One of the shortcomings of the original NIS reports was that the classification "white" was combined with data from "white not of Hispanic origin" and "Hispanic." The assumption was that most children identified to the study as Hispanic would have been classified as white according to Census Bureau race definition.

In a secondary analysis of substantiated maltreatment cases drawn from the NIS data, Hampton (1987) has shown significant differences among blacks, whites, and Hispanics in demographic profiles and in type and severity of maltreatment. Blacks have higher rates of physical neglect and physical abuse than whites and Hispanics (figure 9–1).

This secondary analysis, based on over 400 confirmed cases of maltreatment, weighted to be nationally representative, found that black maltreating families were generally poorer, more likely to be receiving public assistance, and with single-parent mothers with fewer years of formal education. The mothers were less likely to be employed full time and had

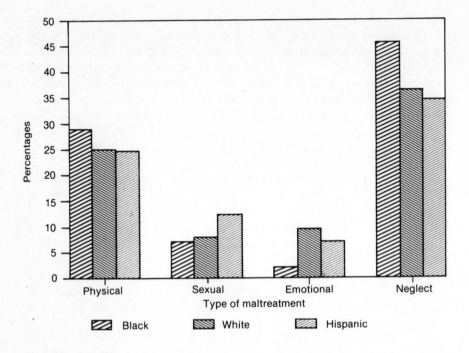

Figure 9–1. Ethnic Differences in Substantiated Child Maltreatment Cases

larger families (Tables 9–1 and 9–2). Controlling for social class reinforces rather than diminishes these observed group differences. Table 9–3 shows a number of differences with respect to type of maltreatment and care-taker problems associated with the maltreatment.

Although the NIS reported no apparent reporting bias due to race in overall study, there is evidence that professionals from at least one report source exhibited bias. Hampton and Newberger (1985) have shown that hospitals tend to overreport blacks and Hispanics and underreport whites. For black and Hispanic families, recognition of alleged child maltreatment almost ensured reporting to CPS.

Physical Abuse

The studies cited addressed general rates of child maltreatment. Although discussions of physical abuse are included, it is important to take a separate look at this form of maltreatment.

In a study of 4,132 cases of child abuse reported to the Los Angeles County Sheriff's Department from 1975 to 1982, Lindholm and Willey

Table 9-1
Ethnicity by Child and Maternal Characteristics for Substantiated Cases

Variable	White	Black	Hispanic	Total
Age of child				
0–5	31.5%	34.5%	45.5%	32.8%[a]
6–12	50.4	49.3	40.8	49.7
13–17	17.8	14.4	13.7	17.0
Sex of child				
Male	50.5	48.9	42.8	49.7
Female	49.5	51.0	57.2	50.2
Mother's education[b]				
0–8 years	13.6	27.1	34.7	16.7
Some high school	47.2	51.5	40.4	47.7
High school graduate or more	39.6	21.4	24.9	35.7
Mother's employment[c]				
Full time	29.5	18.5	27.7	28.0
Part time	64.7	70.5	65.6	65.1
Unemployment	5.8	11.0	6.7	6.9
Mother's age				
19 or under	4.6	7.4	5.4	5.0
20–24	16.5	19.1	21.4	17.2
25–34	20.7	18.4	13.3	20.2
35–44	26.0	29.3	28.3	26.7
45 and older	26.7	19.3	23.9	25.1
Don't know	5.5	6.6	7.8	6.0
Number of children in household				
1	19.0	14.8	20.2	18.6
2	28.3	23.7	30.2	27.5
3	22.9	19.5	27.5	22.3
4	14.8	14.6	10.8	14.8
5 or more	15.1	27.4	11.3	16.8
Father in household				
Yes	56.1	27.0	56.0	51.5
No	43.1	73.0	44.0	48.5
Unweighted N	(3,183)	(746)	(224)	(4,153)
Weighted N	(364,697)	(74,503)	(20,008)	(459,207)

[a]Percentages are based on weighting and may not add to 100 percent because of rounding. Cases with unidentified ethnic status are omitted from all tables.

[b]Excludes 1,330 women for whom data were missing.

[c]Excludes 220 women for whom data were missing.

(1983) report a number of significant differences attributed to ethnic status. Physical abuse was highest in black families, with discipline most often given as the reason for abuse. Differences existed also in the types of physical injury that the children suffered as a result of the abuse. Black

**Table 9–2
Ethnicity by Family Income, Public Assistance Status, Medicaid
Eligibility, and City Size**

Variable	White	Black	Hispanic	Total
Family income[a]				
Less than $7,000	50.1%	74.6%	47.0%	53.7%[b]
$7,000–14,9995	39.9	18.7	41.0	36.8
$15,000–24,999	7.5	4.5	10.5	7.2
$25,000 or more	2.5	2.1	1.5	2.3
Receiving Aid for Dependent Children[c]				
Yes	34.8	62.7	30.0	38.8
No	65.2	37.3	70.0	61.2
Medicaid eligible[d]				
Yes	35.1	59.5	11.4	37.4
No	64.9	40.5	88.6	62.6
City size				
SMSA over 200,000	32.6	47.9	83.8	38.2
Other SMSA	23.6	17.5	13.0	21.9
Non-SMSA	43.8	34.6	3.2	39.9
Unweighted N	(3,183)	(746)	(224)	(4,153)
Weighted N	(364,697)	(74,503)	(20,008)	(459,203)

[a]Excludes 139 cases for whom data were missing.
[b]Percentages are based on weighting and may not add to 100 percent because of rounding.
[c]Excludes 166 cases for whom data were missing.
[d]Excludes 215 cases for whom data were missing

children were most likely to be whipped or beaten and to receive lacerations or scars, whereas white children were more likely to receive bruises. Although blacks constituted only 9.8 percent of the Los Angeles County population, they accounted for 23.8 percent of abuse victims. These data also showed that among whites and Hispanics, males (especially fathers) were the most frequent perpetrators. Conversely, black mothers were more frequently identified as alleged perpetrators. Given the number of female heads of household in the sample, the latter is not surprising. The results indicated that the abusers were more likely to be females in single-parent homes but males in stepparent (consensual or legal) families.

Blacks were also overrepresented in confirmed physical abuse cases in the NIS (Hampton 1985). Compared to others, black victims of assaultive child maltreatment were more likely to be in the 6–12 age group, live in urban areas, have mothers who had completed high school, and suffer more serious injuries. As in the earlier analysis, black victims of assaultive violence were more likely to be in households receiving public assistance.

Table 9–3
Ethnicity by Type of Maltreatment and Problems, Controlling for Income

Variable	White	Black	Hispanic	Total
Type of Maltreatment				
Low-income families[a]				
Physical abuse	18.3%	17.3%	16.3%	18.0%
Sexual abuse	4.4	6.8	7.9	5.0
Emotional injury[b]	12.3	4.5	13.8	10.6
Physical neglect	40.3	53.2	49.4	43.6
Other families				
Physical abuse	32.3	65.4	31.9	35.2
Sexual abuse	10.6	7.1	16.9	10.6
Emotional injury	11.1	3.0	9.2	10.3
Physical neglect	33.9	21.5	21.9	32.2
First-Caretaker Problem				
Low-income families				
Alcohol abuse	16.1	22.7	14.8	17.6
Child rearing	17.7	26.7	20.6	19.9
Caretaker stress	38.6	18.4	38.9	34.0
Other families				
Alcohol abuse	17.9	11.8	19.2	17.5
Child rearing	12.7	12.3	17.3	12.9
Caretaker stress	37.2	45.5	38.3	37.9
Unweighted *N*	(3,183)	(746)	(224)	(4,153)
Weighted *N*	(364,697)	(74,503)	(20,008)	(459,207)

[a]Families with incomes less than $7,000 were included in the low-income category. Fifty-three percent of the families were in this category.
[b]Emotional injuries include both emotional abuse and emotional neglect cases.

Caseworkers report that caretaker stress was highly associated with physical abuse in these families.

More than half (52 percent) of the black victims of assaultive violence suffered injuries from a weapon (for example, knife, gun, stick, or cord). In comparison, only 27.4 percent of white and 44.4 percent of Hispanic assaultive violence victims suffered injuries inflicted by weapons (see table 9–4).

Together the Los Angeles and the NIS data indicate a higher rate of physical abuse among blacks. The Los Angeles study suggests that this abuse is related frequently to parental disciplinary practices. Differences in family structure (specifically, one-parent versus two-parent families) are also noted for their contribution to ethnic differences. Although no socioeconomic status variable was included in this study, one can infer from other variables that a large proportion of these families were poor.

Table 9–4
Demographic Distribution of Assaultive Violence Cases, by Ethnicity

Variable	White	Black	Hispanic	Total
Age of child				
0–5	36.3%	21.6%	41.6%	33.8%[a]
6–12	45.8	59.9	53.4	48.6
13–17	18.0	18.5	5.0	17.5
Sex of child				
Male	55.2	42.9	41.8	52.4
Female	44.8	56.9	58.2	47.6
Mother's education				
0–8 years	4.8	17.5	12.6	7.2
9–11 years	40.7	50.1	62.3	43.1
12 years or more	54.5	32.4	25.2	49.7
Mother's employment				
Employed full time	30.1	36.9	20.0	30.8
Employed part time	63.4	53.9	67.7	61.9
Unemployed	6.5	9.3	12.3	7.3
Number of children in household				
1	23.0	14.3	17.9	21.2
2	32.4	17.5	24.0	29.2
3	20.4	21.1	19.7	20.5
4	14.3	15.6	30.6	15.2
5 or more	9.9	31.5	7.8	13.7
Number of victims				
1	54.2	43.7	74.3	53.1
2	22.3	10.9	6.1	19.5
3	12.8	13.9	1.4	12.5
4	7.3	11.3	18.2	8.5
5	3.4	20.2	0.0	6.3
Father in household				
Yes	68.7	48.7	83.7	65.7
No	31.3	51.3	16.3	34.3
Family income				
Less than $7,000	36.4	43.7	31.2	37.5
$7,000–14,999	48.5	37.8	39.4	46.2
$15,000–24,999	10.5	11.5	24.6	11.3
$25,000 or more	4.6	7.0	4.8	5.0
Role of mother in abuse				
Maltreator	50.5	51.9	22.3	49.6
Not involved	44.3	38.1	72.5	44.3
Don't know	5.2	10.1	5.1	6.1
Severity of abuse				
Serious	9.2	11.7	9.3	9.7
Moderate	57.6	42.8	75.7	55.6
Probable	33.2	45.5	15.1	34.7

Caretaker problems associated with abuse				
Alcohol/drugs	16.8	12.0	8.2	15.6
Physical disability	5.0	.9	0.0	1.2
Child bearing	16.0	23.1	15.1	17.1
Emotional	9.1	13.1	6.3	9.6
Stress	32.3	40.3	51.6	34.5
History of abuse	11.0	3.3	12.5	9.8
Other	9.9	7.4	6.3	9.3
Source of report to CPS				
Law enforcement	14.5	7.9	17.4	13.4
Medical sources	12.2	22.4	12.7	14.1
Schools	20.3	25.2	52.2	22.6
Other	53.0	44.5	17.6	49.9
With implement				
Yes	27.4	52.0	44.4	32.6
No	72.6	48.0	55.6	67.4
Unweighted *N*	(734)	(205)	(37)	(976)
Weighted *N*	(92,008)	(21,654)	(5,008)	(118,671)

[a]Percentages are based on weighting and may not add to 100 percent because of rounding.

The NIS black victims were in fact poor by comparison to nonblack victims, although 37 percent of the mothers were employed full time.

A notable difference exists between the findings from these two studies based on official reports and a study based on self-reports. Using data from a national probability sample of 2,143 families (147 black), Cazenave and Straus (1979) report insignificant differences in attitudes toward slapping and spanking between blacks and whites as measured by a Violence Approval Index. Blacks were less likely to report having actually slapped or spanked a child during the year preceding the study. Black and white respondents, however, reported nearly the same rate of severe parental violence against children.

Cazenave and Straus report that when income and husband's occupation are controlled for, blacks are less likely to engage in child abuse. This finding is directly contrary to the general assumption that blacks are more likely than whites to condone and use physical punishment of children. The authors also indicate that the existence of social supports, particularly from kin, family, and neighbors, may have an independent effect on controlling family violence.

It is beyond the scope of this review to assess fully the differences between these data obtained through self-reports and data obtained from other reporting sources. Each approach has inherent strengths and weaknesses. Among the major drawbacks of the national study (Straus, Gelles, Steinmetz 1980) are the fact that no single-parent families were interviewed, although such families are heavily implicated in violence. Another major drawback is that the sample did not include families with children under the age of 3.

Family Violence

The Straus, Gelles, and Steinmetz study (1980) is generally cited as the primary source of data on the prevalence and incidence of family violence. In terms of overall family violence, they found sibling-to-sibling violence more prevalent than spouse-to-spouse, parent-to-child, or child-to-parent relations. Parent-to-child violence was second in terms of both prevalence and severity.

Severe sibling violence was much more frequent in families in which parents were violent toward their children and toward each other. It occurred in 100 percent of such households compared to only 20 percent of households in which parents did not use violence toward their children or each other (Straus, Gelles, and Steinmetz 1980).

In the same study, Cazenave and Straus (1979) found that black respondents expressed more approval of couple slapping than did white respondents. Black husbands were also more likely to have slapped their wives and engaged in severe violence against them within the study year. Although the rates were relatively low for both groups, the rates for black husbands were three times greater than the rates for whites. There were only modest black-white differences in the prevalence of wife-to-husband violence. Black wives, however, were twice as likely as white to have engaged in severe violence against husbands.

Interspousal violence was highly associated with other forms of family violence in this sample. Straus, Gelles, and Steinmetz (1980) found that women who were victims of severe violence were 150 percent more likely to inflict severe violence on their children than women who were not. These researchers also found that children who were victims of violence from their parents were more likely to use violence against their parents. Among those who had been hit the most by their parents, 50 percent used violence against them, while less than one in four hundred who were hit by their parents was violent toward a parent. These data, along with anecdotal information from battered women's shelters (Fagan and Wexler 1984), indicate that there may be multiple victimization in many households. Battered wives may frequently be involved in the physical abuse of children, and some child and adolescent abuse may be the unintended result of violence between parents.

Summary

Some of the major empirical studies on child maltreatment and family violence were concerned with issues of measurement or estimation of the incidence of intrafamily violence. It is difficult, however, to make a rigorous assessment of this literature because a number of methodological and substantive issues are associated with research on this sensitive topic. Our best guess is that whether researchers use self-reports or some type of official records, the estimates obtained fall significantly below true levels of incidence.

This research has addressed a number of important theoretical issues but has generally discredited an intraindividual approach to domestic violence. The summary evaluation of the psychopathological approach is that the proportion of individuals who batter their family members and suffer from psychological disorders is no greater than the proportion of the general population with psychological disorders (Gelles 1980).

This research has also demonstrated a relationship between exposure to and experience with violence as a child and violent behavior as an adult (Gelles 1980). Although this relationship exists, it is more probabilistic than deterministic.

Investigators have found a consistent relationship between stress and violence, but stress in and of itself does not cause violence. Environmental stress, like childhood exposure to violence, may be a necessary factor in violent relations, but it is not the sole cause of violence. Simplistic, unicausal models are generally dismissed by most who work in this field.

Official statistics on child abuse and wife abuse indicate that women, blacks, minorities, and the poor are overrepresented victims of domestic violence. Research that is not limited to studying officially labeled cases of domestic violence also find relationships between income and family violence (an inverse relationship), race and violence, and minority status and violence (Straus, Gelles, and Steinmetz 1980).

Homicides

Fatal Child Abuse

Homicide of children by their parents or other caretakers represents the most serious form of child maltreatment. Like other forms of maltreatment, child homicides are probably underrecorded by current health statistics (Jason, 1983; Jason, Gilliland, and Tyler 1983). Using data from the FBI's Uniform Crime Reports for 1976 through 1979, Jason and colleagues examined rates for three different categories of child homicide. Neonaticide, infanticide, and filicide refer, respectively, to the murder of children less than a week old, more than 1 week old but less than 1 year old, and more than 1 year old.

During the four-year period from which these data were drawn, black children were victims in 43 percent, 45 percent, and 38 percent of the neonaticides, infanticides, and filicides, respectively. Parents were the offenders in more than two-thirds of neonaticides and infanticides. Rates of homicide by white fathers or stepfathers were 10 percent greater than those by white mothers or stepmothers (an insignificant difference), and rates by black fathers or stepfathers were 50 percent greater than those by black mothers or stepmothers ($p < .001$).

The proportion of parent-perpetrated homicides is inversely related to the victim's age. Homicides of children from 3 years generally were not committed by close relatives of the victim (Jason, Gilliland, and Tyler 1983). The type of weapons used varied with sex of victim and offender but not with race. When use of weapons was stratified by the age of the victim, parents used a higher proportion of firearms than did other offenders.

In 1979, the latest year for which data were analyzed, black children were victimized at a rate 3.7 times that of whites. This analysis considered only cases of law enforcement–recorded homicide; thus it excluded more subtle cases of homicide, concentrating on active, lethal violence (Jason 1983). These data frequently exclude child fatalities associated with neglect (Jackson 1984).

Primary Homicides

The black-white differential in rates of homicide victimization is well documented (Munford et al. 1976; Constantino et al. 1977; Rice 1980; Farley 1980; Mercy 1983; Jason, Flock, and Tyler 1983). In his analysis of homicide trends, Farley (1980) found that among men at the ages of maximum risk of homicide, the rates for nonwhites are eleven times those of whites; among women, homicide rates for nonwhites exceed those of whites. Homicide is the leading cause of death of black men and women aged 25 to 34.

The racial profile of homicide victims changed during the nine-year period 1970–1978. In 1970, 46 percent of these victims were white, and 54 percent were black or of other races; in 1978, 55 percent of victims were white and 45 percent nonwhite (Mercy 1983). Despite the decline in the rate of homicide among blacks, the rate was still 5.6 times higher than for whites.

Several investigators have pointed to the importance of analyzing homicides categorized on the basis of the victim-offender relationship or the precipitating circumstances (Smith and Parker 1980; Jason, Flock, and Tyler 1983). Primary homicide is the most frequent type and generally involves family, friends, or acquaintances (Smith and Parker 1980). These tend to occur within the context of interpersonal relationships with intimates and are often acts of passion (Mulvihill and Tumin 1969). The second type, nonprimary or secondary homicides, generally involves offenders and victims with no prior relationship. They are generally committed in the course of another crime such as robbery or rape but may include gangland slayings.

Between 1976 and 1979, 65 percent of all homicide victims died from assaults not related to another crime. The 1979 rate for black males was 7.3 times that for white males; the rate for black females was 5.8 times that for white females (Jason, Flock, and Tyler 1973). In that year, 6,242 whites and 5,851 blacks were homicide victims.

Using FBI UCR data for 1976–1979, Jason, Flock, and Tyler (1983) report that black female homicide victims were involved primarily with acquaintances (47 percent) and family (43 percent). Sixty-two percent of black male victims were involved in situations with an acquaintance and 20 percent with family. At all ages, the majority of homicides involved family or acquaintances; however, family involvement was least common and involvement with strangers was most common when the victim or offender was a teenager.

The higher proportion of homicides involving friends or acquaintances among blacks may be related to several issues. First, it could reflect the higher proportion of subfamilies and augmented families in the black community. These types often include persons having no consanguinal or legal ties sharing a household (Billingsley 1968). Second, it could reflect the mounting rates of marital dissolution and high rates of single-parent families. In many of these cases, an ongoing relationship may exist with another person that is substantively similar to familial relationships, whether or not the individuals share a common dwelling. Third, these rates might reflect other aspects of the social context of the offender's life-style. The level and severity of family or acquaintance violence may be felt by family or friends, depending on the quantity and nature of time spent with each (Jason, Flock and Tyler 1983).

In his analysis of homicide trends from 1960 to 1975, Farley (1980) reported that almost all of the rise in homicide mortality among nonwhites and a substantial fraction of the rise among whites resulted from the increasing use of firearms. For nonwhite women, approximately 90 percent of the total rise in homicide came about because of the increasing frequency of firearm use. A less dramatic but similar trend was reported for nonwhite men. Farley concluded that if there had been no increases in firearm murders, the homicide rates for nonwhites in the mid-1970s would have been virtually unchanged from the 1960s.

For black offenders, handguns continued to be the weapon of choice in the late 1970s (Riedel 1984; Jason, Flock, and Tyler 1983). Only slight differences were noted between blacks and whites in the distribution of weapons used in homicides. One important difference, however, is that approximately one-third of black female offenders used knives; this proportion was much higher than for any other offender group.

Local studies of the epidemiology of homicide in the United States, which have taken a more in-depth view of homicide, have confirmed the national experience and have found that men, the young, and the non-white population are at greater risk of being homicide victims. There were 578 homicides in Manhattan in 1981, for example. The rate for blacks was 7.7 times that for whites (Tardiff, Gross, and Messner 1986). The discrepancies between the rates for blacks and whites were especially great for drug-related homicides and for homicides involving family members.

An analysis of criminal homicides that occurred from 1970-1979 in the city of Los Angeles found that blacks and whites were more vulnerable to fatal assaults between consensual mates than were Hispanics and Asians (Loya et al. 1986). The homicide rate for blacks during this decade was at least twice as high as for Hispanics and more than three times higher than the other ethnic or racial groups in the study. Blacks were also often victimized as a result of handguns, the most lethal means of death (Loya et al. 1986).

National and local studies reinforce several important points: that blacks have a high rate of homicide; that homicides are primarily intraracial; that the majority of black victims were friends, acquaintances, or relatives of the offender; and that firearms were the weapons most frequently used in homicide cases.

Homicides and Other Violent Behavior

There are three popular but competing models that seek to explain differentials or trends in homicide. The first, a deterrence model, argues that the certainty of punishment, especially capital punishment, minimizes homicide. Ehrlich (1975) argued that capital punishment has a negative effect upon the incentive to commit homicide. His investigation suggested that the elimination of capital punishment was related to a rise in homicide.

One major weakness in this model has been acknowledged: it ignores socioeconomic and demographic variables (Loftin 1977). It also overlooks the fact that most primary homicides are neither psychotic nor premeditated acts. Wolfgang and Ferracuti (1967) estimated that no more than 5 percent of all homicides are planned or intentional. Subsequent research has shown little support for the deterrence model (Loftin 1977; Parker and Smith 1979). There is little useful evidence that raising the costs for violence by inflicting more punishment (or speedier or more severe or more certain punishment) results in less violence (Currie 1985).

The second model relies on cultural variables to account for differences in homicide rates. The subculture of violence thesis argues that certain segments of society have adopted distinctively violent subcultural values (Wolfgang and Ferracuti 1967). These values purportedly provide normative support for violent behavior, thereby increasing the likelihood that hostile impulses will lead to homicidal incidents. Black-white differences in homicide rates are explained in terms of differing value orientations.

More recent research has partially discredited this model. These investigations have shown that a structural poverty index, which combines several socioeconomic variables, is a more powerful predictor of state homicide rates than either race or region (Loftin and Hill 1974; Parker and Smith 1979).

The subculture of violence model fails to explain variations in primary homicide rates; these rates appear to be more highly associated with social structural factors, especially measures of poverty. Racial differences in socioeconomic status are striking, and several studies suggest that poverty may be a more significant factor than race with regard to primary homicides (Loftin and Hill 1974; Bowman 1980; Smith and Parker 1980; Riedel 1984). On the other hand, social structural factors are less important in explaining variations in secondary homicide rates (Smith and Parker 1980; Messner 1983).

The third model, ecologic analysis, incorporates socioeconomic variables and looks at the correlation between these and other factors. Rose (1984) suggests that one should not totally disregard subcultural explanations but look at subculture, socioeconomic status (SES), and urban variables to explain black-on-black homicides.

Within this model, one must first recognize that the black community is quite diverse. This diversity manifests itself not only in economic life, occupational pursuits, and network structures but also in rates of antisocial behaviors. It is evident that risk of homicide victimization varies greatly within the black community. The extent of variation can be related to the nature of a given city's spacial configuration and to the sorting of population along SES and life-style orientations (Rose 1984). Environmental attributes may be associated with inherent risk, promoting activities that may operate independently of external forces.

In his study of black homicides, Rose found that within the black community,

> a set of stable high risk environments could be identified. Nevertheless, the structure of victimization was observed to differ within specific high risk environments. . . . The presence of stable high risk environments seems to suggest the existence of a subculture of violence that is place specific. In those high risk environments where expressive violence represents the modal type, shapes of the southern regional culture of violence predominate; and the cast of participants generally involves persons who have lost hope of ever escaping their marginal status. (p. xx)

This research also found that attempts to explain risk at the neighborhood level, using only structural variables, yielded mixed results. An interaction existed between structural characteristics of a neighborhood and stress levels, such that high stress levels in a high-risk neighborhood were strongly associated with expressive (primary) violence. Structural variables were less likely to explain risk in environments where stress was low to intermediate (Rose 1984).

In addition, the dual labor market system that perpetuates the black population's economic marginality and the role of environment in value formation places many blacks in a position where they are likely to resort to violence to preserve a valued position or relationship or to acquire some valued resource (Bowman 1980; Rose 1984).

Ecologic models hold that homicides are the product of several variables operating at the macrolevel and microlevel. This perspective emphasizes environmental factors for blacks, including poverty, unemployment, substandard housing, stressful life events, and conditions that may render individuals more or less vulnerable. When these factors are added to technological change—the rise in the supply of handguns—one can see at least a partial cause for the increase in black homicide (Farley 1980).

To date, few studies have attempted to test and develop ecologic models for understanding recent homicides in general. During the most recent upsurge in homicide frequency, even fewer studies have devoted exclusive attention to black Americans, the population at greatest risk of victimization (Rose 1984).

Attempts to Identify Possible Links

Certainly no simple cause-effect relationship exists between family violence and homicide in the black community; many intervening and confounding variables are probably present. Although family violence and criminal violence have been investigated separately by sociologists and criminologists, few attempts have been made to integrate the emerging knowledge of violence in the home with other violence research (Fagan and Wexler 1984).

Childhood Exposure to Violence

For both intrafamilial and extrafamilial violence, exposure to violence as a child seems to be an important precursor of adult violence (Gelles 1980; Fagan and Wexler 1984). Violence in one's family of orientation seems to increase the probability of violence not only in one's family of procreation but also outside the family. In a comparison of the characteristics of spouse batterers with those of generally violent men, childhood exposure to violence was the strongest predictor of involvement in both intrafamil-ial and extrafamilial violence, explaining 26 percent of the variance char-acteristics of spouse batterers compared to generally violent men (Fagan, Stewart, and Hansen 1983). These data support a social learning theory of violence.

Fagan, Stewart, and Hansen (1983) suggest that even though there is strong support for the notion of the intergenerational transmission of violence, future research needs to examine the environmental properties that provide such reinforcement and the cognitive processes associated with violent responses in certain situations. Equally important is an understanding of the factors that enable abused children to avoid vio-lence as adults.

Homicides in Response to Violence

Many victims of child or spouse assault respond to the assaultive treat-ment by striking back at the perpetrator. Brown's (1985) comparative analysis of women who kill their abusers and battered women who do not indicate that the significant variables that differentiate these groups de-scribe the man's violent behavior, not the woman's. Here we see that family violence and homicide are directly linked.

The frequency with which family violence leads to retaliative homi-cides rather than leaving the abusive situation has not been well studied. It appears that frequently a link between family violence and homicide is forged when victims of maltreatment attempt to remedy their situation by retaliating. For example, according to Walker (1984), approximately 25 percent of the women serving thirty- to fifty-year sentences at Renz Cor-rectional Facility, Missouri, are there for killing abusive mates. She cites other research conducted with female prisoners that indicates they were being abused at the time they committed other offenses. This female prison population is disproportionately black.

Homicide as Family Violence

Primary homicides and family violence bear a family resemblance. Both appear to be in part products of high-stress, low-resource, and multiple-problem families. In a legal sense, the distinction between family and friends may be more or less artificial. In reality, however, we are dealing conceptually with violence and homicides among intimates. Studies of courtship violence and violence among cohabitants support the broader perspective of violence among intimates.

The specific details about battering yield a catalog of violent acts and injuries (Walker 1984), including hitting, punching, kicking, striking with objects, choking, stabbing, and shooting. Homicides can occur as either an anticipated or unanticipated consequence of any of these acts.

Although inexplicable killings by a previously nonviolent family member do occur, they are rare. Intrafamily homicides are not unpredictable events. The day-to-day reality is that most family murders are prefaced by a long history of assaults (Straus 1985; Hawkins 1986). Homicide among consensual mates may be just one episode in a long-standing syndrome of violence.

In a preliminary study of homicide cases and previous assaultive behavior between January 1983 and June 1984 in Raleigh, North Carolina, Hawkins (1986) obtained data on previous arrests for assault at the house in which the homicide occurred. Of the twenty-three homicide cases, thirteen involved black male victims and four involved four black females. For the four cases involving black females, two households reported to have had at least one previous assault arrest. Two previous arrests were reported for one of the two households. For the thirteen cases involving black male victims, five households were the scene of previous assault arrests. One of these five had two reported arrests (Hawkins 1986).

These statistics are even more disturbing given the short study period. One would suspect that these assaults were part of a history of violent conflict and that the nine arrests in households that were later involved in a homicide reflect an official response to the most severe assaults. Overall these data support previous research that suggests that nonlethal violence is a frequent antecedent of homicide (Browne 1985; Straus 1985).

Social Ecology of Family Violence and Homicide

Fully developed causal models in this field are rare. Although most researchers agree that violence and homicides are the product of a complex, multidimensional process, few have attempted to identify the linking variables at different levels of analysis. Garbarino's ecological model has been utilized to explain the complex nature of child maltreatment (Garbarino and Sherman 1980; Garbarino 1982). The model considers the context in which violent interactions occur and might include questions of environmental (neighborhood or community) quality. It also assesses the cultural, political, economic, and demographic factors that shape the quality of life for families.

From this perspective and work in several other disciplines, we have learned that the extent to which an individual is integrated into local structures of kinship, neighborhood, and community is related to their prospects of mental health, physical well-being, and violence (Currie 1985; Comer 1985). With its focus on the mutual adaptation of persons and environments, this model appears to have some utility for the study of other types of dysfunctional family interactions. An ecologic approach to studying links between family violence and homicide in the black community seems to be a fertile area for additional empirical research.

Conclusion

Are homicides linked to other forms of family violence in the black community? Our review suggests that they appear to be conceptually linked in that they may have a common etiology. Many factors identified by research to date appear to be associated with both processes. In cases when homicide occurs as a direct result of violence or in retaliation to violence, the links may be causal in both directions.

There are many questions the available evidence does not address, but it is clear that the prevention of primary homicides may be affected by efforts to reduce the incidence of family violence. These efforts will require primary prevention techniques, which might include educational programs for parents and children, stress reduction efforts through neighborhood support teams, and family counseling or therapy. Secondary and tertiary prevention techniques will also require implementation.

It is clear that approaches to the problem based on poor conceptual and empirical foundations will do little to reduce black-on-black homicides in the near future. We are challenged to explore the complex set of factors associated with violence among blacks and develop programmatic initiatives with solid financial supports to reduce the immeasurable costs of violence not only to the black community but to the entire nation.

References

American Humane Association. 1986. *Highlights of Office Child Abuse and Neglect Reporting. Annual Report 1984.* Denver: American Humane Association.

Billingsley, Andrew. 1968. *Black Families in White America*. Englewood Cliffs, N.J.: Prentice-Hall.

Blau, J.R., and Peter M. Blau. 1982. "The Cost Of Inequality: Metropolitan Structure and Violent Crime." *American Sociological Review* 47:114–129.

Bowman, Phillip J. 1980. "Toward a Dual Labor-Market Approach to Black-on-Black Homicide." *Public Health Reports* 95, no. 6:555–556.

Browne, Angela. 1985. "Assault and Homicide at Home: When Battered Women Kill." In *Advances in Applied Social Psychology*, vol. 3. Edited by M.J. Saxe and L. Saxe. Hillsdale, N.J.: Lawrence Erlbaum Associates.

Cazenave, Noel, and Murray A. Straus. 1979. "Race, Class, Network Embeddedness and Family Violence." *Journal of Comparative Family Studies* 10:281–300.

Comer, James. 1985. "Black Violence and Public Policy: Changing Directions." In *American Violence and Public Policy*. Edited by Lynn Curtis. New Haven: Yale University Press.

Constantino, Joseph, Lewis Kuller, Joshua Perper, and Raymond Cypess. 1977. "An Epidemiologic Study of Homicides in Allegheny County, Pennsylvania." *American Journal of Epidemiology* 106, no. 4:314–324.

Currie, Elliott. 1985. "Crimes of Violence and Public Policy: Changing Directions." In *American Violence and Public Policy*. Edited by Lynn Curtis. New Haven: Yale University Press.

Ehrlich, I. 1975. "The Deterrent Effect of Capital Punishment: A Question of Life and Death." *American Economic Review* 65:397–417.

Fagan, Jeffrey, and Sandra Wexler. 1984. "Crime at Home and Crime in the Streets: The Relation between Family and Stranger Violence." Paper presented at the National Institute of Justice Workshop on Family Violence as a Crime Problem, October, Washington, D.C.

Fagan, Jeffrey A., Douglas K. Steward, and Karen V. Hansen. 1983. "Violent Men or Violent Husbands? Background Factors and Situational Correlates." In *The Dark Side of Families*. Edited by David Finkelhor, Richard Gelles, Gerald Hotaling, and Murray Straus. Bevery Hills: Sage Publications.

Farley, Reynolds. 1980. "Homicide Trends in the United States." *Demography* 17, no. 2:177–188.

Garbarino, James. 1982. *Children and Families in the Social Environment*. New York: Aldine.

Garbarino, James, and Deborah Sherman. 1980. "High-risk Neighborhoods and High-risk Families: The Human Ecology of Child Maltreatment." *Child Development* 51:188–198.

Garbarino, James, and Aaron Ebata. 1983. "Ethnic and Cultural Differences in Child Maltreatment." *Journal of Marriage and the Family* 39:721–736.

Gelles, Richard J. 1980. "Violence in the Family: A Review of Research in the Seventies." *Journal of Marriage and the Family* 42(November):873–885.

Gil, David. 1970. *Violence against Children: Physical Child Abuse in the United States*. Cambridge: Harvard University Press.

Hampton, Robert L. 1985. "Violence against Black Children: The Current Knowledge and Future Research Needs." Paper presented at the National Institute of Mental Health Staff College Invitational Conference on Research on Violence in the Black Family and Community. September 27, Rockville, Md.

———. 1987. "Race, Class, and Child Maltreatment." *Journal of Comparative Family Studies*, 23, no. 1:113–126.

Hampton, Robert L., and Eli H. Newberger. 1985. "Child Abuse Incidence and Reporting by Hospital: The Significance of Severity, Race, and Class." *American Public Health* 75, no. 1:56–60.

Hawkins, Darnell F. 1986. "Longitudinal-Situational Approaches to Understanding Black-on-Black Homicide." In Department of Health and Human Services, *Report of the Secretary's Task Force on Black and Minority Health*, vol. 5: *Homicide, Suicide and Unintentional Injuries*. Washington, D.C.: Government Printing Office.

Jackson, Aeolian. 1984. "Child Neglect: An Overview." In *Perspectives on Child Maltreatment in the Mid '80's*. Department of Health and Human Service Publication (OHDS) 84-30338. Washington, D.C.: Government Printing Office.

Jason, Janine. 1983. "Child Homicide Spectrum." *American Journal of Diseases of Children* 137(June):578–581.

Jason, Janine, N. Ambereuh, J. Marks, and C. Tyler, Jr. 1982. "Child Abuse in Georgia: A Method to Evaluate Risk Factors and Reporting Bias." *American Journal of Public Health* 72, no. 12:1353–1358.

Jason, Janine, Jeanne C. Gilliland, and Carl Tyler, Jr. 1983. "Homicide as a Cause of Pediatric Mortality in the United States." *Pediatrics* 72, no. 2:191–197.

Jason, Janine, Melinda Flock, and Carl W. Tyler, Jr. 1983. "A Comparison of Primary and Secondary Homicides in the United States." *American Journal of Epidemiology* 117, no. 3:309–319.

Lauderdale, Michael, Al Valiunas, and Rosalie Anderson. 1980. "Race, Ethnicity and Child Maltreatment: An Empirical Analysis." *Child Abuse and Neglect* 4:163–169.

Lindholm, Kathryn J., and Richard Willey. 1983. "Child Abuse and Ethnicity: Patterns of Similarities and Differences." Occasional Paper 18. Los Angeles: Spanish Speaking Mental Health Research Center, University of California.

Loftin, C.K. 1977. "Alternative Estimates of the Impact of Certainty and Severity of Punishment on Levels of Homicide in American States." Paper presented at the annual meeting of the American Sociological Association, Chicago.

Loftin, Colin, and Robert H. Hill. 1974. "Regional Subculture and Homicide: An Examination of the Gastil-Hackney Thesis." *American Sociological Review* 29:714–724.

Loya, Fred, Philip Garcia, John D. Sullivan, Luis A. Vargas, James Mercy, and Nancy Allen. 1986. "Conditional Risks of Homicide among Anglo, Hispanic, Black, and Asian Victims in Los Angeles, 1970–1979." In Department of Health and Human Services, *Report of the Secretary's Task Force on Black and Minority Health*, vol. 5: *Homicide, Suicide and Unintentional Injuries*. Washington, D.C.: Government Printing Office.

Mercy, James A. 1983. "Homicide Surveillance, 1970–1978." *MMWR32* 2ss:9–13.

Messner, Steven F. 1983. "Regional and Racial Effects on the Urban Homicide Rate: The Subculture of Violence Revisited." *American Journal of Sociology* 88, no. 5:997–1007.

_____ . 1982. "Poverty, Inequality, and the Urban Homicide Rate: Some Unexpected Findings." *Criminology* 20:103–114.

Mulvihill, D.J., and M.M. Tumin. 1969. *Crimes of Violence*. Report of the National Commission on the Cause and Prevention of Violence. Washington, D.C.: Government Printing Office.

Munford, Robert, Ross Kazer, Roger Feldman, and Robert Stivers. 1976. "Homicide Trends in Atlanta." *Criminology* 14, no. 2:213–231.

Parker, Robert N., and M. Dwayne Smith. 1979. "Deterrence, Poverty and Type of Homicide." *American Journal of Sociology* 85, no. 3:614–624.

Rice, Dorothy. 1980. "Homicide from the Perspective of NCHS Statistics on Blacks." *Public Health Service Report* 95, 6:550–552.

Riedel, Marc. 1984. "Black-on-Black Homicides: Overview and Recommendations." In *The Criminal Justice System and Blacks*. Edited by Daniel Georges-Abeyie. New York: Clark Boardman.

Rose, Harold. 1984. "Black-on-Black Homicides: Overview and Recommendations." In *The Criminal Justice System and Blacks*. Edited by Daniel Georges-Abeyie. New York: Clark Boardman.

Smith, M. Dwayne, and Robert N. Parker. 1980. "Type of Homicide and Variation in Regional Rates." *Social Forces* 59:146–157.

Spearly, James L., and Michael Lauderdale. 1983. "Community Characteristics and Ethnicity in the Prediction of Child Maltreatment Rates." *Child Abuse and Neglect* 7:91–105.

Straus, Murray A. 1985. "Domestic Violence and Homicide Antecedents." Paper presented at the New York Academy of Medicine, Symposium on Homicide: Public Health Perspectives, October 3–4.

Straus, Murray, Richard J. Gelles, and Suzanne Steinmetz. 1980. *Behind Closed Doors*. New York: Doubleday.

Study Findings. 1981. *National Study of the Incidence and Severity of Child Abuse and Neglect*. Department of Health and Human Services. Publication no. (OHDS) 81-030326.

Tardiff, Kenneth, Elliot M. Gross, and Steven Messner. 1986. "A Study of Homicides in Manhattan, 1981." *American Journal of Public Health* 76, 2:139–143.

Walker, Lenore. 1984. *The Battered Woman Syndrome*. New York: Springer.

Wolfgang, Marvin E., and Franco Ferrauti. 1967. *The Subculture of Violence: Toward an Integrated Theory of Criminology*. London: Tavistock.

10
Black Women Who Kill

Coramae Richey Mann

lack woman offenders were virtually ignored by researchers until
the 1970s, and although studies of female offenders have proliferated in recent years, there remains a dearth of empirical information on females who commit criminal homicide, an appalling situation because of the startling incidence of this crime.

The few studies of criminal homicide that explore gender and race reveal the following ranking in frequency of arrests: black males, black females, white males, white females (Sutherland and Cressey 1978, p. 30). Riedel and Lockhart-Riedel (1984, p. 2) point out, "We are confronted with a paradox at the outset of our inquiry: of the four race and sexual combinations (black males, black females, white males, white females), black females have the second highest rate and yet there is almost no research on the phenomenon." This chapter provides a profile of the black female homicide offender and an analysis of previous research on this topic in conjunction with ongoing field research undertaken in Chicago and Houston.

Definitions and Limitations

Wilbanks (1982) reminds us that some researchers use the terms *murder* and *homicide* as if they were identical. Indeed the Uniform Crime Report arrest categories, as well as law enforcement agencies, identify such offenders under the terms *murder* and *nonnegligent manslaughter*. According to the definitions offered by Wilbanks (1982, p. 153), homicide is the killing of one human being by another; it includes both criminal (murder) and noncriminal (justifiable and excusable) homicide. In concurrence with

This chapter is excerpted from a monograph commissioned by the National Institutes of Health Task Force on Black and Minority Health No. 263 SGX13581 and also includes preliminary findings from a black faculty research grant funded by Florida State University.

Wilbanks, the term I prefer is *criminal homicide,* but the studies I describe and the police department files use *murder, homicide,* and *criminal homicide* interchangeably and thus are reported in those terms.

Another necessary word of caution concerns the data bases used in the studies reported. The Uniform Crime Reports (UCR) collected by the FBI are the most frequently used sources of arrest data available in the United States today, but they do not cross-tabulate by gender and race. Therefore extrapolations from these official statistics must be viewed with caution. Further, in addition to the numerous problems associated with this data source, detailed previously by Hindelang (1974) and Skogan (1974), among others, it should be noted that minorities, especially blacks, are frequently undercounted in the decennial census; therefore race-specific arrest rates are suspect. Finally, it is generally believed in minority communities that police racial prejudice, oversurveillance, and a tendency to arrest lead to more stringent law enforcement in such communities, particularly regarding blacks.

Prison studies, the other common source of homicide information, must also be viewed with caution, since incarceration is the bottom step on the ladder of the criminal justice system and many researchers have found that trip fraught with institutional or other forms of racism at each step (Staples 1975; Pope and McNeely 1981; Georges-Abeyie 1984).

Despite the fallibility of these sources, it is clear that the involvement of black women in criminal homicide is much higher than that of white, Hispanic, Asian, or native American women in the United States.[1] Because homicide is predominantly intraracial, the usual victim of a black female criminal homicide offender is a black male. The murder of black men has reached epidemic proportions; homicide is the leading cause of death among young black males ages 15 to 24 (Mercy, Smith, and Rosenberg 1983). Black males have the highest victim rates of criminal homicide in the country (58.5 per 100,000); black females, at 13.2 per 100,000, rank second (Riedel 1984, p. 53).

Clearly there is an urgent need to obtain an accurate picture of the black female criminal homicide offender, not only because of the seriousness of the crime and the lack of information about this subgroup of offenders but also so that we can understand the underlying factors that contribute to the offense and, it is hoped, to prevent the violence.

This chapter begins with an analysis of identified empirical studies on black female criminal homicide offenders; by definition this analysis excludes works that use anecdotal or case study methods and those cross-jurisdictional studies from the National Center for Health Statistics (NCHS) that contain no information on the offender. The second section describes preliminary findings from data on black women who kill collected from police homicide files in Chicago and Houston.

Empirical Studies of
Female Criminal Homicide Offenders

Fifteen empirical studies focusing on female homicide offenders, spanning a twenty-six-year reporting period (1958–1984), were identified by the iterative search method described by Kleck (1981, p. 783) in his study of racial discrimination in sentencing.[2] Through this process and through data shared by other scholars, I believe that every major empirical study of the offender group has been located. Table 10-1 provides an outline of this material. It shows three studies that describe national rates and/or general trends in male and female homicide (Shin, Jedlicka, and Lee 1977; Wilbanks, 1982; 1983a); three homicide studies in which black female offenders are not identified (Ward, Jackson, and Ward 1969; Rosenblatt and Greenland 1974; Biggers 1979); five studies in which black female homicide offenders are discussed in conjunction with white and/or other offenders, yielding data that made it possible to isolate the black subsample (Wolfgang 1958; Cole, Fisher, and Cole 1968; Gibbs, Silverman, and Vega, 1977; Totman 1978; Wilbanks, 1983b); two studies in which black female offenders, though not separable, nonetheless constituted the largest proportion of the sample, thus enabling these data to be used cautiously (Suval and Brisson 1974; Weisheit 1984); and two studies concerned exclusively with black female criminal homicide offenders (McClain 1982a, b).

The three studies using UCR and/or NCHS data (Shin, Jedlicka, and Lee 1977; Wilbanks 1982, 1983a) are mentioned where appropriate but are not included in this analysis, which focuses on characteristics, circumstances of the offense, and criminal justice data concerned with the offender and her offense. Prison studies (Glick and Neto 1977; Figueria-McDonough 1981; Iglehart 1981) and other relevant data that do not specifically address the crime of homicide are also cited to illustrate pertinent points.

Black women are the most frequently arrested female offenders in cleared murder cases; they also make up the largest proportion of women incarcerated for criminal homicide.

Glick and Neto's (1977, p. 153) widely cited national study of women in jails and prisons reveals a disproportionate number of black women incarcerated for murder (18.6 percent of the black incarceration offenses) in comparison to other racial or ethnic subgroups (whites, 12.9 percent; Hispanics, 8.6 percent; native Americans, 13.4 percent). Similarly, 1979 California prison statistics indicate that black females constituted the highest proportion of total homicide offenders (41.8 percent), followed closely by white females at 38.8 percent (Mann 1984). In the New York State women's correctional system, 80 percent of the women in prison for

Table 10-1
Empirical Studies of Female Criminal Homicide Offenders

Researchers	Year Reported	Data Base[a]		City Study	Prison Study	Time Period	Number of Cases	Number Black	Percentage Black
		UCR	NCHS						
Wolfgang[b]	1958			Philadelphia		1948–1952	93	93	100.0
Cole, Fisher, and Cole	1968				California	1965	111	48	43.2
Ward, Jackson, and Ward	1969				Minnesota	1963–1964, 1968; 1964–1966	179	N.A.	N.A.
Suval and Brisson	1974				North Carolina	1969–1971	87	70	80.5
Rosenblatt and Greenland	1974				Canada (also hospital records)	1970–1971	24	N.A.	N.A.
Gibbs, Silverman, and Vega	1977				Florida	1977	43	26	60.5
Shin, Jedlicka, and Lee	1977	X	X			1940–1974	N.A.	N.A.	N.A.
Totman	1978				California	July–Dec. 1969	50	13	26.0
Biggers	1979				Florida	Two years	32	N.A.	N.A.
McClain	1981			Detroit, St. Louis, Atlanta, Pittsburgh, Houston, Los Angeles		1975	119	119	100.0
McClain[c]	1982			Atlanta	Detroit	1975	9	9	100.0
Wilbanks	1982	X	X			1963–1979	N.A.	N.A.	N.A.
Wilbanks	1983	X				1980	2,412[d]	N.A.	N.A.
Wilbanks	1983			Dade County (Miami)		1980	47[e]	28	59.6
Weisheit	1984				Illinois	1940–1966, 1981–Spring 1983	460	336	73.0

[a]Based on Wilbanks's typology (1982); "anecdotal" studies, the fifth category, is not included.
[b]Black subsample isolated from the total sample.
[c]This subsample is from a 1981 study by McClain.
[d]Although 2,412 reported, figures in Wilbanks's table 1–B total 2,512.
[e]Although 47 reported, figures in Wilbanks's table 1 total 46.

homicide in 1976 were black (Mann 1986); this figure is matched closely by a comprehensive study of women in Michigan prisons, where 71 percent of the incarcerated female homicide offenders in 1978 were nonwhite (Figueria-McDonough 1981, p. 96).

In the twelve studies reported here, the number of subjects ranges from nine black female criminal homicide offenders, who were interviewed (McClain 1982b), to 460 incarcerated female homicide offenders in the most recent study, reported by Weisheit (1984). The latter were admitted to the Illinois State Prison for Women from 1940 to 1966 and from 1981 to the spring of 1983; 73 percent of these offenders were black. With the exception of two studies (Ward, Jackson, and Ward, 1969; Totman 1978), blacks tend to predominate among the homicide offenders in every study where the proportion of black female offenders is known.[3]

Offender Social Characteristics

Age. Prison studies indicate that female criminals tend to be under 30 years of age. (Table 10–2 lists characteristics of offenders.) Glick and Neto (1977, p. 109) report an age range of 22 to 25 years in their national study, with a mean age of 25.7 years for incarcerated black offenders and a slightly higher mean age (28.6 years) for white offenders. This finding is corroborated by the study of female prisoners in Michigan, which reports a modal age of 21 to 24 years (Iglehart 1981, p. 38).

By contrast, the female criminal homicide offender is not young. Wilbanks (1983b) lists a range of 25 to 44 years of age in his description of Miami (Dade County) female homicide offenders. In the studies by Wolfgang (1958), Cole, Fisher, and Cole (1968), and McClain (1981, 1982b), one of which is a subsample from a larger data base, the ages of black female homicide offenders range from 32.6 years (median) to 35.4 years (mean).

Intelligence. Iglehart (1981, p. 42) found that about half the women prisoners in Michigan had IQ scores below normal (0–89), strongly suggesting "that the functioning capabilities of the incarcerated females are severely limited." Her colleague, Figueria-McDonough (1981, pp. 86–87), states, "It is among homicide and assault offenders that a higher relative incidence of women with scores below seventy was found"; only 37 percent of the homicide offenders had IQs that were normal or above. In her examination of subcategories of offenses, Figueria-McDonough suggests that IQ varies directly with the complexity of the illegal act; for example, only 34 percent of the manslaughter cases (about one-half of the homicide commitments) had normal or above-normal IQs, but 48 percent of the first-degree female homicide offenders tested at that level.

Table 10-2
Offender Characteristics

Study	Race (percentage)			Mean Age (years)	IQ	Education (years)	Evidence of Alcohol Use		Evidence of Narcotics Use	
	Black	White	Other				Yes	No	Yes	No
Wolfgang 1968 N = 93	100.0			32.6						
Cole, Fisher, and Cole 1968 N = 111	43.2	41.8	15.0	37.0W 35.4B	88.8W 80.0B	9.6				
Ward, Jackson, and Ward 1969 N = 179	25.0a	64.3	10.7		b		60.0a	40.0	2.0	98.0
Suval and Brisson 1974 N = 97	80.5	19.5		30.0	90.0	9.0	61.1	38.9	1.3	98.7
Gibbs, Silverman, and Vega 1977 N = 43				33.0		c				
First degree	60.5	39.5			108.8		85.7	14.3	85.7	14.3
Second degree	14.3	85.7			94.0		70.0	30.0	75.0	25.0
Third degree	75.0	25.0			92.7		75.0	25.0	75.0	25.0
Totman 1978 N = 50				35.1W 30.6B						
Mate	27.8	55.6	16.6		109.2W 85.6B	10.6W 9.2B				
Child	21.4	71.4	7.1		89.4W 80.0B	10.4W 9.0B				
Biggers 1979 N = 32				35.0	90–100	11.0				
McClain 1982b N = 9	100.0			32.8			12.5	87.5	0.0	100.0

Note: Studies by Rosenblatt and Greenland (1974), McClain (1983), and Weisheit (1984) lacked sufficient data for inclusion in this table, but are described in text where appropriate, as are additional social characteristics not included because of small numbers.

W = white; B = black.

[a] 1963 and 1968 sample.

[b] Scores for 42% of the total 1968 sample (60% of the nonwhite group) fell below 90, 58% fell in the normal range (90–100), and 29% were above 110.

[c] 42.9% of first-degree, 85.0% of second-degree, and 68.8% of third-degree murderers did not have a high school diploma.

Six of the studies under examination here included some measure of intelligence, although reporting methods vary. In the four prison studies where blacks and whites can be compared, whites scored higher on the intelligence tests. (The question of the reliability and validity of these tests will not be addressed here, but readers should keep in mind that such tests have been challenged on racial and cultural grounds.) Cole, Fisher, and Cole (1968) report higher IQs for the white (88.8) than for the black homicide offenders (80.0); both groups tested below the normal range, however. Other instances of less than normal intelligence are seen in the Suval and Brisson North Carolina study (1974), where 69.6 percent of the women, most of whom were black (80.5 percent), had IQs below 90, and in the Totman study in California (1978), which reports both black (80.0 percent) and white (89.4 percent) child killers and black mate killers (85.6 percent) at that level. Ward, Jackson, and Ward (1969) found in their 1968 sample that 42 percent of the women had IQs below 90; 60 percent of the nonwhite group fell below that level.

There appears to be some support for the relationship between IQ and the complexity of the crime, as espoused by Figueria-McDonough (1981). Gibbs, Silverman, and Vega (1977) found that first-degree murderers (primarily white) had the highest average IQs (108.8); second-degree and third-degree murderers, primarily black, had successively lower IQs of 94.0 and 92.7, respectively. A similar finding by Totman (1978) reveals an inverse relationship between IQ and the complexity of the homicide, if one can assume that killing a mate is a more formidable task than killing a child. Mate killers, black and white, had IQs of 85.6 and 109.2, respectively; child killers scored below normal, with IQs of 80.0 (black) and 89.4 (white).

Biggers (1979) in Florida was the only researcher to report IQs in the normal range (90–100) for the entire female homicide offender group, although Ward, Jackson, and Ward (1969) found that more than half (58 percent) of the 1968 California sample attained this level, and 29 percent had IQs over 110.

In sum, three tentative conclusions may be reached concerning the intelligence of the female homicide offenders in the studies under examination: (1) the majority of imprisoned female homicide offenders have less than normal intelligence; (2) black offenders incarcerated for homicide tend to have lower intelligence, as measured by prison-administered IQ tests, than white offenders committed for the same offense; and (3) the IQ of the homicide offender varies inversely with the complexity of the homicide, as suggested by Figueria-McDonough (1981).

Education. In four of the five studies reporting information on years of education attained, female homicide offenders were unlikely to have finished high school; the average number of years completed is nine or fewer. (See table 10–2.) Again, it is possible to make prudent speculations about these data relative to race. It appears that the black offenders achieved fewer years of education because they make up about 80 percent of the sample and the educational level for the sample was found to be fewer than nine years (Suval and Brisson 1974). Support for such a position can be derived from the Totman (1978) findings, where black mate and child murderers are reported to average 9.2 years and 9 years of total education, respectively. Although most *white female homicide* offenders have not completed high school, the average educational levels are higher for both mate killers (10.6) and child killers (10.4) in this group. In addition, Gibbs, Silverman, and Vega (1977) report that the predominantly black second-degree murderers, 85 percent of whom lacked high school diplomas, and the third-degree murderers, 68.8 percent of whom did not finish high school, lag far behind the predominantly white first-degree murderers, only 42.9 percent of whom have less than a high school diploma. It is not far-fetched to assume that black homicide offenders have fewer years of schooling than their white counterparts; Glick and Neto (1977, p. 129) found significant educational differences between white and black female offenders in the national study.

Whatever the offense, it is generally found that incarcerated female offenders have educational achievements below the national average for the population (Iglehart 1981, p. 40) and thus are frequently described as uneducated. The homicide offenders Iglehart cites are no exception. The notion that differences in life circumstances led these women to take other persons' lives suggests strongly that being disadvantaged, poor, and/or members of minority groups must play an important part in reducing life chances, opportunities, and achievements, including educational accomplishments. The often-intolerable life of lower-income individuals, particularly those bearing the additional stigma of racial minority status, can lead to deviant behavior when stress is introduced. Homicide is one reactive behavioral symptom of such a social condition; substance use and abuse are others.

Previous Alcohol and Narcotics Use. A few of the studies of female homicide offenders explored the incidence of alcohol or narcotic use; the findings are mixed. Keeping in mind the small sample, McClain (1982b) reports little evidence of alcohol use (12.5 percent) and no indications of narcotics use among the nine black women studied. The Ward, Jackson, and Ward (1969) study, which used a larger sample, revealed that only 2 percent of the homicide offenders, most of whom were white women (64.3 percent), admitted to narcotics use. Suval and Brisson (1974) offer further corroboration of minimal drug usage in their finding that only 1.3 percent of the female homicide offenders (80.5 percent of them black) used narcotics. A contrasting result is reported by Gibbs, Silverman, and Vega (1977):

they found narcotics histories in 75 percent of both second- and third-degree female murderers and 85.7 percent of the first-degree female murderers. Because these women were imprisoned in Florida, often called the drug capital of the world, this finding may be less incongruous than it seems.

Other Social Characteristics. Additional characteristics of female homicide offenders are not included in table 10–2 because they are reported by only a few of the researchers, but they are mentioned here to add another dimension to the portrait of black women who kill.

National prison studies have indicated that black female offenders are most likely never to have married; whites, by contrast, are most likely to have had serial relationships (Glick and Neto 1977, p. 115). The opposite picture is found in three of the studies explored here, which disclosed only small percentages of single women and extremely high proportions, ranging from 72.9 to 90 percent, of ever-married women and those who cohabited with men. In their North Carolina study, Suval and Brisson (1974) report the highest number of single-women murderers (27.1 percent); in Florida, Biggers (1979) finds that single women are only 12.5 percent of the female homicide offenders. Gibbs, Silverman, and Vega (1977) also found very few single women: 14 percent among first-degree murderers, 10 percent among second-degree murderers, and 12.5 percent among third-degree murderers.

Although three of the studies reporting high proportions of ever-married female homicide offenders differ from other findings on incarcerated women, they may not be incongruous. Because the studies were undertaken in southern Bible belt states, the results may reflect the moral and cultural attitudes of the southern tradition, which includes a double standard for the sexes. In addition, the victim of a female murderer tends to be her mate; therefore such offenders are rarely single.

Contrary to expectations, female homicide offenders do not come from broken homes. The two studies reporting on this subject, which have either predominantly black or all-black samples, found, respectively, that 62.3 percent (Suval and Brisson 1974) and 88.9 percent (McClain 1982b) of the women came from intact homes.

McClain (1982b) reveals that 66.7 percent of the black female homicide offenders studied were unemployed at the time of their offense. This figure coincides with the recent study reported by Weisheit (1984), which included 73 percent black offenders and showed a mean unemployment rate of 63 percent. These figures are somewhat higher than the unemployment percentages reported by Glick and Neto (1977, p. 135) on black (55 percent) and white (50 percent) women unemployed before their incarceration.

In the light of these unemployment statistics, albeit limited to a few studies, and the other dismal social characteristics of this group, it is not surprising that Cole, Fisher, and Cole (1968) report that 81 percent of the white and 90 percent of the black female homicide offenders worked in unskilled occupations before their incarceration. Suval and Brisson (1974) reveal that their entire sample, 80.5 percent of whom were black, occupied that status in the labor force. When we consider the national pattern of minority unemployment, underemployment, and overrepresentation in lower-status jobs in conjunction with the similar lower employment status of all women in the United States, it is clear that black women are discriminated against both for belonging to a minority group and for being females.

Victim Characteristics

Most of the studies examined included information on the homicide victim, but it was limited to the two particulars in table 10-3: the gender of the victim and the relationship between the victim and offender. Despite the paucity of data available, several observations can be made about female homicide offenders in general and specifically about blacks in this category.

There is clear support for the claim that homicide is an intersexual, intraracial, and intrafamilial event. Every researcher included here reported that males, usually adult males, were the primary target of homicide. The proportions of men as the victims of women ranged from 61 percent (Ward, Jackson, and Ward 1969) to the 97.9 percent indicated by Wilbanks (1983) in Dade County (Miami), Florida. A comment is in order about the McClain (1982b) findings, which reveal a difference of slightly more than ten percentage points between male (55.6 percent) and female homicide victims (44.4 percent). These data are based on only nine cases from Atlanta and Detroit, however, and could reflect idiosyncrasies of the sampling, particularly because the six-city sample from which these cases were selected (McClain, 1981) includes 85.5 percent male victims. On the other hand, there are indications that black females tend to kill friends more than white female homicide offenders do; these friends could be females. In analyzing the victim-offender relationships in table 10-3, for example, it is noted that among the second-degree murderers (who are mostly black) in the Gibbs, Silverman, and Vega (1977) study, 40 percent of the victims were friends and acquaintances; so were 34.2 percent of all the black subjects in McClain's larger study and 33.3 percent in her subsample. Many of the victims in the larger McClain sample could be women; they are clearly women in the subsample, as evidenced by the fact that male and child victims account, respectively, for only 55.6 and 11.1 percent of the victims.

Table 10-3
Victim Characteristics
(percentages)

	Victim Characteristics				Victim-Offender Relationship			
	Adult Male	Adult Female	Husband-Lover	Child	Family	Friend or Acquaintance	Stranger	Other/ Unknown
Wolfgang 1958	86.5	13.5	20.7		46.7	21.8	3.3	7.7
Cole, Fisher, and Cole 1968								
White				20.0	47.0		33.0	
Black				12.0	56.0		31.0	
Ward, Jackson, and Ward 1969	61.0[a]	16.0	35.0[a]	19.0		18.0	8.0	20.0
Suval and Brisson 1974	84.0	11.0		5.0				
Rosenblatt and Greenland 1974					87.5	8.3		4.2
Gibbs, Silverman, and Vega 1977								
First degree					71.4	14.3	14.3	
Second degree					40.0	40.0	20.0	
Third degree					56.3	18.8	25.0	
Totman 1978			72.0	28.0				
Biggers 1979			78.0				12.5	9.4
McClain 1981	85.5[b]	14.5	49.7	2.5	5.1	34.2	8.5	
McClain 1982	55.6[b]	44.4	55.6	11.1		33.3		
Wilbanks 1983	97.9[b]	2.1	61.7	8.5		14.9	8.5	6.4
Weisheit 1984			45.0	9.0	3.0	29.0	11.0	3.0

[a]1963 and 1968 samples.
[b]Sex of victims only, since child victims are not identified.

The intraracial nature of homicides is indicated in the victim-offender relationships. It appears that most of the victims of female homicide offenders are either husbands, lovers, family members, friends, or acquaintances. In American society today, the personal closeness implied by these descriptions is usually limited to members of the same racial or ethnic group, even if we allow for the slight possibility of an interracial marriage.

Two of the twelve studies reporting the victim-offender relationship consist of all black female homicide offenders. These investigations, reported by Wolfgang (1958) and McClain (1981), are separated by more than two decades but reveal some intriguing similarities. Both researchers collected city data and took samples of similar sizes: Wolfgang from Philadelphia ($N = 93$) and McClain from Detroit, St. Louis, Atlanta, Pittsburgh, Houston, and Los Angeles ($N = 119$).

Wolfgang and McClain also report almost identical victim gender characteristics: males were the most likely victims, 86.5 and 85.5 percent, respectively. These two studies diverge, however, when the victim-offender relationship is examined. In 1958 Wolfgang reported that 67.4 percent of the homicides were "family affairs" (husband-lover, family), but only 57.3 percent of the victim-offender relationships (husband-lover, child, family) in the McClain study were so identified in 1981. A closer inspection of the two sets of statistics indicates that only 20.7 percent of the victims in the Wolfgang study were husbands or lovers of the offenders. No children were victims, but other family members were (46.7 percent). This configuration seems to have changed by 1981, when McClain reported that 49.7 percent of the homicide victims were husbands or lovers, 2.5 percent were children, and only 5.1 percent were other members. Such drastic changes suggest that black women may be growing more violent toward those closest to them, or those whom they most love. It is also conceivable that black women are simply becoming more violent. The latter position is supported somewhat by an examination of the Wolfgang and McClain data on friend-acquaintance and stranger homicides, both of which show impressive percentages. In Wolfgang's sample, black female homicide offenders killed their friends or acquaintances in much lower proportions (21.8 percent) than the women in McClain's sample (34.2 percent). In addition, stranger-victim homicides were reported by Wolfgang at only 3.3 percent, compared to 8.5 percent by McClain. By 1968, Cole, Fisher, and Cole found ten times the Wolfgang incidence for stranger-victim homicides among both white females (33 percent) and black females (31 percent) in California. The predominantly black second- and third-degree female murders identified in the Florida study by Gibbs, Silverman, and Vega (1977) also show high percentages of stranger victimization (20 and 25 percent, respectively). Since Wolfgang's study, not one of the researchers has uncovered a percentage less than two and one-half times Wolfgang's percentage for this category of victim.

Offender Characteristics during Crime

Premeditation. As table 10–4 shows, female homicide offenders generally do not preplan the murders. Half (50 percent) of the first-degree murders reported by Gibbs, Silverman, and Vega (1977) were premeditated; slightly less than half (46 percent) were planned according to Ward, Jackson, and Ward (1969). The large proportion of unknown cases (38 percent), however, makes this statistic questionable; in the subsample of the totally black population McClain (1982b) examined, 66 percent of the homicide offenders denied premeditation in the killings. This figure tends to coincide with those for second-degree (61.1 percent) and third-degree murders (80 percent) in Gibbs, Silverman, and Vega (1977) who were disproportionately black; they claimed that they did not plan the murders. Although only three of the studies reported on this variable, they appear to support the notion that black women do not plan their homicides in advance.

Offender's Role. The typology that Ward, Jackson, and Ward (1979, p. 116) used outlines the roles women can play in the commission of violent crimes:

> the *conspirator*, who instigates or has knowledge of the crime but does not participate in committing the criminal act itself; the *accessory*, who plays a secondary role in committing the crime—acting as lookout, driving a getaway car, carrying weapons, tools, or the proceeds of robberies and burglaries; the *partner*, who participates equally in all aspects of the crime; and finally, the woman as the *sole perpetrator* of the crime.

From the eight studies that describe the role of the homicide perpetrator, it appears that a woman who kills acts alone. The proportions of sole perpetrators, seen in table 10–4, range from 71.4 percent (Gibbs, Silverman, and Vega 1977) to 96.4 percent (Suval and Brisson 1974); black female homicide offenders fall at the higher end of the range (94.1 percent), according to the findings reported by McClain (1981). Acting as partners in homicide runs a far second to acting alone.

Alcohol Involvement. A few of the cases noted whether the homicide offender, the victim, or both were under the influence of alcohol. In the present analysis, this category is reported separately from other possible reasons given for the homicide, including whether the offender "blamed"

Table 10-4
Offense Characteristics (Offender)
(percentages)

	Premeditated			Offender's Role					Alcohol Involvement				Rationale-Motive								
	Yes	No	Unknown	Sole	Partner	Conspirator	Accessory	Other	Offender	Victim	Both	Don't Know	Claims Innocence	Self-Defense Justifiable	Multiple	Alcohol-Drug Influence	Psychological-Emotional	Other's Fault	Accident/Trivial	Economic	Other/Unknown
Wolfgang 1958									19.8	3.1	43.8			50.6					4.3/31.2	8.6	5.41
Cole, Fisher, and Cole 1968 White				87.0				13.0	60.0												
Black				94.0				6.0	62.0												
Ward, Jackson, and Ward 1968	21.0[a]	46.0	33.0	77.0[a]	16.0	3.0	3.0						13.0[a]	24.0	8.0	5.0	9.0	3.0	17.0/-		21.0/-
Suval and Brisson 1974				96.4					45.8				21.6								
Rosenblatt and Greenland 1974				91.7			8.3		91.7												Altruism
Gibbs et al. 1977 First degree	50.0	50.0		71.4	28.6				71.4			28.6	28.6	14.3			28.6		5.91/-		
Second degree	38.9	61.1		80.0	20.0				63.2			17.6	11.8	17.6			35.3		6.71/-		
Third degree	20.0	80.0		75.0	25.0				56.3					33.3		6.7	40.0				
Totman 1968														Self-preservation			Revenge				
McClain 1981				94.1	4.2		1.2		20.0					11.1		11.1	44.4				
McClain 1982	33.4	66.6										22.2									11.1/-
Wilbanks 1983				91.5						46.2				21.3			59.6			8.5	8.5/2.1
Weisheit 1984				79.4										21.0			30.0 Revenge	1.6		24.0	24.0/-

[a]1963 and 1968 samples.

a substance for her deed. The reasons are classified under "rationale-motive" in table 10–4.

The studies vary considerably as to whether the homicide offender admitted to alcohol involvement at the time of the crime. The two studies concerned exclusively with black female homicide offenders suggest very little connection between the use of alcohol and the homicide. Wolfgang (1958) reports that only 19.8 percent of the blacks recalled alcohol involvement and that both the female offender and her victim allegedly were under the influence in 43.8 percent of the incidents. Similarly, McClain (1981) finds that one-fifth (20 percent) of the black female homicide offenders were under the influence of alcohol at the time of the homicide. Such findings are not surprising since female homicide offenders reported a low incidence of alcohol and narcotics abuse.

In the light of this observation, however, we may ask whether black female homicide offenders are less likely than their white counterparts to introduce the influence of alcohol as an excuse, or rationalization, for the homicide, because the remainder of the studies indicate fairly extensive alcohol involvement in the crime (from 45.8 percent to 91.7 percent). An examination of the motives given for the homicide helps partially to answer such an inquiry.

Rationale or Motive. In only three studies (Ward, Jackson, and Ward 1969; Gibbs, Silverman, and Vega 1977; McClain 1982b) did the homicide offender admit that the influence of alcohol and/or drugs contributed to the victim's death. The very small proportions (5 percent, 6.7 percent, 11.1 percent, respectively) suggest that although alcohol or drugs were used by the offender and/or the victim during the homicide, the female homicide offender did not regard this use as a principal cause of the offence.

Although various reasons are proffered for the homicide, the most frequent causes seem to be psychological or emotional. In the present analysis, this category includes anger and revenge, which appear more frequently to be the justification for black female homicide offenders. In the McClain (1982b) subsample, 44.4 percent of the subjects listed this reason. This rationale is also implied in studies with large proportions of black offenders, such as Weisheit (1984), who lists revenge as the primary motive in 30 percent of the cases, or Gibbs, Silverman, and Vega (1977), who find that second-degree (35.3 percent) and third-degree murderers (40.0 percent) cited psychological motivations for their crimes.

Self-defense, "self-preservation," and other forms of justifiable action were the second most frequent reasons given for killing another person, according to seven studies of female homicide. Wolfgang's (1958) black female subgroup listed self-defense in 50.6 percent of the cases, but only 11.1 percent of McClain's (1982b) black subsample cited self-defense as the motive. Claiming innocence may be another way of stating that the homicide was justifiable, but there is no way to verify this from the data reported by Ward, Jackson, and Ward (1969), Suval and Brisson (1974), and Gibbs, Silverman and Vega (1977). By the same token, more detailed information might allow us to determine that the women who stated that the homicide was someone else's fault would also be classified as basically innocent (see Ward, Jackson, and Ward 1969; Weisheit 1984).

Again, we might presume that the studies that list economic reasons as the rationale for the homicide actually refer to homicides committed during a felony such as a robbery, but insufficient information precludes this supposition.

Offense Characteristics

Most of the studies examined here contained some information on the type of weapon or the method of killing, but little attention was paid to other factors associated with the crime under consideration—for example, the location, if outdoors (bar, street, alley), and whether the homicide took place in a residence. Table 10-5 presents information about the offense characteristics reported.

Weapons and Methods. With few exceptions, firearms (handguns, shotguns, pistols, rifles) were the preferred weapons of most female homicide offenders. Biggers (1979, p. 6) notes that the women murderers in her Florida study were familiar with violence whether at home or in their neighborhoods. Thus "guns were considered 'safe' weapons because attack or defense could be made from a safe distance," and the women who used this type of weapon "either carried guns with them or had easy access to them in their own homes." It has also been pointed out that gunfire is impersonal because the injury may be inflicted from a distance, whereas beating, stabbing, and strangulation involve personal contact (Blackbourne 1984). Poisoning is another homicide method historically regarded as peculiar to women, undoubtedly because of the distance between victim and offender. Interestingly, only two studies (Totman 1978; Weisheit 1984) reported the use of poison. Totman (1978) indicates that 7.1 percent of the child murders involved poison, not an unusual finding in a parent-child homicide. The incidence of poisoning reported by Weisheit (1984) is extremely low: less than 1 percent.

Another stereotype—that of black women (and men) as cutters, slashers, and stabbers—may have originated with findings reported some years earlier by Wolfgang (1958), who noted that black women tend to use knives more often than guns in homicides. Table 10-5 shows that the majority of black female homicide offenders (67.7 percent) in his study did

Table 10-5
Offense Characteristics

	Type of Weapon or Method Used					Homicide Located in Residence of					Location in Residence					Outside Residence		
	Firearm	Knife	Hands[a]	Poison	Other-Unknown	Offender	Victim	Both	Other	Away from Residence	Living Room	Bedroom	Kitchen	Stairs or Hall	Other	Bar	Street	Other/Unknown
Wolfgang 1958	22.5	67.7	2.2		7.5						9.2	25.7	29.4	9.2		3.7	12.8	10.1/-
Cole, Fisher, and Cole 1968																		
White	37.0	32.0	13.0		18.0													
Black	31.0	48.0	6.0		15.0													
Rosenblatt and Greenland 1974	50.0		50.0															
Gibbs, Silverman, and Vega 1977																		
First degree	100.0																	
Second degree	73.7	15.8			10.6													
Third degree	62.5	31.3			6.3													
Totman 1978																		
Mate	61.0	25.0			14.0	64.0		14.0	22.0		13.7	19.6	5.9		23.5	5.9	5.9	13.7/11.8
Child			71.5	7.1	21.5													
McClain 1982a	72.6	23.0	2.7		1.1	47.0			15.4	37.6						2.6	29.0	6.0/-
McClain 1982b	66.7	11.1	11.1		11.1													
Wilbanks 1983	59.6	25.5	14.9				59.0		25.6							2.1	10.6	12.8/-
Weisheit 1984	44.0	40.5	?	0.007		In the home (not identified) 63.0												

[a]Includes beating, clubbing, strangling.
[b]1963 and 1968 sample.

choose knives as weapons. Cole, Fisher, and Cole (1968) also indicate that knives were the most frequent weapon (48 percent) used by black women in homicides. Since 1977, however, it has become apparent that firearms are now preferable to other weapons or methods for both black and white women who kill. It is particularly notable that 72.6 percent of the black women in the six-city study by McClain (1981) and 66.7 percent in the subsample (1982b) opted for guns in committing their homicides.

The three studies thus clearly identify black female homicide offenders separately from whites and suggest that black women are less inclined than white to use hands, feet, pipes, baseball bats, clubs, and other hand-held clubbing instruments as methods of killing. Wolfgang (1958) finds that only 2.2 percent used this means of homicide; Cole, Fisher, and Cole (1968) report a 6.0 percent incidence, or half the white proportion (13 percent); and McClain (1981) notes that only 2.7 percent of black female homicide offenders used their hands to commit homicide.

Location of the Homicide. The paucity of data in these studies precludes an accurate knowledge of where a woman elects to commit murder, but the information in table 10–5 suggests that the site is the residence of either the victim, the offender, or another person. Wolfgang (1958) found that the kitchen was the most common homicide location in the home (29.4 percent), possibly reflecting the high incidence of knife homicides he found among the black female offenders. Twenty years later, Totman (1978) reported the bedroom as the most frequent known homicide location (19.6 percent) in mate homicides, possibly because the gun is kept there.

Very few female homicide offenders commit their offenses away from the residence—on the street or in an alley, parking lot, automobile, or bar, for example. It is notable that McClain (1981) reports the street as the locale in 29 percent of the black female homicide cases, almost three times the percentage found by Wilbanks (1983b) and nearly five times the frequency among mate killings according to Totman (1978).

Criminal Justice Experience

The final data, seen in table 10–6, describe the female offender's experience with the criminal justice system. The most abundant findings, concerning previous arrests, are reported by nine of the studies. Unfortunately, it appears that the fate of the offender after apprehension was overlooked, ignored, or unavailable to most of the researchers.

Previous Arrests. After a careful analysis of each of the studies that reported the offenders' arrest histories, a curious pattern appears, differentiating white and black female homicide offenders. Research including

Table 10-6
Criminal Justice Offender Information
(percentages)

| | Previous Arrests | | Court Disposition | | | Prison Sentence (Years) | | | | | | | |
	Yes	No	Guilty	Dismissed or Acquitted	Other	1-3	4-8	9-15	15-30	30-Life	Life	Death	None
Wolfgang 1958	51.6	48.4	66.3	27.2	6.5								
Cole, Fisher, and Cole 1968													
White	66.0	33.0											
Black	81.0	19.0											
Ward, Jackson, and Ward 1969	20.0[a]	80.0											
Suval and Brisson 1974	27.1	72.9											
Rosenblatt and Greenland 1974	16.7	83.3				25.0	25.0	25.0		25.0			
Gibbs, Silverman, and Vega 1977													
First degree									14.3	85.7			
Second degree							5.0	20.0	35.0	40.0			
Third degree						12.5	37.5	43.8	6.3				
Totman 1978													
Mate	65.0W	35.0W											
	90.0B	10.0B											
Child	10.0W	90.0W											
	33.3B	66.7B											
McClain 1982	62.5	37.5											
Wilbanks 1983			63.0	18.5	18.5	41.2[b]	17.6[c]	17.6[d]		11.8			

[a] 1968 sample.
[b] Up to 5 years.
[c] 6-10 years.
[d] 11-20 years.

only blacks and those instances in which blacks can be examined apart from whites seems to indicate that black female homicide offenders have been involved in the criminal justice system more frequently than their white counterparts. Wolfgang (1958), for example, shows that slightly more than half (51.6 percent) of the black female homicide offenders had previous arrests. This finding is also noted by McClain (1982), who found 62.5 percent in this category, Cole, Fisher, and Cole (1968), who report 81 percent, and Totman (1978), who lists 90 percent black female mate killers with previous arrests. Although Totman found lower proportions of child killers than mate killers with previous criminal records, nonetheless the black women who killed their children (33.3 percent) were three times more likely to have previous arrests than white women who committed the same offense (10 percent). On the other hand, Suval and Brisson (1974) report a sample with 80.5 percent black offenders, but the previous arrest history of the group is only 27.1 percent. In addition, Totman (1978) records 65 percent of the white mate killers with prior arrests. Obviously no definitive statement can be made about this phenomenon, but it appears that black female homicide offenders have had more previous contact with the criminal justice system.

This finding is not surprising because minority women, like minority men, find themselves entangled more frequently in the law enforcement net for a number of reasons: more surveillance by the police in minority communities, police prejudice against minorities, wide police discretion regarding arrests, and the many ills and conditions in the social structure that contribute to deviance and are found more frequently in poor and minority neighborhoods.

Court Disposition and Sentencing. Only two studies report on the dispositions of the courts in female homicide cases. Wolfgang (1958) found that 66.3 percent of the black female homicide offenders were found guilty, while 27.2 percent were dismissed or acquitted. More recently, Wilbanks (1983b) reports that 63 percent of the women were found guilty and 18.5 percent dismissed or acquitted in a sample that consisted of 59.6 percent black and 40.4 percent white female homicide offenders. If these two studies may be used as guideposts, it seems that little change in the court dispositions of female homicide cases has taken place in twenty-five years.

Women who commit homicide do not appear to receive excessively long prison sentences. As seen in table 10–6, only the Florida study reported by Gibbs, Silverman, and Vega (1977) suggest harsh sanctions: 14.3 percent of the first-degree murders (85.7 percent of whom are white) were sentenced to fifteen to thirty years in prison, and 85.7 percent received prison terms of thirty years to life. It is curious, however, that the proportion of fifteen- to-thirty-year sentences for second-degree murderers (35 percent) in the Gibbs, Silverman, and Vega sample (which is 65 percent black) is twice that for first-degree murderers. Finally, in the studies examined, none of the women who committed homicide received a death sentence.

Ongoing Field Research

Field research is currently underway in three cities with large homicide rates: Chicago, Houston, and Atlanta. (New York City was dropped from the study because it lacks centralized homicide files.) The selection of these cities resulted from an examination of the UCR for 1979 and 1983. These years were selected for analysis because the UCR crime trends are reported in five-year periods, thus making it possible to note any changes in arrests for murder over that time span.

In 1979 the national murder rate was 9.7 per 100,000; by 1983 it had dropped to 8.3 per 100,000. The fifteen states that had a murder rate of 10.0 per 100,000 in 1979 were ranked according to their rates; the Metropolitan Statistical Areas (MSAs) with the largest rates within those states were then ranked to determine the urban areas with the highest incidence of murder. An identical analysis of the 1983 UCR data was made, and ten states were found to fit the criterion. The objective was to obtain MSAs with the largest numbers of black female criminal homicide offenders and simultaneously to select those that could provide a regional picture of the phenomenon. Thus the aforementioned cities were chosen. Preliminary data received from the target cities reveal the numbers and proportions of female criminal homicide offenders by race whose cases were cleared by the police in 1979 and 1983. (See table 10–7.)

A survey instrument was designed to record data from the police department homicide files in the three cities that had centralized files. Chicago and Houston have been visited to date, and random samples totaling 114 cases have been collected.

Regardless of the city or year, black women are found predominantly in cleared murder cases. These offenders represent from 61 percent (Houston, 1983) to 87 percent (Atlanta, 1983) of the women arrested for murder. The finding that black women are arrested disproportionately for murder in Atlanta, Chicago, and Houston coincides with the results of the studies previously reviewed. It is interesting to note the proportions of black women among total murder arrestees in these cities, which range from a low of 8.8 percent (Houston, 1979) to 14.2 percent (Atlanta, 1983). White female murders, on the other hand, range from only 1 percent of those arrested (Chicago, 1983) to 5.2 percent (Atlanta, 1979). Stated

Table 10-7
City Study: Cleared Murder Cases of Female Offenders, by Race

City and Year	Totals		Black		White		Hispanic		Other	
	N	(%)	N	(%)	N	(%)	N	(%)	N	(%)
Atlanta 1979	29	(100.0)	21	(72.4)	8	(27.6)				
% of all murders (N = 155)		(18.7)		(13.5)		(5.2)				
Atlanta 1983	23	(100.0)	20	(87.0)	3	(13.0)				
% of all murders (N = 141)		(16.3)		(14.2)		(2.1)				
Chicago 1979	99	(100.0)	84	(84.9)	13	(13.9)	2	(2.0)		
% of all murders (N = 808)		(12.3)		(10.4)		(1.6)		(0.3)		
Chicago 1983	81	(100.0)	68	(84.0)	7	(8.6)	5	(6.2)	1	(1.2)
% of all murders (N = 729)		(11.1)		(9.3)		(1.0)		(0.7)		(0.1)
Houston 1979	89	(100.0)	62	(69.7)	18	(20.2)	9	(10.1)		
% of all murders (N = 702)		(12.7)		(8.8)		(2.6)		(1.3)		
Houston 1983	77	(100.0)	47	(61.0)	21	(27.3)	9	(11.7)		
% of all murders (N = 471)		(16.4)		(10.0)		(4.5)		(1.9)		

another way, the highest proportion of total murder arrests for white females is less than the lowest proportion for black females in the cities under examination.

Aggregated data for Chicago and Houston in 1979 and 1983 indicate that 78.9 percent of the female criminal homicide offenders whose cases were cleared were black, 11.4 percent were white, and 9.6 percent were Hispanic.[4]

The ages of these female offenders range from 12 to 61 years, with a median age of 29.8 (mean, 32.1 years). This finding is in keeping with previously described studies, which show that female criminal homicide offenders are not young.

A much larger proportion than expected were single (37.3 percent), an equal percentage were married (37.3 percent), and 22.9 percent were once married (widowed, divorced, separated). A majority of the female criminal homicide offenders in these two cities were mothers (76.8 percent); the most frequent number of children was two (28.1 percent).

Contrary to the findings in other studies, which generally report that incarcerated female offenders, particularly homicide offenders, have less education than the national average, 46.7 percent of the women arrested for murder in the two cities had twelve years of schooling and 13.3 percent reported eleven years of education.

Only 41.2 percent were employed at the time of the offense. Thus the unemployment percentage of 58.8 percent for this offender group is close to the figures reported in the other studies.

Further evidence that homicide is intersexual, intraracial, and intrafamilial was found in the city study: 83.3 percent of the victims were male; the victims tended almost exclusively to be of the same race (black, 78.9 percent; white 10.5 percent; Hispanic, 10.5 percent); and only 5.4 percent of the victims were strangers, while 18.9 percent were acquaintances. The victims, who ranged in age from under a year to 70, had a median age of 33.5 years (mean, 33.98 years).

The women who murdered in Chicago and Houston acted alone (91.2 percent) and tended not to plan the murder (62.3 percent). Almost half the cases claimed self-defense as a motive (45.6 percent). Over one-third (34.7 percent) of the female homicide offenders had been drinking before the murder, as had 59.8 percent of the victims, but only 9.6 percent of the offenders and 4.1 percent of the victims indicated drug involvement at that time.

Characteristics of the offense in Chicago and Houston coincide with the findings in the other studies. The weapon of choice is a firearm (57.5 percent), followed closely by a knife (35.4 percent). The living room predominates as the scene of the murder (33.8 percent); the bedroom ranks second (23 percent) and the kitchen (17.6 percent) third. Although the greatest number of murders took place in November, eleven each were committed in January, February, March, April, and July. Saturday was the most frequent day for the offense (23.5 percent), with Sunday next in frequency (19.1 percent) and Friday third (13.2 percent), suggesting that murder is a weekend offense for these women.

A majority of these female offenders had no felony arrest history (76.9 percent) or convictions (78.3 percent). A larger proportion had previous misdemeanor arrests (44.6 percent) and convictions (43.9 percent). Interestingly, 61.9 percent of the victims had previous arrest records.

Although 93.5 percent of the female criminal homicide offenders in Chicago and Houston were charged with first-degree murder, only 28 percent were sentenced to prison. Those who went to prison received eight years for the most part (42.5 percent). Eight years was also the usual probation sentence (59.2 percent). This finding supports previous research indicating that women who commit homicide do not receive excessively harsh sentences.

Summary and Conclusions

Arrest statistics demonstrate that black female homicide offenders rank second, next to their black brothers, in the incidence of taking another human life. Part of this problem may be attributed to institutional racism in the criminal justice system, which leads nonwhites to be processed more extensively than whites for the commission of offenses. The deplorable conditions in minority communities—poor housing, lack of health care, unemployment, underemployment, racial discrimination, and many other social ills—no doubt contribute substantially to the minority crime problem. Nonetheless, the findings from the current study suggest that the disproportionate involvement of black females in homicide cannot be explained totally by either institutional racism or defects in the social structure. Explanation is needed for the fact that black women make up only about 11 percent of the female population in the United States but are arrested for almost three-fourths of the murders committed by females.

Homicide among blacks in the United States is believed to have reached epidemic proportions. Because homicide is an intraracial event, it is obvious that blacks are slowly eliminating each other almost to the point that one could speak of black-on-black genocide. Blacks accused and convicted of murder, when imprisoned, add to the growing and disproportionate minorities in the correctional systems. I cannot explain why this is happening; I hope that a profile of the black female homicide offender is the first step in addressing the problem of black violence.

This chapter includes information acquired from an exhaustive search of the literature on female homicide offenders, supplemented by more recent arrest data obtained from urban areas that contain large numbers of blacks and that are believed to represent a partial regional sampling of the country: Atlanta (South), Chicago (Midwest), and Houston (West and Southwest).[5]

The analysis is based on fifteen empirical studies focusing on female homicide offenders between 1958 and 1984. Three of these studies included identifiable black subjects; where possible, the black female offenders were isolated in the others. Throughout this analysis, the data on white homicide offenders were invaluable for comparison.

Black females tend to predominate among homicide offenders: they constitute about 73.6 percent of the female arrests for murder; white women average only 17.5 percent of such offenders. Both groups tend to be older than the typical female offender in the general prison population. Most incarcerated women are under 30 years of age, but the woman who kills, black or white, tends to be over 30.

Like other incarcerated women, female homicide offenders are reported to have lower intelligence (as measured by IQ tests) and concomitantly lower educational attainments. Black female homicide offenders were found to have lower IQs and fewer years of completed education than white women who committed the same offense. The IQs of the female homicide offenders varied inversely with the complexity of the homicide, a finding first noted by Figueria-McDonough (1981).

With little education and less than normal intelligence, it is not surprising to find that females who commit homicide are more likely, when employed, to have occupations at lower-status levels, such as service jobs. This finding is more obvious among black female homicide offenders.

Previous studies of incarcerated female offenders have shown that U.S. prisons are occupied mostly by single women; black women occupy an unmarried status more frequently than whites and other minority groups. In the present examination, the opposite tendency was found: female homicide offenders, regardless of race, were more likely to have been married or at least cohabiting with men. Because most of the studies were undertaken in southern states, marital status may be indicative of mores and social standards peculiar to the South.

Another social characteristic frequently ascribed to female offenders is that they are products of broken homes. Overall, and again irrespective of race, this was not found to be true of female homicide offenders.

One of the stereotypes of females who commit crimes is that they are "fallen women." Many references have been made to the madonna-whore dichotomy, which suggests that there are "good" women and "bad" women. The good women adhere to the double standard by being housewives and mothers. The bad women are the whores, the sexually promiscuous or deviant, the criminals. The studies examined in this chapter belie the myth of the fallen woman by finding little reported incidence of sexual promiscuity or homosexual activity among the female homicide offenders. Although reported in two of the studies, sexual promiscuity and homosexuality were denied more frequently by black women than by the white women questioned about such behaviors.

It is often felt that in the commission of murder, the offender and possibly also the victim are under the influence of alcohol or drugs. This investigation found little support for such a contention among the women examined in the studies available. Not only was there little indication of alcohol or narcotics use among female homicide offenders, it was also unlikely that these offenders would offer substance abuse as an excuse for the homicide, though a small proportion of the studies indicated that they were under the influence at the time of the crime.

In keeping with other studies of homicide, it was found clearly that homicide is intersexual, intraracial, and intrafamilial. Female homicide offenders (and blacks are no exception) tend to kill their mates or other members of their families close to them. Black women, however, tend to kill friends and acquaintances more often than do their white counterparts, and there are indications that these victims may be other females. Women, as a rule, are involved only infrequently in homicides of strangers, which typically result from the commission of other crimes, such as robbery or burglary.

Women do not tend to plan the murders they commit. Black female homicide offenders are even more unlikely to premeditate their homicides than white females incarcerated for this crime, according to the studies that report on this topic. Further, unlike those who commit other offenses such as burglary or robbery, black female offenders who kill are more likely than white homicide offenders to be the sole perpetrators, rather than accessories or partners to the event. The data suggest that the reason for this finding is apparently related to the rationale or motive given for the homicide. Psychological or emotional reasons for committing murder, typically anger and revenge, are given most frequently by black women. Data from Chicago and Houston corroborate this finding by indicating that arguments or altercations are the most frequent apparent motives indicated in murder. Among the female homicide offenders examined, self-defense is the second most frequent reason given, which indicates further some degree of emotionality and suggests that an altercation between the victim and offender led to the event.

Women, including blacks, tend to kill their victims in the home with firearms. Earlier studies had suggested that black female homicide offenders were more likely to use knives or other cutting instruments as murder weapons, but this choice of method has been replaced over time by guns, which are considered "safe" and impersonal because of the distance they put between the perpetrator and the victim.

This analysis indicates that black women who murder have been involved previously in the criminal justice system more frequently than their white counterparts. The previous arrest history of the offenders is the indicator for this finding, but because the results differ across the studies reporting such data, this suggestion is somewhat speculative. Even if verification could be documented, it would not be surprising because black people in general are more frequently victims of police surveillance and harassment. These actions result in more arrests and ultimately in more sentencing.

On this last point, a few of the studies hint that once convicted, black female homicide offenders are more likely to receive harsher sentences than white females who commit the same crime. The controversy over race and sentencing is still a part of the criminological dialogue; it is suggested here that black women offenders, like their black brothers, are treated differently by the criminal justice system.

A great deal of research on this topic is needed before any definitive statements can be made about the black female homicide offender. Studies on this topic are few, and those available vary in research focus and results. Through a minute examination of every available study of the black female who murders, this chapter has attempted to compile a profile of this offender group. The dearth of such studies prohibits a complete portrait of the black female homicide offender, but at least a snapshot has been provided.

Notes

1. High homicide rates among American blacks are not paralleled among African blacks (Shin, Jedlicka, and Lee 1977) or among African black women. Women in African countries are more likely to commit property crimes than crimes of violence, and female homicide rates there are negligible (Ebbe 1984).

2. A comprehensive assessment of the published scholarly empirical research on female criminal homicide offenders was undertaken through an examination of sociological, criminological, and psychological abstracts. The references listed in each of the identified books and studies were then examined until all avenues of information were exhausted. Each study was examined for data on black criminal homicide offenders; where possible, these data were extracted.

3. The Ward, Jackson, and Ward prison study included only 25 percent black women from two states, Minnesota and California, which have relatively small numbers of blacks in the general population. California was also the location of the Totman prison study, which lists the data by victim (mate or child), a fact that

may explain the low percentages of blacks found (27.8 and 21.4 percent, respectively).

4. Cross-tabulations by city or race have not been performed because the data are still being cleaned, and some missing data have not been received. Therefore the following frequencies apply to the combined sample of 114.

5. Efforts are underway to include additional cities in order to provide an eastern and western perspective.

References

Biggers, T.A. 1979. "Death by Murder: A Study of Women Murderers." *Death Education* 3:1–9.

Blackbourne, B.D. 1984. "Women Victims of Homicidal Violence." Unpublished paper.

Brown, L. 1983. "Annual Report 1983 Homicide Divisions." Houston, Tex.

Brzeczek, R.J. 1979. *Murder Analysis 1979.* Chicago: Chicago Police Department.

Cole, K.E., G. Fisher, and S.R. Cole. 1968. "Women Who Kill." *Archives of General Psychiatry* 19:1–8.

Deming, R. 1977. "The Black Female Criminal." In *Women: The New Criminals.* Edited by R. Deming. New York: Thomas Nelson and Sons.

Ebbe, O. 1984. "The Correlates of Female Criminality in Nigeria." Unpublished paper.

Figueira-McDonough, J. 1981. "Profiles of Female Offenders." In *Females in Prison in Michigan, 1968–1978: A Study of Commitment Patterns.* Edited by J. Figueira-McDonough, A. Iglehart, R. Sarri, and T. Williams. Ann Arbor, Mich.: School of Social Work and the Institute for Social Research.

Georges-Abeyie, D. 1984. *The Criminal Justice System and Blacks.* New York: Clark Boardman Company.

Gibbs, D.L., I.J. Silverman, and M. Vega. 1977. "Homicides Committed by Females in the State of Florida." Paper presented at the annual meeting of the American Society of Criminology, Atlanta, Ga.

Glick, R.M., and V.V. Neto. 1977. *National Study of Women's Correctional Programs.* U.S. National Institute of Law Enforcement and Criminal Justice. Washington, D.C.: Government Printing Office.

Hindelang, M.J. 1974. "The Uniform Crime Reports Revisited." *Journal of Criminal Justice* 2:1–17.

Iglehart, A. 1981. "Personal and Social Characteristics of Female Offenders." In *Females in Prison in Michigan, 1968–78: A Study of Commitment Patterns.* Edited by J. Figueira-McDonough, A. Iglehart, R. Sarri, and T. Williams. Ann Arbor, Mich.: School of Social Work and the Institute for Social Research.

Jason, J., L.T. Strauss, and C.W. Tyler. 1983. "A Comparison of Primary and Secondary Homicides in the U.S." *American Journal of Epidemiology* 117, no. 3:309–319.

Jones, A. 1980. *Women Who Kill.* New York: Holt, Rinehart and Winston.

Kleck, G. 1981. "Racial Discrimination in Criminal Sentencing." *American Sociological Review* 46:783–805.

Lewis, D.K. 1981. "Black Women Offenders and Criminal Justice." In *Comparing Female and Male Offenders*. Edited by M. Warren. Beverly Hills: Sage Publications.

McClain, P.D. 1982a. "Cause of Death-Homicide: A Research Note on Black Females as Homicide Victims." *Victimology* 7:204-212.

———. 1982b. "Black Female Homicide Offenders and Victims: Are They from the Same Population?" *Death Education* 6:265-278.

McGuire, Robert J. 1977. *Homicide Analysis*. New York: Office of Management Analysis, Crime Analysis Section.

Mann, C.R. 1981. "The Minority Woman Offender in the Criminal Justice System." Paper presented at the annual meeting of the American Society of Criminology, Washington, D.C.

———. 1984. *Female Crime and Delinquency*. University: University of Alabama Press.

Mann, C.R. 1986. "The Black Female Criminal Homicide Offender in the United States." Pp. 145-183 in Department of Health and Human Services, *Report of the Secretary's Task Force on Black and Minority Health, Volume 5: Homicide, Suicide, and Unintentional Injuries*. Washington, D.C.: U.S. Government Printing Office.

Mercy, J.A., J.C. Smith, and M.L. Rosenberg. 1983. "Homicide among Young Black Males: A Descriptive Statement." Paper presented at the annual meeting of the American Society of Criminology.

Messner, S.F. 1983. "Sex Differences in the Societal Arrest Rate: A Cross-National Test of the Theory of Structural Strain." Paper presented at the annual meeting of the American Society of Criminology.

Napper, G. Information received in 1985 from Commissioner Napper, Atlanta.

National Association for the Advancement of Colored People (NAACP). 1985. "Death Row, U.S.A." New York: NAACP Legal Defense Fund.

Pope, C.E., and R.L. McNeely, eds. 1981. *Race, Crime and Criminal Justice*. Beverly Hills: Sage Publications.

Rasko, G. 1976. "The Victim of the Female Killer." *Victimology* 1:396-402.

Rice, F., Jr. 1983. *Murder Analysis 1983*. Chicago: Chicago Police Department.

Riedel, M. 1984. "Blacks and Homicide." In *The Criminal Justice System and Blacks*. Edited by G. Daniel. New York: Clark Boardman Company.

Riedel, M., and L. Lockhart-Riedel. 1984. "Issues in the Study of Black Homicide." Paper presented at the annual meeting of the American Society of Criminology, Cincinnati, Ohio.

Rose, H.M., and P. McClain. 1981. *Black Homicide and the Urban Environment*. Washington, D.C.: Center for Studies of Minority Group Mental Health, National Institute of Mental Health.

Rosenblatt, A., and C. Greenland. 1974. "Female Crimes of Violence." *Canadian Journal of Criminology and Corrections* 16:173-180.

Shin, L., D. Jedlicka, and E.S. Lee. 1977. "Homicide among Blacks." *Phylon*, pp. 398-407.

Skogan, W.G. 1974. "The Validity of Official Crime Statistics: An Empirical Investigation." *Social Science Quarterly* 55:25-38.

Staples, P. 1975. "White Racism, Black Crime, and American Justice: An Application of the Colonial Model to Explain Crime and Race." *Phylon* 36:14-22.

Sufrin, M. 1984. "Female Felons, Lady Killers, and Other Women in Crime." *Genesis* (November): 25-27.

Sutherland, E.H., and D.R. Cressey. 1978. *Criminology*, 10th ed. Philadelphia: Lippincott.

Suval, E.M., and R.C. Brisson. 1974. "Neither Beauty nor Beast: Female Criminal Homicide Offenders." *International Journal of Criminology and Penology* 2:23-34.

Totman, J. 1978. *The Murderers: A Psychosocial Study of Criminal Homicide*. San Francisco: R. and E. Research Associates.

U.S. Department of Justice. 1980. *Uniform Crime Reports for the United States*. Washington, D.C.: Government Printing Office.

––––––. 1984. *Uniform Crime Reports for the United States*. Washington, D.C.: Government Printing Office.

Ward, D.A., M. Jackson, and R.E. Ward. 1969. "Crimes of Violence by Women." In *Crimes of Violence*. Edited by D. Mulvihill and M. Tomin. National Commission on the Causes and Prevention of Violence. Staff report 11-13. Washington, D.C.: Government Printing Office.

Weisheit, R.A. 1984. "Female Homicide Offenders: Trends over Time in an Institutionalized Population." *Justice Quarterly* 1, no. 4:471-489.

Wilbanks, W. 1982. "Murdered Women and Women Who Murder: A Critique of the Literature." In *Judge, Lawyer, Victim, Thief: Women, Gender Roles, and Criminal Justice*. Edited by N.H. Ratter and E.A. Stanko. Boston: Northeastern University Press.

––––––. 1983a. "Female Homicide Offenders in the U.S." *International Journal of Women's Studies* 6 no. 2:302-310.

––––––. 1983b. "The Female Offender in Dade County, Florida." *Criminal Justice Review* 8, no. 2:9-14.

––––––. 1984. *Murder in Miami*. New York: University Press of America.

––––––. 1985a. "Is Violent Crime Intraracial?" *Crime and Delinquency* 31, no. 1:117-128.

––––––. 1985b. "Criminal Homicide Offenders in the U.S.: Black vs. White." In *Black Suicide and Homicide*. Edited by R. Davis and D. Harokin.

Wolfgang, M.E. 1958. *Patterns in Criminal Homicide*. Philadelphia: University of Pennsylvania Press.

Wyrick, E.S., and O.H. Owens. 1977. "Black Women: Income and Incarceration." In *Blacks and Criminal Justice*. Edited by C. Owens and J. Bell. Lexington, Mass.: Lexington Books.

Young, V. 1980. "Women, Race, and Crime." *Criminology* 18:26-34.

IV
Special Issues

11
Devalued Lives and Racial Stereotypes: Ideological Barriers to the Prevention of Family Violence among Blacks

Darnell F. Hawkins

Because a large proportion of all interpersonal violence among blacks, as among other groups, occurs within the family context, the black family is a likely target for an emphasis on violence intervention. Black family violence can be reduced. Social researchers and policymakers have so far largely concentrated on the more or less technical aspects of violence prevention: the perfection of methodologies for identifying high-risk groups and individuals, assessing the effectiveness of intervention strategies, and similar concerns. In this chapter, I examine one of the least explored problems: the constraining influence of certain ideological currents on the perceived feasibility or possibility of successful prevention. Only if these ideological barriers are seriously confronted and discarded will rates of family violence among blacks be lowered.

Ideological Barriers

Efforts to intervene in domestic violence among blacks must confront three major ideologically based barriers. The first derives from the noninterventionist sentiments historically associated with family violence in the United States. Such sentiments, despite some diminution in recent years, still persist. Further, despite increasing public concern and legislation sometimes requiring intervention in domestic disputes, the prevention of family violence among blacks faces still other race-specific ideological barriers. One such barrier derives from the historical devaluation of black life in the United States. The other is a product of stereotypical views of the normality of violence among blacks. Both are interrelated and emanate from historical patterns of racism and oppression in American society. In this chapter I discuss these race-specific ideological currents and their significance for past and present efforts to intervene in black family violence. Much of the attention is focused on the impact of these beliefs and values on the actions of public officials who are likely to be in a position to devise and implement strategies for the prevention of family violence, among them, law enforcement and judicial authorities, medical doctors, psychologists-counselors, public health officials, social workers, and similar professionals.

Five arguments are important to this discussion:

1. In comparison to whites, the persons and lives of blacks are less valued in American society.
2. The devaluation of black life is evidenced in many ways but is perhaps most apparent in the sentencing of criminal defendants.
3. Linked to the devalued status of blacks is a stereotyped view of violence as more normal among blacks than among whites.
4. This view of the normality of black violence has also been associated with a more limited law enforcement and judicial response to acts of violence in the black community than that found in the white community.
5. Both the devalued status of the black victim and the acceptance of violence as normal among blacks pose significant barriers to the intervention into and prevention of family violence within the black community.

These observations are not new, of course. Similar themes have been proposed by various analysts of black-white relations throughout much of U.S. history. But these beliefs have particular relevance given increased governmental efforts at violence prevention.

It may be argued that the devalued status of blacks in American society is not unique. That is, other nonwhite minority groups and perhaps the entire lower class itself (whites and nonwhites) can be described as devalued in comparison to whites and persons of higher social class status. Marxist and other class-based theoretical approaches suggest that the devalued status of blacks derives from their position in the class structure. It is beyond my scope here to debate the merits of such an argument. I do not argue for the uniqueness of the social status of blacks in American society, although an argument could certainly be made for such. Similarly, much of the evidence of the devalued status of blacks I provide could well be applicable to other subgroups in the United States.[1]

Like other social phenomena, the devalued status of blacks and the perception of violence as normal among them are both ideological constructs and also potentially empirically assessable social facts. To understand fully the impact of these phenomena on the prevention of family violence among blacks, we must take a sociology of knowledge approach. Social scientists have described the operation of these phenomena within the larger American society. But social science itself has been greatly affected by the same racial bias that it seeks to analyze. Social scientists have also been involved in efforts to overcome the racial bias that produces the results from the devaluing of black life and views of the normality of violence among blacks. The major emphasis in this chapter is on social science as both an analyst and embodiment of these phenomena. I believe that the ideological barriers I describe are evident in both social scientific thought and in opinions held by the American public. I also believe that a truly critical and reflexive social science may be one step toward the solution of the problems posed by these barriers to the prevention of family violence within the black community.

The Cheapness of Black Life: Proof and Causes

Predictably, much of the proof or evidence offered by observers to show the cheapness of black life in the United States involves the crime of homicide. Two major observations or conclusions have been widely reported. First, it has been suggested that the fact that the rate of homicide and other interpersonal violence is considerably higher among blacks than among whites is itself an indication of an undervaluing of life within the black community. That is, blacks themselves do not value their own lives or the lives of others of their race. One result is frequent acts of interpersonal aggression. Over the last fifty years, considerable debate has ensued over the question of whether this social-cultural condition is the result of slavery and racial oppression or a carry-over from the African heritage of black Americans. An early analyst of homicide, Brearley (1932), argued that the disproportionate incidence of black homicide may stem from both racial oppression and African cultural traditions. He says,

> His historical background may also help to explain the Negro's attitude toward the taking of human life. In central Africa, his ancestral home, both birth and death rates were high, and violent death was frequent and often unpunished, especially if the victim were a slave. A lack of regard for the person and personality of others seems to have been almost characteristic of central African culture. When the Negro was brought to

America as a slave, his owners did little to encourage high esteem for the sanctity of life. On the contrary, they often treated the Negro as if he were only a relatively valuable domestic animal, disciplining him by corporal punishment, using his wives and daughters as concubines, and increasing the instability of his family by the sale or exchange of its members. This background may influence the traditions and attitudes of the Negro of today and decrease his regard for the sacredness of human life. (pp. 113–114)

This view of causes of black homicide has been frequently restated by subsequent researchers even in more recent years (see Curtis 1975). Silberman (1978), on the other hand, argues that the propensity to violence among blacks is not part of the cultural heritage American blacks brought from Africa. Instead he concludes that "violence is something black Americans learned in this country" (p. 123). Despite the disagreement over the exact origins of high rates of black violence, such violence is frequently used to argue for the existence of a value system among blacks that is characterized by a lack of regard for the sacredness of life. Further, this belief underlies subculture of violence theory (Wolfgang and Ferracuti 1967) and is also a basis for a view of the normality of violence among blacks. In this instance (as proof of devalued lives) researchers appear to follow the line of argument depicted in the diagram:

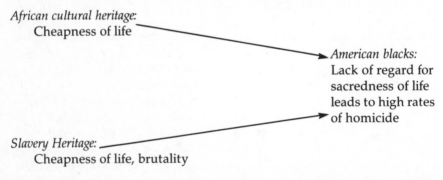

African cultural heritage:
Cheapness of life

American blacks:
Lack of regard for
sacredness of life
leads to high rates
of homicide

Slavery Heritage:
Cheapness of life, brutality

The second source of proof offered by social scientists for the cheapness of black life is similar. Emphasis, however, is placed not on the values and behavior of blacks themselves but rather on the actions of whites toward blacks. Further, much less emphasis is placed on historical antecedents. This view holds that the devaluation of black life stems mainly from white oppression and is best observed in the actions of public officials, especially those within the system of criminal justice. Proponents of this view generally document the culpability of whites in fostering a system of justice that values the lives of whites more than those of blacks even in recent years.

Some of the first observations regarding this kind of devaluing of black life within an official bureaucratic context come from studies of the sentencing of black and white murderers.[2] In attempting to probe the question of whether black criminal defendants are more harshly punished than white defendants, researchers have noted a significant race-of-the-victim effect. One of the earliest empirical investigations was done by Johnson (1941). He proposed that the four black-white homicide offender-victim dyads could be ranked in seriousness from most to least serious as follows: (1) Negro versus white, (2) white versus white, (3) Negro versus Negro, (4) white versus Negro. He reported that data on court prosecutions in Virginia, North Carolina, and Georgia between 1930 and 1940 confirmed this ordering of offenses. Myrdal (1944, p. 551) used this and similar studies to conclude:

> In criminal cases the discrimination does not always run against a Negro defendant. It is part of the Southern tradition to assume that Negroes are disorderly and lack elementary morals, and to show great indulgence toward Negro violence and disorderliness "when they are among themselves." . . . As long as only Negroes are concerned and no whites are disturbed, great leniency will be shown in most cases. . . . The sentences for even major crimes are ordinarily reduced when the victim is another Negro. Attorneys are heard to plead in the juries: "Their code of ethics is a different one from ours." . . . Leniency toward Negro defendants in cases involving crimes against other Negroes is thus actually a form of discrimination. . . . For offenses which involve any actual or potential danger to whites, however, Negroes are punished more severely than whites.

Myrdal's and Johnson's conclusions were based on observations in the South during the 1930s and before. Thus it is reasonable to ask how generalizable their conclusions are—to the non-South and to the present time.

Empirical studies of criminal justice outcomes report that these findings and conclusions are applicable to other areas of the United States and are descriptive of decision-making patterns even in recent years. Wolfgang and Riedel (1973) and LaFree (1980) reported that rape sentencing during the 1970s showed an offender-victim pattern similar to that described by Johnson (1941). In addition a long list of studies have shown a comparable racial pattern for not only homicide and rape but also assault and robbery (Garfinkel 1949; Zimring, Eigen, and O'Malley 1976; Myers 1979; Radelet 1981; Baldus, Pulaski, and Woodworth 1983; Paternoster 1983). Radelet, Baldus et al., and Paternoster report that even during the 1970s and 1980s, the killer of a white (regardless of race) is much more likely to be sentenced to death than the killer of a black. In summarizing these findings, Kleck (1981, p. 799) says, "There appears to be a general pattern of less severe punishment of crimes with black victims, especially in connection with the imposition of the death penalty."

The differential punishment of crimes involving black and white victims likely begins with the actions of law enforcement officials. Although there have not been many empirical studies of this aspect of law enforcement, several researchers have suggested that the race of the victim and offender is a factor affecting police decision making. Banton (1964, p. 173) quotes the captain of police detectives in a southern town during World War I: "In this town there are three classes of homicide. If a nigger kills a white man, that's murder. If a white man kills a nigger, that's justifiable homicide. If a nigger kills a nigger, that's one less nigger." Johnson (1941), and Myrdal (1944) noted that this kind of racial bigotry was characteristic of the police response to black crime during the 1920s, 1930s, and 1940s. Investigations conducted after the urban riots of the 1960s suggest that similar bias has existed during more recent years.

The kinds of empirical findings reported in the research on sentencing have led a number of researchers to speak of black victims of homicide and other crimes as devalued victims (Kleck 1981; Hawkins 1983; Petersen and Hagen 1984). Thus, racist perceptions by public officials of the value of black life have led to differential treatment of black and white offenders and victims.

Hawkins (1983) suggests that the devalued status of the black victim affects the actions of a wide range of officials who respond to violent behavior or other crime: police, health care workers, prosecutors, judges, juries, and others. The devalued status of the black victim also has relevance for understanding the attitudes of public officials toward family violence among blacks. Crime statistics document the fact that a large proportion of all assaults and homicide among blacks, as among nonblacks, occurs within the context of the family. Lundsgaarde (1977) noted that homicide offenders who murdered members of their family received less punishement than those who killed nonfamily. The literature on the devalued status of the black victim suggests that among black and white domestic murderers, blacks will receive less punishment than whites.[3]

The underpunishment of blacks who offend against other blacks is not just a finding from social science research. It is an often-discussed problem within the black community itself.[4] Many analysts have noted that the seeming vigilantism among blacks that often leads to assault or homicide results partly from their inability to rely upon the criminal justice system to settle disputes and dispense justice fairly. If homicide is a means of dispute resolution in the absence of more appropriate and less violent means (Levi 1980), then the high rate of criminal violence among blacks is a direct result of the devaluing of black life by officials within the American system of criminal justice.

These observations highlight the mixture of social fact and racial stereotype that has shaped public attitudes and policy toward blacks in the United States. On the one hand, blacks have historically been depicted as adhering to lesser moral standards than whites. The high rate of black homicide is used as proof of such moral bankruptcy. On the other hand, the acceptance of this viewpoint by public officials leads to patterns of intervention and law enforcement that in many instances may exacerbate already high levels of violence among blacks. Thus, the undervaluing of black life may represent a formidable barrier to current efforts to reduce violence, including family violence, within the black community. So may concomitant perceptions of the normality of violence among blacks, a common theme in American social thought and social science theory. This theme too is reflected in statements and behaviors of public officials in response to homicide in the black community and has been documented in social science research.

The Normality of Violence among Blacks

David Sudnow published in 1965 a particularly significant study of some of the sociological features of the criminal code in a public defender's office. The study represented a pioneering effort designed to look at the actual practice of criminal case processing by public defenders at such practices as plea bargaining and other forms of sentence determination. An equally significant result of the investigation was his finding that public defenders tended to use a system of social typing for crimes and criminal offenders. They justified such typing on the basis of their on-the-job experiences, which taught them that some kinds of offenders were likely to repeat the same offense while others were not repeat violators. If the latter were repeat violators, they were said to do so less frequently. Sudnow used the term *normal crimes* to describe "those occurrences whose typical features, e.g., the way they usually occur and the characteristics of persons who commit them (as well as the typical victims and typical scenes), are known and attended by the P.D." He goes on to say that for any of a series of these offense types, the public defender "can provide some form of proverbial characterization" (1965, p. 260).

Sudnow provides several examples of such proverbial characterizations. Most involved typing of the social class and/or race of the offender and victim. Such typings may have served the purpose of expediting the public defender's and prosecutor's processing of large numbers of cases, but the potential for bias and discrimination in such characterizations is obvious. Swigert and Farrell (1977), who explored this aspect of criminal typing in their study of homicide processing, concluded that a stereotype of the homicide offender as a "normal primitive" existed among court-appointed diagnosticians of homicide in a large urban jurisdiction in the northeastern United States. This classification represented a conception of criminality that combined both race and class characteristics. They cite the following description, developed by the diagnostic clinic they studied, as the basis for the homicide criminal typing:

> While treated as a diagnostic category, the designation "normal primitive" constitutes a *social* description of a group of people whose behavior, *within their own social setting,* is best described as normal. The "normal primitive" comes largely from the foreign-born and black populations. Their lives are characterized by impoverished economic conditions which, as with their behavior, may be described as "primitive." Occupational achievements center around unskilled, menial labor, and these careers are often sporadic. *Educational levels are minimal and testing indicates borderline to low-average intelligence. While the children of the foreign-born do acclimate to a less "primitive" existence, the offspring of the black population seem unaffected by improved educational and social opportunities.*
>
> The personality characteristics of the "normal primitive" are childlike or juvenile, the behavior and attitude of being similar to that of an eight- to twelve-year old boy. At the same time, acceptance as a *man* by this group is very important. In this regard, the "normal primitive" is sensitive and takes offense to any question of his masculinity.
>
> Interaction among such individuals often occurs in bars where arguments readily result in aggressive encounters. Compelled to fight any challenger of his masculinity or courage, the "normal primitive" protects himself by carrying a lethal weapon.
>
> In summary:
>
> The primitive man is comfortable and without mental illness. He has little, if any, education and is of dull intelligence. His goals are sensual and immediate—satisfying his physical and sexual needs without inhibition, postponement or planning. There is little regard for the future—extending hardly beyond the filling of his stomach and the next payday or relief check. His loyalties and identifications are with a group that has little purpose in life, except surviving with a minimum of sweat and a maximum of pleasure. He has the ten-year old boy's preoccupation with prowess and "being a man." Unfortunately, he lacks the boy's external restraint and supervision so that he is more or less an intermittent community problem and responsibility. (Cited by Swigert and Farrell 1977, p. 19; emphasis in original)

Swigert and Farrell found that this conception of the normal primitive had significant consequences for the assignment of public counsel, denial of bail, and a plea of guilt before the judge. The lack of legal resources resulted in more severe sanctions awarded by the court. Swigert and Farrell, however, did not control for race of the victim as a factor in the punishment.[5] I propose that the conception they describe is characteristic of the beliefs of many public officials, including police, public defenders, prosecutors, judges, and others in the criminal justice system. It is also evident among the larger public. Variants of this theme are found in social scientific theory. I suggest further that this conception of the etiology of criminal violence and the characteristics of typical offenders and victims represents a substantial, but often unacknowledged, barrier for assaultive violence and homicide prevention efforts, especially among blacks.

Swigert and Farrell's study (1977) and my own earlier work (1983) have suggested that the normal primitive criminal conception is quite similar to and may have some of the same flaws and consequences as the popular social scientific description of members of the subculture of violence. Such descriptions can be found in the earlier work of Pittman and Handy (1964) and Wolfgang and Ferracuti (1967). Such descriptions undoubtedly reflect a sincere effort on the part of social researchers to provide some explanation, albeit largely based on description, for the extremely high rates of violence among certain segments of the population. But there are problems caused by this form of explanation. One is a conclusion by researchers that to the extent that violence results from social values, it is predictable and more or less normal among persons within certain subcultural groupings, such as blacks and lower-class whites. Swigert and Farrell (1977) argue that such subcultural explanations may be largely a function of the effectiveness with which the stereotype of the violent criminal has been applied by the legal system. But in most instances, the view of violence as normal among blacks leads to the same pattern of official response that has been linked to the devalued status of blacks: less intervention and punishment.

Bernstein, Kelly, and Doyle (1977) reported an unexpected finding in their study of felony sentencing in New York State. White defendants, as well as defendants who had been employed for longer periods of time, were more severely sentenced than nonwhites and persons who were unemployed or employed for shorter periods. In interviews, Bernstein, Kelly, and Doyle found that the judges and prosecutors who handled the cases assumed that nonwhites commit crimes because their subculture accepts such behavior; hence offenses of nonwhites seemed less pernicious to them. Their expectations for white defendants, on the other hand, were higher and failure to meet such expectations appeared more noxious—thus, the more severe sanction (1977, p. 753).

In a similar vein, I have suggested (1983, pp. 426–427) that the official view of violent behavior as normal among blacks, especially among lower-class blacks, also affects the etiology of black homicide. Violent behavior of all types is considered normal among such persons and therefore ultimately unpreventable; hence the police, who are repeatedly called upon to investigate incidences of violent behavior within the black community, make few efforts at prevention. The view of the normality of violence among blacks affects both punishment and intervention and prevention efforts. As in the instance of devalued lives, this view is perhaps best illustrated by looking at the attitudes and behavior of the police.

Police and other law enforcement agents often are able to pinpoint high crime blocks and neighborhoods. They may also believe that they are able to identify individuals or types of individuals who commit or are perceived to commit acts of criminal violence. In fact, since police perceptions of crime often greatly influence defense and prosecutorial decision making, Swigert and Farrell's clinic description of the normal primitive may be largely a restatement of police views of the homicidal criminal. Police views of the typical assault and homicide offender are remarkably similar to the clinical description. Police perceptions may be accurate descriptions of reality in some cases, but in others, they may merely reflect biases found in the larger society.[6] In addition, their views often reflect more directly a kind of "those people will always do that sort of thing" sentiment that is only implicit in Swigert and Farrell's clinical description and in the ideas of subculture of violence theorists. Such a remedying of these larger societal problems is seen as necessary before criminal violence can be successfully prevented or reduced. They often question the effectiveness of remedial approaches to violence prevention that do not address these larger societal causal factors. There is much validity to such an approach, but the result is sometimes a conclusion that little, if anything, can be done to prevent violence among deprived groups in American society as it is currently structured. Another result is that whites and the middle class are considered more likely targets of intervention than blacks and the lower class.

I believe that to a large extent, the ideological currents I have described characterize the thinking and actions of many of the government officials, practitioners, and social researchers who are attempting to address the problem of assaultive violence and homicide among the poor and blacks in the United States. Thus a view of the inevitability and unpreventability of violence among certain population groups is part of the ideological baggage many people bring to discussions of violence prevention. That set of values is as much a part of American society as is the excessive violence among certain subgroups in the population at which current prevention efforts are directed. Indeed the view that violence among blacks is unpreventable has been a common theme in public discourse and social scientific writings for more than a century.[7]

New Themes, Old Conclusions

It may be argued that many would-be intervenors in family violence among blacks today have disavowed racist perceptions of the devalued black victim and the normality of black violence. Rather than blame the victim, they highlight the social structural conditions under which blacks live in the United States: poverty, inequality, racism, deprivation, and similar factors in the genesis of criminal violence among blacks.[8] The problem with such extreme emphasis on these factors is that adherents believe that these larger societal problems must be remedied before criminal violence can be successfully prevented or reduced. There is much validity to such an approach, but the result is sometimes a conclusion that little, if anything, can be done to prevent violence among deprived groups in American society as it is currently structured. Another result is that whites and the middle class are seen as more likely targets of intervention than blacks and the lower class.

In summary the prevention and reduction of family violence within the black community may be impeded by the following kinds of ideologically based barriers:

1. The devalued status of the black victim and the view that violence is normal among blacks are reflected in a pattern of unequal legal response to black and white victims of violence.

2. This unequal treatment by police, judicial officials, and others is not only evidence of the devalued status of the black victim of violence; it may also contribute to further violence. To the extent that commonly occurring acts of minor violence are not investigated and major acts of intraracial violence go unpunished, patterns of vigilantism may emerge among blacks. Some evidence suggests that this may be a factor contributing to the high rates of violence in the black community.

3. The idea that violence is more or less normal, and hence inevitable, within the black community may affect the behavior of many potential intervenors outside the legal arena. If social service personnel, public health officials, counselors, and others share this view of black criminality, they may believe that their intervention efforts are futile and instead aim their work at the middle class and whites rather than lower-class blacks.

4. The belief that a high rate of violence among blacks is inevitable and normal is partly grounded in racial stereotype. It is also a product of observations made by social scientists who have sought to explain disproportionate levels of violence within the black community. These social scientific conceptions, as well as racial bias, often are used to support conclusions that the prevention of violence among blacks will be largely unsuccessful absent major changes in the political economy or black subcultural values.

Preventing Black Family Violence

The devalued status of blacks in the United States is well documented, as are continuing perceptions of the normality of violence within the black community. Both ideological currents have relevance for the protection afforded black victims of violence and also for the successful reduction of rates of violence among blacks. Since a disproportionate amount of such violence occurs with the home, these ideological barriers have particular relevance for efforts to prevent family violence.

Historically black women and children have been afforded less protection from abuse within the family than any other groups within American society. White women and children have also been underprotected but much less so than blacks. Unless persisting ideological constraints are confronted and challenged, increasing official intervention in domestic violence will merely result in an unequal race-of-victim-based pattern of intervention similar to that found in the handling of nonfamily criminal violence. That is, black and poor victims of family violence may be ignored and most prevention efforts targeted at the white middle class. The avoidance of this kind of pattern may rest on careful consideration of the following kinds of concerns.

First, the greater frequency of homicide within the black community or among the poor in general does not itself suggest that such behavior is more normative or accepted. Homicide is still relatively infrequent even among poor blacks and represents an unacceptable form of behavior, as it does in other groupings within U.S. society or in other societies.

Second, homicide and other forms of violent behavior are preventable to a large extent, as a number of researchers have suggested (Wolfgang and Ferracuti 1967; Allen 1980; Hawkins 1983, 1984). Since a large proportion of homicides among blacks occur among family members, the prevention and reduction of black family violence must be a top priority given present concern for the reduction of black homicide.

Finally, a promising form of prevention may focus on research and policies that consider situational aspects of the genesis of crime. These largely involve the design, management, or manipulation of the immediate environment in order to reduce opportunities for crime and to increase risks of detection (see Clarke 1983). These strategies of intervention place less emphasis on individual motives and malevolence or social structural factors and more emphasis on more manipulatable aspects of the social environment.

Notes

1. Explanations for the devalued status of blacks that emphasize the political economy may be extremely useful for providing a historical perspective. For instance, during slavery, blacks were valuable property. Landowners frequently intervened to stop the execution for capital crimes of slaves whom they owned. It

was only after state legislatures passed laws providing for the reimbursement of owners for executed slaves that such intervention subsided (Higginbotham 1978). Under these circumstances, the lives of slaves were valuable. Nevertheless, there is considerable evidence that black-on-black offenses were more leniently treated than black-on-white offenses during slavery. After slavery ended, blacks became a surplus population to a large extent, and their lives became much less valuable to white authorities.

2. Most of the discussion in this chapter addresses the problem of the devaluation of black life as it is evidenced in official decision making within formal organizations. Of course, the cheapening of black life in American society is a product of the larger system of value. Evidence can be found in a variety of social settings and throughout much of the history of the United States. A major contributor to (or reflection of) the devalued status of blacks has been the criminal law itself. Although the race-of-victim effects described in this chapter are due to extralegal sources of bias, during slavery the criminal law itself provided for differential punishment based on the race of the offender and victim. For instance, Mangum (1940) and Higginbotham (1978) note that in the antebellum South and North, statutes provided harsher penalties for certain crimes when committed by blacks than when committed by whites. Other laws made certain acts crimes only if they were perpetrated by blacks. Thus, it may be argued that the findings of Johnson (1941) and subsequent investigations merely reflect a continuation of historical patterns.

3. Researchers have not generally made such racial comparisons. That is, they have not categorized homicides as domestic versus nondomestic to ascertain levels of punishment by race. This has been partly due to small sample sizes in some studies. Nevertheless, the findings of Johnson (1941) and others would support an expectation of racial differences in the punishment of domestic homicides, as well as homicides committed against nonfamily.

4. That is, blacks are acutely aware of the double standard for the punishment of crime based on the race of the victim. A similar concern for this phenomenon is shown in black folklore. Charles Owens (1977, p. 3) cites a black folktale, "A Fine for Killing Two Negroes," from the work of Dorson (1967), as representative of black views of the low value of black life in the United States.

5. While Swigert and Farrell (1977) found that the conception of the normal primitive led to a more punitive response, they failed to distinguish between intraracial and interracial offenders. As the studies of racial disparities in sentencing show, blacks are likely to be treated more leniently when they kill other blacks.

6. Kephart (1957, pp. 88–93) reported that in a survey of police officers in Philadelphia, 75 percent overestimated the actual percentage of arrests involving blacks made in the districts to which they were assigned.

7. Immediately after the Civil War and well into the twentieth century, high rates of black crime, including homicide, were cited by some writers as proof of the genetic and/or social depravity of the black race; see Otken (1894).

8. For example, there have appeared several radical critiques of subcultural theorizing in recent years. Foremost among those providing such critiques have been researchers labeled as conflict theorists. In addition, some researchers have

begun to explain high rates of black homicide and other violence by using models that describe the "internal colonialism" that characterizes the conditions under which blacks in the United States live. These more social structure–oriented explanations are important advances but still leave unresolved some of the problems of homicide prevention.

References

Allen, Nancy H. 1980. *Homicide: Perspectives on Prevention.* New York: Human Sciences Press.

Attorney General's Task Force on Family Violence. 1984. Washington, D.C.: Department of Justice.

Baldus, David C., Charles Pulaski, and George Woodworth. 1983. "Comparative Review of Death Sentences: An Empirical Study of the Georgia Experience." *Journal of Criminal Law and Criminology* 74(Fall):661–753.

Banton, Michael. 1964. *The Policeman in the Community.* London: Tavistock.

Bard, Morton. 1969. "Family Intervention Police Teams as a Community Mental Health Resource." *Journal of Criminal Law, Criminology and Police Sentence* 60, no. 2:247–250.

Berk, Sarah F., and Donileen R. Loseke. 1981. "'Handling' Family Violence: Situational Determinants of Police Arrest in Domestic Disturbances." *Law and Society Review* 15, no. 2:315–346.

Berstein, Ilene Nagel, William R. Kelly, and Patricia A. Doyle. 1977. "Societal Reaction to Deviants: The Case of Criminal Defendants." *American Sociological Review* 42(October):743–755.

Brearly, H.C. 1932. *Homicide in the United States.* Chapel Hill: University of North Carolina Press.

Calvert, R. 1974. "Criminal and Civil Liability in Husband-Wife Assaults." In *Violence in the Family,* pp. 88–90. Edited by S. Steinmetz and M. Straus. New York: Harper & Row.

Centers for Disease Control. 1983. *Homicide Surveillance Summary: 1970–78.* Atlanta, Ga.: Violence Epidemiology Branch, Center for Health Promotion and Education, Public Health Service, U.S. Department of Health and Human Services.

Clarke, Ronald V. 1983. "Situational Crime Prevention: Its Theoretical Basis and Practical Scope." In *Crime and Justice: An Annual Review of Research,* 4:225–256. Edited by Michale Tonry and Norval Morris. Chicago: University of Chicago Press.

Curtis, Lynn A. 1975. *Violence, Race and Culture.* Lexington, Mass.: Lexington Books.

Davison, T. 1978. *Conjugal Crime: Understanding and Changing the Wifebeating Pattern.* New York: Hawthorne Books.

Dennis, Ruth E. 1979. "The Role of Homicide in Decreasing Life Expectancy." In *Lethal Aspects of Urban Violence.* Edited by Harold M. Rose. Lexington, Mass.: Lexington Books.

Dexter, Lewis Anthony. 1958. "A Note on Selective Inattention in Social Science." *Social Problems* 61(Fall):176–182.

Dobash, R.E., and R. Dobash. 1979. *Violence against Wives.* New York: Free Press.

Dorson, Richard. 1967. *American Negro Folktales.* Greenwich, Conn.: Fawcett Publications.

Dunn, Christopher S. 1976. *The Patterns and Distributions of Assault Incidence Characteristics Among Social Areas.* Analytic Report 14, Law Enforcement Assistant Administration, National Criminal Justice Information and Statistics Service. Washington, D.C.: Government Printing Office.

Farley, Reynolds. 1980. "Homicide Trends in the United States." *Demography* 17 (May):177–88.

Field, Martha H., and Henry F. Field. 1973. "Marital Violence and the Criminal Process: Neither Justice nor Peace." *Social Science Review* 47(June):221–240.

Garfinkel, Harold. 1949. "Research Note on Inter- and Intra-racial Homicides," *Social Forces* 27:369–381.

Gelles, R. 1980. "Violence in the Family: A Review of Research in the Seventies." *Journal of Marriage and the Family* 42(December):873–885.

———. 1982. "Domestic Criminal Violence." In *Criminal Violence,* pp. 201–235. Edited by Marvin E. Wolfgang and Neil Alan Weiner. Beverly Hills: Sage.

Hawkins, Darnell F. 1983. "Black and White Homicide Differentials: Alternatives to an Inadequate Theory." *Criminal Justice and Behavior* 10(December):407–440.

———. 1984. "Sociological Research and the Prevention of Homicide Among Blacks." Paper prepared for the Black Homicide/Mental Health Workshop, Washington, D.C., June 14–16.

———. 1985. "Black Homicide: The Adequacy of Existing Research for Devising Prevention Strategies." *Crime and Delinquency* 31(January):83–103.

Higginbotham, A. Leon. 1978. *In the Matter of Color-Race and the American Legal Process: The Colonial Period.* New York: Oxford University Press.

Johnson, Guy B. 1941. "The Negro and Crime." *Annals of the American Academy of Policial Science* 217:93–104.

Kephart, William M. 1957. *Racial Factors and Urban Law Enforcement.* Philadelphia: University of Pennsylvania Press.

Kleck, Gary. 1981. "Racial Discrimination in Criminal Sentencing: A Critical Evaluation of the Evidence with Additional Evidence on the Death Penalty." *American Sociological Review* 46(December):783–805.

LaFree, Gary. 1980. "The Effect of Sexual Stratification by Race on Official Reactions to Rape." *American Sociological Review* 45:842–854.

Langley, R., and R.C. Levy. 1977. *Wife Beating: The Silent Crisis.* New York: E.P. Dutton.

Levi, Ken. 1980. "Homicide as Conflict Resolution." *Deviant Behavior* 1(April–September):281–307.

Lundsgaarde, Henry P. 1977. *Murder in Space City: A Cultural Analysis of Houston Homicide Patterns.* New York: Oxford University Press.

Magnum, Charles. 1940. *The Legal Status of the Negro.* Chapel Hill: University of North Carolina Press.

Myers, Martha A. 1979. "Offended Parties and Official Reactions: Victims and the Sentencing of Criminal Defendants." *Sociological Quarterly* 20:529–540.

Myrdal, Gunnar. 1944. *An American Dilemma.* New York: Pantheon.

Otken, Charles H. 1894. *The Ills of the South.* New York: G.P. Putnam's Sons.

Owens, Charles E. 1977. "What Price Justice." Introduction to *Blacks and Criminal Justice.* Edited by Charles E. Owens and Jimmy Bell. Lexington, Mass.: Lexington Books.

Parnas, R. 1967. "The Police Response to Domestic Disturbance." *Wisconsin Law Review* 1967:914–960.

Paternoster, Raymond. 1983. "Race of Victim and Location of Crime: The Decision to Seek the Death Penalty in South Carolina." *Journal of Criminal Law and Criminology* 74:754–785.

Peterson, Ruth D., and John Hagan. 1984. "Changing Conceptions of Race and Sentencing Outcomes." *American Sociological Review* 49(February):56–70.

Pittman, D.J., and W. Hardy. 1964. "Patterns in Criminal Aggravated Assault." *Journal of Criminal Law, Criminology, and Police Science* 56(December):488–497.

Radbill, S. 1980. "Children in a World of Violence: A History of Child Abuse." In *The Battered Child,* pp. 3–20. 2d ed. Edited by R. Helfer and C. Kempe. Chicago: University of Chicago Press.

Radelet, Michael L. 1981. "Racial Characteristics and the Imposition of the Death Penalty." *American Sociological Review* 46(December):918–927.

Rose, Harold M. 1978. "The Geography of Despair." *Annals of the Association of American Geographers* 68:453–464.

———. 1981. *Black Homicide and the Urban Environment.* U.S. Department of Health and Human Services, National Institute of Mental Health. Washington, D.C.: Government Printing Office.

Roy, M., ed. 1977. *Battered Women.* New York: Van Nostrand Reinhold.

Ryan, William. 1971. *Blaming the Victim.* New York: Pantheon.

Shin, Yongsock, Davor Jedlicka, and Everett S. Lee. 1977. "Homicide among Blacks." *Phylon* 38(December):398–407.

Silberman, Charles E. 1978. *Criminal Violence–Criminal Justice: Criminals Police, Courts, and Prisons in America.* New York: Random House.

Star, B. 1980. "Patterns of Family Violence." *Social Casework* 61(June):339–346.

Stark, R., and J. McEvoy. 1970. "Middle Class Violence." *Psychology Today* 4 (November):52–65.

Straus, Murray A. 1974. Foreword to *The Violent Home: A Study of Physical Aggression between Husbands and Wives* by R.J. Gelles. Beverly Hills: Sage.

Straus, Murray A., R.J. Gelles, and S.K. Steinmetz. 1980. *Behind Closed Doors: Violence in the American Family.* Garden City, N.Y.: Doubleday, Anchor Books.

Sudnow, David. 1965. "Normal Crimes: Sociological Features of the Penal Code in a Public Defender Office," *Social Problems* 12(Winter):255–276.

Swigert, Victoria, and Ronald A. Farrell. 1977. "Normal Homicides and the Law." *American Sociological Review* 42(February):16–32.

U.S. Department of Health and Human Services. 1980 Public Health Service. Office of Health Research, Statistics and Technology. National Center for Health Statistics. National Center for Health Services Research. *Health United States: 1980.* 1981. DHHS Publication (PHS)81–1232. Washington, D.C.: Government Printing Office.

———. 1981. *Public Health Reports.* Washington, D.C.: U.S. Government Printing Office.

Wolfgang, Marvin, and Franco Ferracuti. 1967. *The Subculture of Violence: Towards an Integrated Theory in Criminology.* London: Tavistock.

Wolfgang, Marvin, Franco Ferracuti, and Marc Riedel. 1973. "Race, Judicial Discretion, and the Death Penalty." *Annals of the American Academy of Political and Social Science* 407:119–133.

Zimring, Franklin E., Joel Eigen, and Sheila O'Malley. 1976. "Punishing Homicide in Philadelphia: Perspectives on the Death Penalty." *University of Chicago Law Review* 43:227–252.

12

Research Issues Relating to the Causes of Social Deviance and Violence among Black Populations

Coramae Richey Mann
Velma LaPoint

T
he criminal justice system works through three separate agencies—the police, the courts, and corrections—to apprehend, adjudicate, treat, or incarcerate lawbreakers. Megargee (1975) suggests that selective factors operate at each stage of the criminal justice process, factors that are reflected in the small number of arrests resulting in convictions and the smaller number of convicted persons incarcerated in correctional facilities. Although criminal justice decisions and procedures generally operate to decrease the number of individuals enmeshed in the system, the opposite effect is observed in minority group and low-income persons processed by the system (Christianson 1984; Megargee 1975; Owens 1980).

Data indicate that blacks are highly overrepresented among perpetrators of common law crimes. Although most arrests for deviant behavior are made for less serious offenses, the analysis of the causes of deviant behavior emphasizes violent offenses. Most of the theories and the concomitant research address the causes of deviant behavior by attempting to analyze the violent behavior of blacks. This chapter therefore will focus on contemporary perspectives and theories that attempt to explain violent crime among blacks; such behavior is the primary concern of both criminal justice officials and private citizens.

This chapter will have a sociological and criminological emphasis rather than a psychological orientation. Research on the causes of illegal deviant behavior has only recently drawn attention from psychologists, who have not found the field attractive in the past. In addition, psychologists have not been involved in the study of criminal behavior because such behavior, unlike many other dysfunctional behaviors, is seldom defined by clinical professionals or behavioral researchers. The arresting officer, prosecutor, judge, or jury determines the status of each individual case (Pacht and Strangman 1980). Sociologists, however, have focused closely on crime and delinquency, particularly because only a few universities have schools or departments of criminology or criminal justice (Pacht and Strangman 1980).

Monohan and Splane (1980) have raised another significant issue regarding the limited, but growing, role of psychology in research and theoretical formulations of crime. They state that the disciplinary conflict between sociologists or criminologists and psychologists has minimized the role, and consequently the influence, of psychology. Criminologists, for example, have been reluctant to rely upon the individual as the unit of analysis in research, whereas the individual is generally the focus of psychologists. Psychologists and criminologists also differ frequently regarding the level of intervention. The level of causal analysis, whether individual or systemic, relates to the level of intervention, both preventive and rehabilitative. Such differences maintain interdisciplinary disputes; Monohan and Splane (1981) offer suggestions for reconciliation.

This chapter examines: 1) definitions of behavior that violates laws of society and some of the responses to this behavior; 2) subcultural and contracultural perspectives on criminal and delinquent behavior; 3) the types of research methods commonly used in criminological research; 4) interpretative issues to illustrate how these methodological procedures relate to the validity, reliability, and generalizability of research findings; and 5) research and social policies relating to black individuals who are labeled deviant. Finally, we will suggest future considerations and directions in an effort to improve research on the causes of deviant behavior among blacks. We will close the chapter with recommendations of topics that need investigation, methods that could be employed in research, and support for the argument that black researchers should be involved prominently in research on social deviance among blacks.

Definition of
Social Deviance, Criminality, and Delinquency

Social deviance is a label referring to behavior that differs from a given norm or standard of behavior. According to Theodorson and Theodorson (1969):

> Deviance is a common phenomenon in the life of every human being (even in the so-called "simple societies"). It is always defined from the point of view of a particular normative structure, and in a complex society where there are a multiplicity of groups and conflicting normative standards, each member of the society is at some time liable to be considered deviant by one standard or another. Often deviance simply

involves conformity to the standards of a subgroup rather than those of the dominant social group. The consequences of deviance from normative standards are varied and may range from a frown to imprisonment or confinement for mental illness. However, people who deviate from social norms are not necessarily (or necessarily considered) mentally ill nor does deviance necessarily entail mental illness. The despised deviant from a particular society or social system may be regarded as a martyr or saint by another ethical philosophy or historical period. Thus deviance is not inherent in specific behavior or attitudes but rather is a phenomenon of human interaction in a particular normative setting (p. 111).

A definition of social deviance implies that certain standards, rules, norms, or laws are presumed to be accepted by consensus in society. The violation of these somewhat intangible and loosely defined proscriptions results in the ascribed status of deviance (Reid 1979).

Criminologists focus on those forms of deviant behaviors that violate a law, statute, or ordinance in society. Under this definition, a deviant act is any act defined by law as being criminal when committed. Juvenile delinquency is included in the general concept of deviancy and criminality, but it is limited to deviant activities of a defined age group (Trojanowicz 1978). The age group is defined by the jurisdiction in which the youth is located; each state determines the age at which a minor becomes an adult and enforces its laws accordingly. Thus, behaviors that are defined as deviant or criminal may not only vary from state to state but from situation to situation.

In this chapter the terms *deviant* and *criminal* are used interchangeably, while *delinquency* refers to the deviant behavior of juveniles. In addition, we wish to clarify our use of the term *commission of a crime*. From our perspective, arrest or conviction by criminal justice personnel does not necessarily mean that the arrested individual committed the crime. Therefore, when we refer to deviant, criminal, or delinquent behavior, such behavior either may have been only alleged or may have actually occurred.

The behavior of an individual who violates laws is defined and determined initially by lawmakers and law enforcement personnel. Thus, arrest statistics illustrate the incidence of serious crime among blacks. Arrest figures compiled by the Federal Bureau of Investigation for 1983 and reported by the Uniform Crime Reports (UCR) reveal that blacks constituted 35.7 percent of all arrests made for index crimes (U.S. Department of Justice 1984): criminal homicide, forcible rape, robbery, aggravated assault, burglary, breaking and entering, larceny-theft, motor vehicle theft, and arson (Mann 1984a). The UCR for 1983 indicate that blacks accounted for 49.6 percent of the persons arrested for murder and nonnegligent manslaughter (criminal homicides), 48.9 percent of those arrested for rape, 62.5

percent for burglary, 33.3 percent for larceny theft, 32.3 percent for auto theft, and 23.3 percent for arson. In 1983, black individuals constituted 47.5 percent of the arrests for violent crime but only 32.7 percent of the arrests for property crime (U.S. Department of Justice 1984). These figures show clearly the disparate proportion of black arrests: blacks constitute only about 13 percent of the U.S. population but about 27.3 percent of all persons arrested in 1983 (U.S. Department of Justice 1984). Self-report studies (Elliot and Ageton 1980) and victimization studies (Hindelang 1978) report similar results.

Since the mid-1960s, the arrests of females have not varied by more than five percentage points as a proportion of total arrests. In 1960, females accounted for 10.7 percent of the total number of arrested persons; by 1983, they made up only 16.6 percent of that total (U.S. Department of Justice 1984). Today's female crime problem mirrors the female crimes of past years; the type of offenses for which females are arrested did not change substantially from 1960 to 1983. In 1970 violent female offenders were only 10.2 percent of the total; murder and nonnegligent manslaughter were the most frequent violent offenses (13.7 percent), compared to 10.8 percent of violent crime arrests and 13.3 percent for murder in 1983. Within the crime index, arrested female offenders constitute one-fourth (25.4 percent) of those who committed serious crimes (Mann 1984a). Because the UCR does not report arrests by sex and race, it is difficult to determine the prevalence of black women in female crime, but a few individual studies support the notion that black females are at least as deeply involved in crime as their male counterparts.

Although most arrests are made for less serious or nonindex crimes, efforts to explain crime focus on violent offenses or personal crimes rather than on property crimes, where there is usually no victim. Many theories and studies attempt to analyze the behavior of blacks arrested for serious or violent crime.

Individuals convicted of the more serious violent crimes are more likely to be incarcerated. According to Megargee (1975), those who are imprisoned—that is, those who are convicted of the more serious crimes—represent a very small, highly biased sample of the population of individuals committing deviant acts:

> The more intelligent, skilled, and experienced criminals are most likely to avoid detection; of those identified by the police, those with the best of connections, the greatest financial resources, the most stable work and family backgrounds, the fewest prior offenses, and the whitest skins are most likely to avoid arrest, conviction, and imprisonment. (p. 4)

A leading black sociologist, Robert Staples (1976), presents a similar perspective on deviant behavior among blacks. Beginning with a general definition of crime as an act committed in violation of a law that prohibits it, Staples delineates four types of crimes: (1) ordinary crimes (such as traffic violations, some forms of sexual conduct, falsification of information on employment or loan applications); (2) political crimes (including failure to enforce laws that prohibit racial discrimination in employment, housing, and education); (3) corporate crimes (for example, misrepresentation in advertising, violation of trust, and gambling); and (4) underclass crimes (for example assault and robbery).

In general, Staples (1976) states that the manner in which crimes are defined determines how the problem of crime is perceived, who is arrested for criminal behavior, and what remedies are used to reduce crime. Given the overrepresentation of blacks arrested for certain crimes, the dominant racial group defines as criminal those acts that fit its purpose and classifies as criminal an individual who commits certain kinds of illegal acts. Other such acts are exempted from prosecution because they are not perceived as criminal or threatening to society. Because one group has the power to define and determine what constitutes criminal behavior and how such behavior is to be treated (including punishment), strong disparities exist in the seriousness of a crime and the responses to a given category of crime (Staples 1976).

Similar views are expressed by Alvin J. Bronstein, director of the National Prison Project of the American Civil Liberties Union. An advocate of the rights of incarcerated individuals, Bronstein states that criminal justice personnel should deemphasize their concern with traditional crime (such as activities by burglars, muggers, and bank robbers). Although such crimes are costly, they do not threaten the fabric of society and will never be affected by overreliance on incarceration as punishment. Intentional manufacture of unsafe products, theft from consumers due to price rigging, and pollution of the environment from industrial production are the kinds of crime that require societal attention (McCombs 1982).

Finally, Cullen and coworkers (1985) ask whether empirical reality exists or whether consensus regarding crime is due to methodological artifact. They are concerned that "in the prevailing social climate, there is the very real risk that criminological research can be employed to legitimate expressly punitive justice policies" (Cullen et al. 1985, p. 113).

Theories and Research on the Causes of Social Deviance among Black Populations

Theories of deviance can be categorized in numerous ways (Trojanowicz 1978; Thio 1978; Reid 1979); the following brief overview is limited to theories relevant to explaining deviance among blacks. The most widely noted theories in this vein are subcultural theory and its stepchild, contracultural theory, both natural outgrowths of the positive school of criminology.

The classical school of criminology embraced the social contract concept: (1) an individual and society have certain responsibilites to each other (Reid 1979); (2) humans operate under free will; and (3) punishment is a deterrent that should fit the crime (Reid 1979). This concept ushered in the Age of Enlightenment in criminological thought and legal process and facilitated an end to the atrocities of the Middle Ages.

As the classical school responded to the conditions existing in the Middle Ages, the positive school, which developed in the latter part of the nineteenth century, arose in response to the classical orientation of rational and consistent prosecution and punishment (Trojanowicz 1978) and the pervading emphasis on legal structure. Positivists believed that criminology should focus on an examination of the individual and his or her criminal behavior through the use of newly developed empirical methodologies. Thus, according to Reid (1979):

> The positivists rejected the harsh legalism of the classical school and substituted the doctrine of determinism for that of free will. They focused on the constitutional, not the legal aspect of crime, and they emphasized a philosophy of individualized, scientific treatment of criminals, based upon the findings of the physical and social sciences. (P. 136)

This emphasis on the application of scientific methods to the study of criminal behavior originated in Italy, spread to France, and readily became the major approach of American behavioral scientists. Later the focus turned from the individual offender to the impact of social structure and process on the individual offender.

In the last decade of the nineteenth century, the French sociologist Emile Durkheim published his classical work, *The Division of Labor in Society*. He coined the term *anomie*, a state that emerges in a society because of the increased division of labor and the increased heterogeneity that develops as a result of social evolution (Landen 1973). Durkheim found that fragmentation, disorganization, and loss of social control took place in complex, evolving industrializing societies and resulted in a loosening of the norms, social isolation, loneliness, and loss of identify for the individuals in such societies. Such a state of anomie provides the milieu for the flourishing of crimes and other antisocial behavior (Reid 1979).

Although Durkheim coined and defined *anomie*, the American sociologist Robert Merton developed it, largely as a reaction to the Freudian psychoanalytic theory of deviance based on biological, libidinal, and animalistic desires (Thio 1978) and to extant biological theories that attributed human behavior to inherited traits (Reid 1979). In 1938, Merton pointed to the influence of the social structure and its contribution to crime. According to this perspective, American society stresses success as an important cultural value, a goal that each American, regardless of class level, aspires to achieve. Yet the institutionalized means to attain success are not available to everyone, particularly not to members of the lower class. Therefore, to attain success, lower-class people must resort to illegitimate means. Although social deviance also occurs at other socioeconomic levels, the Mertonian perspective of anomie provides the foundation for the subcultural theories of deviance. This body of theories originated in attempts to explain juvenile delinquency and only later was applied to adult groups.

Studies of adult criminality have concentrated on male populations, particularly on those who commit violent crimes. Because black men are represented disproportionately in official crime statistics, theories regarding violent crime are attached more frequently to this population. Foremost among these is the subculture of violence theory outlined by Wolfgang and Ferracuti (1967), who examined 588 cases of criminal homicide committed in Philadelphia from 1948 to 1952. They reported the following homicide rates per 100,000 in the population by race and gender of offender: black males, 41.7; black females, 9.3; white males, 3.4; and white females, 0.4. The 20- to 24-year-old age group predominated, with a rate of 12.6 per 100,000, but whereas males of both races committed criminal homicides more frequently in their twenties, "Negro males in their early sixties kill as frequently as do white males in their early twenties" (Wolfgang 1970, p. 54).

The subculture of violence theory, which Amir (1970) later applied to rape, appears to be "the most influential contemporary explanation among criminologists interested in the determinants of violence" (Carey 1978, p. 275). Briefly, Wolfgang and Ferracuti state that a subculture differs from the dominant culture, or larger value system, in having a social value system of its own that conflicts with the wider, central culture. In addition to personality variables, which determine whether the subcultural values will be transmitted, Wolfgang and Ferracuti suggest that the values learned in the subculture include "a potent theme of violence . . . that makes the lifestyle, the socialization process, the interpersonal relationships, and individuals living in similar conditions" (p. 140). On the basis of these findings, Wolfgang and Ferracuti conclude that the subculture of violence is the basic cause of high homicide rates in black communities.

Because this perspective focuses on urban black males' values as different from and more violent than the values of the dominant culture, Ball-Rokeach (1973) points out that incarcerated offenders who participate in violent, aggressive behavior should differ from a sample of American men. Her findings did not support the subculture of violence theory; her national survey disclosed no accepted values of violence and those who rejected them. She concludes that violence may be linked to one or more situational variables such as access to weapons, conflict within the group, alcohol, population density, or rapid social change (Ball-Rokeach 1973). This study, however, neglected to examine meaningfully the research of black and white social scientists who have explored the black community as a subculture. Cole (1970) describes the subculture of black Americans as consisting of three subdivisions relating to values that are shared with the dominant culture, shared with other oppressed peoples, and unique to black individuals. She finds that the data concerning the black subculture are concentrated consistently and overwhelmingly on one black life-style, which she terms "street life-style," to the neglect of the diversity of other life-styles within black communities in the United States.

The violent contraculture theory appears to challenge the previous formulations of a black subculture of violence and focuses on a group of lower-class males who are violence prone and in conflict with the dominant culture (Wolfgang and Curtis 1972; Curtis 1974, 1975, 1976). The authors concluded that the black subculture of poverty does acquire more characteristics in common with the dominant culture but is actually a renegade contraculture within that group that perpetrates the crimes of violence. Although this contraculture in the black community has been isolated because of "residential segregation, economic deprivations, and racial discrimination," the authors refer to "reaction formation" by young black males against "matriarchs in broken families" (Wolfgang and Curtis 1972).

Among those who assume that black males from a low socioeconomic class become violent because they lack adequate male role models, three salient socioeconomic facts are neglected (Mann and Selva 1978). First, the extended family, in which other relatives or in-laws live in the same household with the primary family, exists in appreciable numbers among blacks. Second, male role models also exist in the augmented family, which includes household members not related to the family, such as roomers, lodgers, and boarders, and has been estimated at more than one-half million (Billingsley 1971). Third, black communities are replete with adult male models, both within and outside households. Hannerz (1972) points out that males have no monopoly on teaching other males about masculinity; black mothers, grandmothers, aunts, and sisters also impart information about the behavior expected of men.

Historically, theories of deviance among females have been biologically or psychologically based, with an assumption that a female must be innately deviant to engage in criminal activity. For decades women were regarded as capable of committing only the crimes of prostitution, abortion, or infanticide; therefore they were dismissed as the focus of attention in criminological research except for offenses related to sexual taboos (Lombroso and Ferrers 1916; Dalton 1960a, 1960b; Cowie, Cowie, and

Slater 1968; Konopka 1966; Herskovitz 1969; Mann, 1984a). In the 1970s, however, sociological and criminological theorists turned from chromosomes, hormones, penis envy, menopause, masculine protest, and other physiological and psychogenic-based issues to economic and sociological explanations of female deviance similar to those proffered by the many researchers who explored the causes of male deviance and delinquency.

The women's movement as a causative factor in female crime has also been the subject of considerable controversy among contemporary theorists. Space limitations prohibit a thorough examination of these views; therefore our discussion is limited to the position of Freda Adler (1975), who addresses specifically crime among black females.

Adler believes that females imitate males in the desire for the same goals and in the adoption of male roles to achieve them (Mann 1984a). She sees crime as linked to opportunity: girls today are adopting male roles and committing more male-oriented juvenile crimes such as gang membership, drinking, fighting, and stealing. The causes of such misbehavior are found in the social structure of Western society, its urbanization, and the blockage of opportunities for females. Racial differences in female criminality, according to Adler, are rooted in the impact of slavery on the black family in the United States. Economic sanctions applied to the black male after emancipation led to a sex role reversal among black women, who had to assume the role of household head, which was denied to their men. To meet family financial obligations, the black woman had to resort to deviance. Because of her position of equality to the black man, the black woman is also more equal to her black brother in crime; thus her crimes are dissimilar to the criminal behavior exhibited by white female offenders (Adler 1975).

Despite various explanations for arrest differences between blacks and whites, few scholars have attempted to address the alleged differences between the criminality of white women and that of black women. Many of the factors operating in black communities have been thought to affect black males and black females equally. The subcultural perspectives can be counted among those factors, although black females are generally considered more prone to violate public order statutes such as prostitution, drinking, and drug abuse. Overall, the patterns of black male and black female crime are thought to be more similar than the criminal patterns of their respective white counterparts (Adler 1975).

In a recent review and statistical analysis of forty-four studies concerned with the relationship between gender and criminality, Smith and Visher (1980) suggested a significant convergence in male and female involvement in deviance/criminality for nonwhites but no discernible pattern for whites. In addition, white males commit more crimes and more deviant acts than white females, and this difference seems to remain constant over time. In contrast, Smith and Visher believe that the deviant behavior of black females is becoming more like that of black males. This position supports Adler's basic argument for the greater similarity between the economic and social roles of black men and black women.

Young's (1980) analysis of National Crime Survey data on personal victimization, which are independent of official statistics, tends to refute two of Adler's basic assumptions about black female crime. Young first challenges Adler's contention that black female criminality exceeds that of white females by a much greater margin than the criminality of black males exceeds that of white males. She reports that the same ratio of black male criminals to white male criminals (2:1) held true for black female criminals when compared to white females (Young 1980). Second, contrary to Adler's hypothesis that crime patterns for black males and females are more alike than crime patterns for white males and females, Young's data show that the pattern of crime according to sex is more similar among whites than among blacks. She concludes, however, that there is no simplistic answer to the question of whether female offenders differ by race.

Most of the theories and research on juvenile delinquency have been devoted to studies of boys. Although the following discussion is not exhaustive, it is compatible with the approach of exploring the theories and research that focus on black populations. The major elements underlying these examples are ethnicity and lower socioeconomic status.

Early research studies, such as Thrasher's (1936) classical study of Chicago gangs and Shaw and McKay's (1942) systematic analyses of gang activity and the distribution of delinquency, were forerunners of the statistical-ecological studies that focused on lower-income areas, where deviance was considered endemic. Merton's theory of anomie and theories of delinquent subculture by Cohen (1955) and Cloward and Ohlin (1960) grew out of these earlier studies with little empirical evidence of their own. Gibbons (1976), for example, states that Cohen described gang delinquency with broad strokes and related comparatively small areas of factual data with large amounts of speculation.

Albert Cohen (1955) substituted the concept of status for Merton's success as the cultural value sought in American society; the lower-class child is denied the attainment of this goal because the yardstick for measuring status is defined by success in school. Lower-class boys (girls are not included) are unable to meet the middle-class standards of behavior and performance established by the middle-class system (Thio 1978). Thus, as a result of status frustration, they set up their own status-earning, competitive system—a delinquent subculture—in which the criteria for status attainment, delinquent activities, are the opposite of middle-class criteria. Cohen is describing a group function as the reaction to the inability to attain societal goals.

These brief descriptions show that there are more similarities than differences between the perspectives of Merton and Cohen. Both theorists state that society has defined certain aspirations (success or status) that are to be obtained and has blocked or failed to provide avenues of achievement to individuals of lower socioeconomic backgrounds. As a consequence, members of lower socioeconomic backgrounds may resort to deviance as an avenue to achievement.

Cloward and Ohlin (1960) also assign the deviant label to the lower class, but they simultaneously introduce the idea of illegitimate opportunity. According to this perspective lower-class boys not only have limited opportunities for attaining success in legitimate ways, but they have no guarantees of access to illegitimate avenues of success.

In contrast, Walter Miller (1976) does not attribute the delinquent behavior of individuals from lower socioeconomic backgrounds to the blockage from access to success. He designates the status of being lower class as the causal factor in deviance:

> There is a substantial segment of present-day American society whose way of life, values, and characteristic patterns of behavior are the product of a distinctive cultural system which may be termed "lower-class." (p. 144)

> A large body of systematically interrelated attitudes, practices, behaviors, and values characteristic of lower-class culture are designed to support and maintain the basic features of the lower-class way of life. (p. 154)

Miller's (1976) perspective of delinquency is based on research on one-sex street-corner peer groups in a lower-class community whose prevalence and stability are associated closely with the female-based household. In such households, men are either absent or are present only sporadically and are uninvolved in the economic support or socialization of the youthful family members. The implication is that such a family configuration affects adversely a boy's sex role identification. This situation is counteracted by the street group and its activities, which function to restore a sense of being a man. Miller's emphasis on the female-headed household (single-parent family) has found some support in the analyses of black family life offered by the Department of Labor report (frequently referred to as the Moynihan report [1965]), and in the social control (bonding) theory of Hirschi (1969) and other control theorists.

Miller's (1976) assumptions about lower-class black males can be criticized on the ground that his descriptions seem to be most applicable to some urban residents, particularly blacks, and not to other lower-class groups, such as residents in Italian or Chinese areas (Gibbons 1976). In addition, in this era of mass communication, it stretches the imagination to assume, as Miller does, that the lower-class culture he described can exist in a pure form without influence by other class-level standards (Trojanowicz 1978). Finally, self-report studies of delinquency committed by other economic class levels have found few racial differences (Williams and Gold 1978). Thus, the difference between the self-reported criminal involvement of white and black respondents is either minimal or nonexistent, as contrasted to reports in official statistics (McNeely and Pope 1981).

The social control theory of delinquency developed by Travis Hirschi (1969) is rooted in Durkheim's theory of anomie, since the basic concept focuses on the individual's bond to society. When a juvenile's ties to conventional society are weakened or broken, the potential for delinquent activity is increased.

Although Hirschi's theory does not directly discuss the issue of the single-parent family, attachment to parents is an important variable in his perspective on delinquency causation. Control theory has received a good deal of empirical support, but it too has problems. Hirschi's study used a sample of California urban youth. Although many of his findings were replicated by Hindelang (1978) in a rural sample from New York State, Hindelang failed to verify a positive relationship between the attachment to parents and attachment to friends and delinquency (Reid 1979).

Single-parent families headed by females and families characterized by conflict have historically been alleged to cause female delinquency, largely because adolescent female deviance has been viewed as sexual misbehavior (Gibbons 1976). According to this perspective, because the female is deprived of affection in the home, she seeks it outside the home through a sexual relationship. Runaway and delinquent females have been viewed as sexually delinquent because of conditions in the family, particularly in the single-parent family.

In a study of adjudicated delinquents, Datesman and Scarpetti (1975) concluded that female delinquency and single-parent families are related largely because of moral offenses. Contrary to previous notions that pathological consequences of single-parent families fall more heavily on black children than on white children, they found that the relationship between gender and single-parent families for blacks was not significant for either personal or property offenses. They suggest that the black female is insulated more securely from delinquency because she is socialized into a traditional male role in a black matrifocal family system.

Austin (1978) criticizes the Datesman and Scarpetti study on the basis of the small numbers of their sample. Through the use of a stratified sample of 5,545 youth, Austin examined the effects of father absence on delinquency, according to race and gender. His findings indicate that only white females experienced detrimental effects. Black females from single-parent families appeared to be less vulnerable than females from white single-parent and two-parent families or females from black two-parent families.

Although social control theorists do not analyze the relationship between single-parent families and delinquency, the notion of bonding, particularly to the family, suggests such a perspective. Subcultural theorists, notably Miller (1976), point to the broken home, the single-parent home, or the female-headed home as providing a potential environment for delinquency. At the family level of analysis, black households appear to have been singled out and are considered generally disorganized, pathological, disintegrated, and prone to deviance and crime (Debro and Headly 1981). It is presumed that without a father in the home, the child will fail; black homes are more prone to being fatherless, and thus black children are more likely to be delinquent (U.S. Department of Labor 1965). The usual argument is that the black male lacks positive role models in the absence of a father in the home.

Whether researchers refer to a female-headed household, a broken home, a father-absent family, a single-parent home, or a female-dominated family (terms commonly used or implied in subcultural and anomie theories), these terms are not defined operationally except by the fact that one parent is not present in the home. This condition is described as more characteristic of the lower class than of the middle class, especially among black families. The quality or adequacy of the home, however, has been overlooked, yet a two-parent home can be fraught with problems that could lead to delinquency, and a single-parent home can provide a nurturing environment that could prevent delinquency. Nevertheless, the trend has been to consider single-parent families as a cause of delinquency.

Wilkerson (1976) has identified problems with the causal formulation. First, the term *single parent* is ambiguous and broadly defined. A family that has lost a parent to death may have dynamics different from a family in which a parent has deserted. Second, there is evidence that children from single-parent families may be more likely to be involved in the juvenile justice system than those from allegedly stable nuclear families. A third problem, which is ancillary to official processing, is a tendency for delinquency studies to rely on official data when unofficial sources may be equally pertinent to the relationship between single-parent families and delinquency. As a result of these oversights and methodologically deficient studies, Wilkerson concludes that we do not know to what extent single-parent family status contributes to delinquency; the literature is divided on this subject. (For a more detailed analysis of research on

children in single-parent families, with particular attention to the relationship between female-headed single-parent families and juvenile delinquency, Herzog and Sudia [1973] offer a classical review of the literature.)

The delinquent subculture theories in general have placed a great
deal of emphasis on lower-class crime and delinquency through the use of
official statistics, which consistently overrepresent persons from the lower
class. Furthermore, because research on communities in the United States
has shown that the lower class is most vulnerable to law enforcement and
judicial action (Quinney, 1980), these statistics are largely unreliable and
of questionable validity. Many of these theories have been tested on
institutionalized populations; studies on noninstitutionalized populations
reveal that social class is not a significant factor in deviance because most
youngsters commit deviant acts but are never processed through the
juvenile justice system (Reid 1979).

If, as anomie theorists believe, a great part of the problem is due to
blocked opportunities to success or status goals based on middle-class
aspirations, lower-class people must have such aspirations. Yet there is no
firm evidence to support the contention that lower-class people have the
same level of aspirations as middle- or upper-class people; on the contrary, it has been demonstrated that lower-class people are realistic about
their status and have a significantly lower level of success values (Thio
1978). Thio also states that according to anomie theory, blacks would have
the same kind of cultural or success goals as whites; this position negates
the notion of a pluralistic American society in which minority groups may
have their own cultural values.

Research Methods Used in Studies

Behavioral scientists use many different approaches and methods to
study social deviance among black populations. Some methods have
inherent limitations when employed with any population; others are
limited by the influence of racial, ethnic, and class factors.

Social science investigators conducting research on the causes of social
deviance are predominantly white and middle class (Brown 1974; National
Minority Advisory Council on Criminal Justice 1982), yet the subjects of
such research are typically black. Thus research has a negative connotation
to many prospective black research populations. Georges-Abeyie's (1984)
literature review of minorities in the criminal justice system presents an
excellent critique of the majority-generated research on blacks enmeshed
in that system and of the "nature and extent of negative perceptions held
by racial and ethnic minorities in regard to the system itself" (p. 125).
Frequently these perceptions are due to negative behavioral assessments,

often unwarranted, that emanate from findings and interpretations of research (Boykin 1979; Williams 1980). Participation in research is usually voluntary; furthermore, many research designs require participants to reveal factual, often intimate, information about themselves, either verbally in interviews or behaviorally in observations.

According to Reid (1979), the experimental method of research used primarily in experimental psychology is not used as frequently in sociology and criminology because of difficulties in establishing matched experimental and control groups and controlling intervening variables. In an effort to be objective, researchers have emphasized the use of official statistics from courts, the UCR, and other measurable data such as victimization surveys. Self-report studies have also been viewed as more empirical than the more qualitative types of research, such as interviews and field studies.

Official Statistics

Many problems are associated with the reported measures used to describe arrest data, particularly the FBI's UCR, although the UCR is considered the most acceptable source of such statistics in the United States. Although the FBI collects these data nationally under congressional mandate, state and local governments are not obligated to report such data (Reid 1979). These statistics are often manipulated to present the police in a favorable light (Brown 1974).

Sutherland and Cressey (1978) give six reasons why crime known to the police is not a sufficient index of crime:

1. The number of crimes known to the police is surely smaller than the actual crime rate because most persons do not report crimes.

2. The accuracy of such reports is related to the degree of honesty, efficiency, and consistency of those reporting.

3. The differences in types of offenses and the corresponding attention result in differential recording of offenses.

4. The quantity of personnel, the degree of expertise, and the degree of effort exerted by law enforcement agencies affect the volume of crime known to the police.

5. The fifty states and the District of Columbia vary in their classifications of crime, and such variations affect the number of crimes known to and reported by police.

6. Arrest and crime rates are confounded with fluctuations in the census.

Data from official crime statistics are particularly prone to bias. According to Feldman (1977), official statistics give the impression that the typical criminal is young, male, working class, and black. He states, however, that in the United States, certain groups of the population are more likely than others to proceed from one stage of the criminal justice system to other stages. It is likely, for example, that lower-class individuals, who are also disproportionately black, are more likely to be observed and scrutinized in any violation of the law than their middle- or upper-class, typically white counterparts. It follows that the likelihood of detection will be higher for offenses committed by members of the so-called more criminal class.

McNeely and Pope (1981) state that inferences made from arrest, conviction, and prison data to the general rates of criminality are uncertain because selection bias by law enforcement personnel may account for the disproportionate number of black arrests. One glaring problem inherent in such data bases is that the U.S. Census Bureau consistently undercounts black males, the population most considered at risk for crime. In 1970, for example, the census apparently undercounted by 18 percent black men in the 30- to 34–year-old age group (Skogan 1981). If the data base is undercounted, the computed rates will be inflated; this is generally the case for black males.

Victimization Surveys

Victimization surveys are another type of study used in research on the causes of social deviance. Research participants are asked questions regarding whether they have been criminally victimized, the characteristics of the crime and the offender, and the extent of reporting the offense(s) to legal authorities (Pope 1981). These surveys may be administered nationally by the National Opinion Research Center (NORC) or the National Crime Survey conducted by the U.S. Census Bureau.

The methodological limitations of victimization surveys also raise questions regarding the accuracy of the reported volume of crime. Because some victimization surveys rely on self-reports of past events through personal contact or telephone interviews, the findings are subject to the vagaries of the participants. A recent analysis of the measurement issues involved in this kind of crime reporting suggests that retrospective reports are subject to four kinds of errors: (1) the interviewees may not recognize a crime or may be ignorant of what a crime is; (2) they may forget or may not tell of the criminal incidents; (3) their recall may be inaccurate or incomplete; or (4) "differential productivity" might exist among respondents (that is, some people respond better than others). Findings from victimization surveys are also affected by procedural factors, such as panel bias, attrition, and variations in styles and techniques (for example, telephone or personal interviews) of recording (Skogan 1981).

Self-Reports of Crime

In contrast to victimization surveys, some studies use respondents who are perpetrators of social deviance. Although most of these self-report studies from 1950 to 1960 queried juveniles, this method of uncovering hidden or unreported crime has also been used with adult populations. Self-reports have many of the same drawbacks as victimization surveys, particularly concerning the respondents' reliability in veracity and in recollection of events. Furthermore, self-report studies of juveniles tend to involve only minor infractions of the law instead of more serious offenses.

Field Studies

A third approach is the field study, or the study in a natural setting. The most commonly used field method is participant observation, in which the researcher blends with the environment under study and often lives in the community to observe the actions of its inhabitants. Systematic observation, a more structured method, usually employs an operationally defined checklist either alone or in conjunction with participant observation, since the latter technique relies heavily on field notes.

Observational studies are frequently criticized for being qualitative, subjective, and biased, particularly by those in the criminological discipline who emphasize scientific empiricism. Participant observation is subject to such problems, especially when the information is gathered from those convicted of crime. Such subjects may change their behavior if they believe that a publication will be an outcome of the study. The researcher may also become absorbed in the life-styles of those being observed and become less objective. Finally, questions of ethics arise regarding confidentiality and trust. Ethical problems are introduced by not informing subjects that they are being observed and by disguising entry into the groups. Yet if the researcher does identify self and purpose, this knowledge may influence the participants.

Additional issues relating to the influence of racial, cultural, and class differences in self-report and field studies are relevant to research with black populations. Many black participants have negative attitudes toward social science research that may influence verbal and behavioral responses. Distrustful attitudes toward research, for example, may interfere with honest verbal disclosure of information in self-reports. Similarly, black respondents may modify their behavior when queried or observed by white investigators whose backgrounds differ from theirs in many ways.

Sampling Procedures

Another area of methodological problems is sampling bias. Researchers generally study individuals who have been processed by personnel in the criminal justice system; others may also be involved in the commission of crime but may have avoided processing. A major question, according to Pacht and Strangman (1980), is which group should be selected for study. Frequently the apprehended group is more convenient for investigation because it represents a captive, available population. The use of such groups supports the assumption that offenders who are arrested or institutionalized are representative of offenders in general. This is not the case, however; factors account for a given individual's being processed or not processed.

Another problem of using institutionalized populations in research is the dualistic fallacy (Reid 1979). It is assumed that there are two mutually exclusive groups of individuals, criminals and noncriminals, whose behavior is distinguishable. According to this fallacy, each of two groups is considered homogeneous; studies can compare them on a given trait and conclude that the findings represent differences between the two groups. Reid states, however, that studies using this assumption have no scientific validity because they do not discriminate between those who commit crimes and those who do not.

A third problem related to sampling of institutionalized populations is the assumption that offenders are unchanged by their institutionalization (Feldman 1977). Assessments of incarcerated persons are an amalgam of the influences experienced before the offense and institutionalization and those experienced during incarceration.

A final problem related to sampling bias is sample size. Samples are supposed to be representative of the population and large enough to represent that population. Most research on deviance, however, uses extremely small populations scattered throughout the country. Self-report studies are typically unrepresentative of the general population because in many cases they rely upon those who volunteer to participate (Reid 1979). Furthermore, the proportion of black respondents in such samples has been small (McNeely and Pope 1981). Because victimization studies are a form of self-report, they are also subject to errors related to sample size. The National Crime Survey of Cities, for example, based its estimates of rape victimizations in Philadelphia on only twenty-nine interviews with rape victims (Skogan 1981).

As one black researcher points out in this criticism of macrosocietal-level etiological factors in homicide studies, "the inattention of past researchers to the more immediate, situational determinants of homicide may be more problematic" (Hawkins 1985, p. 95). Preliminary findings from Chicago and Houston in an ongoing field study of female criminal homicide offenders, for example, reveal that black family violence resulting in murder was usually precipitated by a domestic argument or fight that did not necessarily involve alcohol, a presumption usually made in cases of black violence (Mann, 1986).

This discussion of methodological problems is not exhaustive; researchers in social deviance also conduct studies without comparison groups, undertake few longitudinal studies, rarely conduct follow-up studies, and tend to focus on single-factor causality to the neglect of multiple-factor approaches. In sum, research on the causes of social deviance lacks the methodological rigor requisite to empirical study, particularly in regard to black populations.

Interpretive Issues and Applications of Research

Problems also exist in the interpretation of findings and conclusions from such research. These interpretations have implications for policies and interventions regarding the control and treatment of social deviance among black populations.

First, interpretive issues are evident in the light of the racial, cultural, and class differences between researchers and subjects of research. Researchers, who are predominantly white and middle class, do not appear to be aware of the social reality—the environmental context—of the black populations (Boykin 1979; Williams 1980). Georges-Abeyie (1984, p. 141) cites "the myopic vision of sociological and criminological theories and research which treats black ghettos and slum-ghettos as monolithic ethnic/-racial entities (and thus blacks as one ethnic group)." This failing is also prominent in research on the causes of social deviance among black populations (Brown 1974; Comer 1985; National Minority Advisory Council on Criminal Justice 1982; Takagi 1980).

The overrepresentation of black individuals in official crime statistics illustrates how faulty interpretations can be made when the environment of black populations is not considered. The racial, cultural, and class backgrounds of black individuals influence officials' decisions on whether and how individuals will be processed by the criminal justice system. This factor must be considered in the interpretation of official statistics.

Individuals processed in the criminal justice system are generally those studied in research; thus issues relating to sampling procedures raise questions about the validity and generalizability of research findings. According to Feldman (1977), researchers should attempt to achieve representativeness of samples in research on the causes of social deviance. He suggests that studies of self-reported offenders are less subject to bias than those from official statistics. Moreover, because institutionalization affects behavior, it is preferable to study nonincarcerated convicted offenders or, better, nonconvicted, self-reported offenders. When sampling bias is minimized, problems of interpretation are minimal and findings are more useful.

Issues relating to limitations of self-reporting and field studies raise serious questions about the validity of the verbal and behavioral responses of research participants. In an attempt to overcome such limitations, repeated samplings of verbal or behavioral responses across settings and time may yield a more stable measure of variables.

Another interpretive issue is raised by many of the methods commonly used in research on social deviance. Much of the research is descriptive, with emphasis on field and self-report studies, but it is impossible to control many important variables in field studies. As a related problem, ethical considerations prevent the creation of laboratory experiments to isolate certain variables involved in many criminal acts.

Several studies have examined the relationships among variables, race, and crime. The most commonly used statistical analytic method is coefficient correlation, which determines the degree to which these relationships exist. Although correlations may exist, they create problems in the interpretation of data. Frequently researchers interpret high correlations as indicative of causal relationships. Yet although a correlation exists between two variables, it does not mean that a causal relationship also exists (Reid 1979).

In addition to these interpretive difficulties, other problems exist in policy and program development. Although these topics will not be discussed thoroughly in this chapter, we refer readers to the report by the National Advisory Council on Criminal Justice (1982).

Research and Social Policies

Although blacks are more often the victims of crime than whites and although their rates of arrest, conviction, and incarceration are disproportionate to their numbers in the population, they have been virtually excluded from critical decision-making positions in research, where definitions and explanations of social deviance are formulated, and in social policies and programs, where decisions are implemented regarding the prevention and control of social deviance (for example, correctional programs and community-based crime control programs). The exclusion of blacks from these areas has far-reaching implications. The National Minority Advisory Council contends, for example, that political and race-related factors explain why violent crime among blacks is the focus of inquiry, control, and treatment. In contrast, the council finds society responsible for the lack of emphasis on white-collar crimes (among them, bribery, embezzlement, and consumer fraud), although the rate of crime in this category for whites is double the rate among blacks. Official statistical procedures use only two racial categories for white-collar statistics. According to the report, minority group individuals are overrepresented among those arrested and imprisoned for social deviance, but they are not responsible for most of the crime committed in the United States.

Virtually no existing data can explain this discrepancy, except that those in decision-making positions choose to focus on crimes committed more frequently by blacks and other minority groups. White-collar crime has not been the major focus of research on the causes of social deviance; consequently it is not the focus of public concern, prevention, or control. This analysis corroborates the perspectives of Staples (1976), who indicated discrepancies in definitions of crime and societal responses.

Directions for Future Research

Several scholars have asserted the need for prominent involvement by black social scientists at all levels of research on social deviance among black populations. Such involvement is needed to counteract the ethnocentric bias—racial, cultural, and class—perpetuated in research on social deviance (Brown 1974; Comer 1985; Hilliard 1980; King 1978; National Advisory Minority Council on Criminal Justice 1982; Owens 1980; Swan and Street 1974; Takagi 1981).

It is asserted that black or other minority-group behavioral scientists can offer a black or minority-group perspective in research on social deviance among blacks. Takagi (1981) states that a minority perspective on research takes into consideration race and social deviance from the standpoint of the minority-group individual. Concurring with this perspective, the National Minority Advisory Council on Criminal Justice (1982) states:

> Because of the disproportionate number of minorities whose lives are touched almost daily by the criminal justice system, either as victims, or as offenders, this report has been written according to the definitions and concerns of minorities. This process is necessary because minorities are no longer passive objects of study; minorities are fairly capable of defining themselves. (pp. xxii–xxiii)

Similar views were presented by leading black scholars at a federally sponsored research conference on violence among black families and communities (National Institute of Mental Health 1985). Scholars proposed both macro- and micro-oriented conceptualizations and definitions of violence and deviance among blacks. The analysis focused on historical, cultural, and political factors that affect black family life, including economic and racial discrimination. The scholars also related these theoretical issues to research methodology and to policy and program issues that could reduce and control violence and deviance among blacks. A black or minority group perspective is not incompatible with many standard empirical analytical research procedures (Akbar 1981; Boykin 1979; Takagi 1981).

There is a need to investigate theories that are relevant to research on the causes of social deviance among black populations (Brown 1974; Debro and Headly 1981; Comer 1985; Takagi 1981). As indicated in our review, scholars have tended to focus on cultural or subcultural theories at the expense of other plausible theoretical formulations. This emphasis has led to a focus on single-factor relationships of causality to the neglect of multiple-factor analysis.

Owens (1980) finds no consensus of perspectives on the causes of black social deviance among the few black investigators in this area of research. He states, however, that in general, the research emphasizes the interaction of the individual with the social, economic, and political systems. Both individual and external environmental factors are responsible for deviant behavior.

Similarly Pacht and Strangman (1980) state that no single all-encompassing theory of social deviance will ever be developed in the field. They consider it more likely that several small theories will be developed to explain the various categories of deviant behavior. Explanations of social deviance will require interdisciplinary efforts.

Monohan and Splane (1980) indicate disputes among psychology, criminology, and sociology in research on social deviance. They state that this research requires sociologists who use psychological variables and psychologists who are aware of the social roots of individual processes. As psychologists become more proficient in research on social deviance, nonprogrammatic, single-variable research will decrease.

James Comer (1985), a leading black psychiatrist, is highly critical of single-factor models that attempt to explain violence and deviance among blacks. He sees a need for a conceptual framework that deals with multiple factors to explain why similar conditions have different outcomes within a particular family, among families in the same community and social network, and among blacks of similar income levels. Comer believes that epidemiology and human ecology are highly relevant disciplines because they focus on a web of causation rather than seeking primary causes of violence and deviance and because they examine individuals and families embedded in social networks that generate both prosocial and antisocial behavior. He suggests that the conceptual model should look at violence and deviance among blacks by considering African cultural foundations, the role of slavery, and contemporary social, economic, and political conditions that affect black individuals in the context of their families, communities, and the larger society.

Research is also needed to analyze the effects of discrimination in stages of the criminal justice system, in the light of selective factors in operation by personnel. The analysis should include the attitudes and backgrounds of personnel (National Minority Advisory Council on Criminal Justice 1982). Mann (1980, 1984b), for example, conducted court observational studies on the influence of extralegal or social factors (among them, race, appearance, dress, and demeanor) on judicial decisions relating to the status of juvenile offenders and female felony offenders.

A third important area is comparative research on social deviance among black populations within different geographical locations in the United States (Swan and Street 1974). These studies may reveal many geographical influences (such as historical and community) as related to socially deviant behaviors. Such studies would strengthen data bases relating to black populations, particularly if they use similar research designs and measures. International studies of deviance among black populations of African descent are also needed. Such studies would have immense value, particularly in relation to cultural definitions of deviance and factors that influence such behavior.

A fourth area of needed research concerns crime and delinquency among black females, who are overrepresented among all females in the criminal justice system (Glick and Neto 1977; Mann 1984a). In addressing research issues on women, Rafter and Natalizia (1981) agree with the need to obtain more data on females in all areas. They suggest that for some purposes, studies should not use male comparison groups until firm data bases for women have been established. Specifically, they see a need to examine relationships between rates of crime by women and women's access to employment during specific historical and economic periods, and relationships between criminal justice institutions and other institutions that exert social control over women, such as the welfare system. Such studies have particular relevance to black females.

Fifth, there is a need for research on deviance among black youth, who are also overrepresented in the criminal justice system. Several scholars have suggested that when institutions (for example, education and social service) fail to meet the needs of black youth, they will appear as perpetrators of delinquency and crime in the juvenile justice system and later in the adult justice system (Gibbs 1984; Washington and LaPoint, in press).

Finally, several black scholars indicate a need for research on blacks who are not labeled as deviant and enmeshed in the criminal justice system (Bell-Scott and McKentry 1986). Research studies on deviance could include such persons as comparison groups. Woodsen (1983) suggests that research be conducted to evaluate how black families and communities effectively help their own community members reduce and control delinquency and crime.

Within these suggested studies of social deviance, the methodological limitations should be addressed as they relate to types of research designs, sampling, and data collection procedures. To reduce various types of biases, investigators must use appropriate research techniques and procedures relevant to research on black populations.

Takagi (1981), Akar (1981), and Boykin (1979) suggest that field or ethnographic approaches with participant-observer data collection techniques be undertaken in research on black populations. Such designs could include an analysis of structures (history, politics, and economics) and cultures (ways of thinking and behaving that embody ideas, beliefs, values, and prescription). Within the current paradigm, observations within naturalistic settings should precede experimental manipulations (Akbar 1981). Boykin (1979) also recommends an ethnographic orientation, which would yield a better phenomenological understanding of the experiences of black individuals. Although ethnographic or field studies with participant-observer techniques have inherent problems, several scholars suggest that these approaches are no less biased than other, more controlled, research approaches that profess scientific objectivity (Akbar 1981; Boykin 1979; National Minority Advisory Council on Criminal Justice 1982; Takagi 1981). Regarding objectivity, Barry and Philip (1984) state that among the blacks they reviewed, a value orientation toward race and race relations was implicit in all theoretical approaches to social deviance.

These theoretical approaches would also influence methodological approaches. Barry and Philip (1984) state:

> Although objectivity may be a desirable goal of research and planning, it is at best elusive, and at worst a stumbling block in the way of understanding. Adherence to a supposedly objective research paradigm may, in fact, result in failure to examine important causal relations and may . . . lead to value-laden conclusions. (P. 30)

In the light of the strong recommendation that black behavioral scientists should be involved prominently in research on social deviance among black populations, issues exist regarding financial support for black social scientists. The National Advisory Council on Criminal Justice (1982) states:

> While White researchers have used the bulk of research grants and contracts to conduct investigations into the problem of minority crimes as systemic injustices, crime has increased on all levels and the conclusions of these social scientists have added confusion rather than clarity to these complex problems. Programs have been designed based on such research, yet cities and prisons explode in disorder. While the federal

response to crime has been to support, through grants, more guns, tanks, and sophisticated technology, equally as deadly and dangerous are the ideas and research of some nonminority researchers and social scientists. While minority on minority crime has become an extreme danger in minority communities, the greatest portion of educational and research moneys have gone to nonminority researchers and institutions. Federal support in this crucial area has not been equal to the problems in crime and criminal justice adversely affecting minority communities. (P. xxxviii)

The council strongly urges federal, state, and local governments to support more research by minority group investigators on issues in social deviance.

There are many unresolved issues in definition, theoretical formulation, methodology, and interpretation of research on the causes of social deviance. Black social scientists must become involved prominently at all levels of the research. There are important relationships among research and social policy regarding social deviance among black populations. Given the serious nature of this problem, in which blacks are overrepresented both as victims and as perpetrators of social deviance but underrepresented in the administration of justice, social scientists have an undisputed responsibility to obtain factual information through research.

References

Adler, F. 1975. *Sisters in Crime: The Rise of the Female Criminal*. New York: McGraw-Hill.

Akbar, N. 1981. "Our Destiny: Authors of a Scientific Revolution." In *The Fifth Conference on Empirical Research in Black Psychology*, pp. 1–10. Edited by M. McAdoo, H. McAdoo, and W.E. Cross. Department of Health and Human Services, National Institute of Mental Health. Washington, D.C.: Government Printing Office.

Amir, M. 1970. "Forcible Rape." In *Crime in America*. Edited by B.J. Cohen. Itaska, Ill.: F.E. Peacock Publishers.

———. 1981. *Patterns of Forcible Rape*. Chicago: University of Chicago Press.

Austin, R.L. 1978. "Race, Father-Absence and Female Delinquency." *Criminology* 15:487–504.

Ball-Rokeach, S.J. 1973. "Values and Violence: A Test of the Subculture of Violence Thesis." *American Soiological Review* 38:736–749.

Bell-Scott, P., and C.D. McKentry. 1986. "Black Adolescents in Their Families." In *Adolescents in Families*, pp. 410–432. Edited by G.K. Leigh and D.W. Peterson. Cincinnati, Ohio: South-Western.

Billingsley, A. 1971. "The Structure and Functions of Negro Family Life." In *Readings in the Sociology of the Family*. Edited by B.N. Adams and T. Welrath. Illinois: Markam.

Boykin, A.W. 1979. "Black Psychology and the Research Process: Keeping the Baby But Throwing Out the Bath Water." In *Research Directions of Black Psychologists*, pp. 85–103. Edited by A.W. Boykin, A. Franklin, and J.F. Yates. New York: Russell Sage Foundation.

Brown, L.P. 1974. "The Impact of Crime and the Criminal Justice System on the Black Community: An Overview." In *Social Research and the Black Community: Selected Issues and Priorities*, pp. 88–98. Washington, D.C.: Institute for Urban Affairs and Research, Howard University.

Carey, J.T. 1978. *Introduction to Criminology*. Englewood Cliffs, N.J.: Prentice-Hall.

Chapman, J.R. 1980. *Economic Realities and the Female Offender*. Lexington, Mass.: Lexington Books.

Christianson, S. 1984. "Our Black Prisons." In *The Criminal Justice System and Blacks*, pp. 259–270. Edited by D. Georges-Abeyie. New York: Clark Boardman.

Cloward, R.A., and L.E. Ohlin. 1960. *Delinquency and Opportunity: A Theory of Delinquent Gangs*. Glencoe, Ill.: Free Press.

Cohen, A.K. 1955. *Delinquent Boys: The Culture of the Gang*. New York: Free Press.

Cole, J.B. 1970. "Negro, Black, and Nigger." *Black Scholar* 1, no. 8:40–44.

Comer, J.P. 1985. "Black Violence and Public Policy." In *American Violence and Public Policy*, pp. 63–86. Edited by Lynn A. Curtis. New Haven: Yale University Press.

Cowie, J., V. Cowie, and E. Slater. 1968. *Delinquency in Girls*. London: Heinemann.

Cullen, F.T., B.G. Link, L.F. Travis III, and J.F. Wozniak. 1985. "Consensus in Crime Seriousness: Empirical Reality or Methodological Artifact?" *Criminology* 23:99–118.

Curtis, L.A. 1974. *Toward a Cultural Interpretation of Forcible Rape by American Blacks*. Washington, D.C.: Bureau of Social Science Research.

———. 1975. *Violence, Race and Culture*. Lexington, Mass.: Lexington Books.

———. 1976. "Rape, Race and Culture: Some Speculations in Search of a Theory." In *Sexual Assault: The Victim and the Rapist*. Edited by M.J. Walker and S.L. Brodsky. Lexington, Mass.: Lexington Books.

Dalton, K. 1960a. "School Girls' Behavior and Menstruation." *British Medical Journal* 2:1647–1649.

———. 1960b. "Menstruation and Crime." *British Medical Journal* 2:1647–1649.

Datesman, S.K., and F.R. Scarpetti. 1975. "Female Delinquency and Broken Homes: A Reassessment." *Criminology* 13:33–55.

Debro, J., and B. Headly. 1981. "Research on Minority Communities: Toward an Understanding of the Relationship between Race and Crime." Manuscript.

Elliot, D.S., and S.S. Ageton. 1980. "Reconciling Race and Class Differences in Self-reported and Official Estimates of Delinquency." *American Sociological Review* 45:95–110.

Feldman, M.P. 1977. *Criminal Behavior: A Psychological Analysis*. New York: John Wiley.

Felice, M.R., and D.R. Offord. 1971. "Girl Delinquents—A Review." *Corrective Psychiatry and Journal of Social Therapy* 17:18–33.

Georges-Abeyie, D. 1984. "The Criminal Justice System and Minorities—A Review of the Literature." In *The Criminal Justice System and Blacks*, pp. 125–126. Edited by D. Georges-Abeyie. New York: Clark Boardman.

Gibbons, D.C. 1976. *Delinquent Behavior*. Englewood Cliffs, N.J.: Prentice-Hall.

Gibbs, J.T. 1984. "Black Adolescents and Youth: An Endangered Species." *American Journal of Orthopsychiatry* 54, no. 1:6–21.

Glick, R., and V. Neto. 1977. *The National Study of Women's Correctional Programs.* Publication 027–00028. Washington, D.C.: Government Printing Office.

Hannerz, V. 1972. "What Ghetto Males Are Like: Another Look." In *Black Psyche.* Edited by S.S. Guterman. Calif.: Gendessary Press.

Hawkins, D.F. 1985. "Black Homicide: The Adequacy of Existing Research for Devising Prevention Strategies." *Crime and Delinquency* 31:83–103.

Herskovitz, H.H. 1969. "A Psychodynamic View of Sexual Promiscuity." In *Family Dynamics and Female Sexual Delinquency.* Edited by O. Pollock. Calif.: Science and Behavior Books.

Herzog, E., and C.E. Sudia. 1973. "Children in Fatherless Families." In *Review of Child Development Research,* vol. 3: *Child Development and Social Policy,* pp. 141–232. Chicago: University of Chicago Press.

Hilliard, T.O. 1980. "Applications of Psychology and the Criminal Justice System: A Black Perspective." In *Black Psychology,* pp. 456–468. Edited by R.L. Jones. New York: Harper & Row.

Hindelang, M.J. 1978. "Race Involvement in Common Law Personal Crimes." *American Sociological Review* 43:93–109.

Hirschi, T. 1969. *Causes of Delinquency.* Berkeley: University of California Press, 1969.

Hirschi, T., and H.C. Selvin. 1967. *Delinquency Research: An Appraisal of Analytic Methods.* New York: Free Press.

King, L. 1978. "Social and Cultural Issues in Psychopathology." *Annual Review of Psychology* 29:405–433.

Konopka, G. 1966. *The Adolescent Girl in Conflict.* Englewood Cliffs, N.J.: Prentice-Hall.

Krisberg, B., I. Schwartz, G. Fishman, Z. Eisikovits, and E. Guttman. 1986. *The Incarceration of Minority Youth.* Minneapolis: Center for the Study of Youth Policy, Hubert H. Humphrey Institute of Public Affairs, University of Minnesota.

Landen, W.A. 1973. "Emily Durkheim." In *Pioneers in Criminology.* Edited by H. Mannheim. New Jersey: Patterson Smith.

Lombroso, G., and W. Ferrers. 1916. *The Female Offender.* New York: Appleton.

McCombs, P. 1982. "ACLU Unit Winning Fight for Reform in Nation's Prisons." *Washington Post,* May 24, p. A2.

McNeely, R.L., and C.E. Pope. 1981. *Race, Crime, and Criminal Justice.* Beverly Hills, Calif.: Sage.

Mann, C.R. 1979. Unpublished proposal. Graduate Minority Fellowships for the School of Criminology, Florida State University. Department of Health and Human Services Higher Education Act—Graduate and Professional Opportunities Program.

———. 1980. "Courtroom Observations of Extra-Legal Factors in the Juvenile Court Disposition of Runaway Boys: A Field Study." *Juveniles and Family Court Journal* 31, no. 4:43–52.

———. 1984a. *Female Crime and Delinquency.* University: University of Alabama Press.

_____. 1984b. "Race and Sentencing of Female Felons: A Field Study." *International Journal of Women's Studies* 7:160–172.

_____. 1986. "Women Murders and Their Motives: A Tale of Two Cities." Paper presented at the annual meeting of the Academy of Criminal Justice Sciences, Orlando, Fla.

Mann, C.R., and L.H. Selva. 1978. "The Myth of the Black Rapist." Paper presented at the annual meeting of the Southwestern Sociological Society, Houston, Texas.

Mannle, H.W., and P.W. Lewis. 1979. "Control Theory Re-Examined: Race and the Use of Neutralizations among Institutionalized Delinquents." *Criminology* 17:58–74.

Megargee, E.I. 1975. *Crime and Delinquency.* New York: General Learning Press.

Miller, W.B. 1976. "Lower Class Culture as a Generating Milieu of Gang Delinquency." In *Juvenile Delinquency.* Edited by R. Giallombardo. New York: John Wiley.

Monohan, J., and S. Splane. 1980. "Psychological Approaches to Criminal Behavior." In *Criminological Review Yearbook,* pp. 17–47. Edited by E. Bittner and S.L. Messinger. Beverly Hills: Sage Publications.

National Institute of Mental Health. 1985. "Proceeding of Annual Invitational Conference on Research on Violence in Black Families and Communities." Manuscript. Rockville, Md.: Staff College, National Institute of Mental Health.

National Minority Advisory Council on Criminal Justice. 1982. "Toward Equal Justice Now." Washington: Government Printing Office.

Nobles, W.W. 1980. "African Philosophy: Foundations for Black Psychology." In *Black Psychology,* pp. 23–36. Edited by R.L. Jones. New York: Harper & Row.

Owens, C. 1980. *The Mental Health of Black Offenders.* Lexington, Mass.: Lexington Books.

Pacht, A.R., and E.G. Strangman. 1980. "Crime and Delinquency." In *New Perspective in Abnormal Psychology,* pp. 353–375. Edited by A. Kazdin, A. Bellack, and M. Hersen. New York: Oxford University Press.

Pope, C.E. 1981. "Blacks and Juvenile Crime: A Review." In *Blacks, Crime and Criminal Justice.* Edited by D. Georges-Abeyie. New York: Clark Boardman.

Quinney, R. 1980. *The Social Reality of Crime.* Boston: Little, Brown.

Rafter, N.H., and E.M. Natalizia. 1981. "Marxist Feminism: Implications for Criminal Justice." *Crime and Delinquency* 27:81–98.

Reid, S.T. 1979. *Crime and Criminology.* New York: Holt, Reinhart and Winston.

Sample, B.C., and M. Philip, Jr. 1984. "Perspectives on Race and Crime in Research Planning." In *The Criminal Justice System and Blacks,* pp. 21–35. Edited by D. Georges-Abeyie. New York: Clark Boardman.

Shaw, C., and H.D. McKay. 1942. *Juvenile Delinquency and Urban Areas.* Chicago: University of Chicago Press.

Skogan, W.G. 1981. *Issues in the Measurement of Victimization.* Washington, D.C.: Department of Justice.

Smith, D.A., and C.A. Visher. 1980. "Sex and Involvement in Deviance/Crime: A Quantitative Review of the Empirical Literature." *American Sociological Review* 45:691–701.

Staples, R. 1976. *Introduction to Black Sociology.* New York: McGraw-Hill.

Sutherland, E.H., and D.L. Cressey. 1978. *Criminology.* Philadelphia: J.B. Lippincott.

Swan, A., and L. Street. 1974. "Crime and Social Policy: The Politics of Race." In *Social Research and the Black Community: Selected Issues and Priorities,* pp. 112–119. Washington, D.C.: Institute for Urban Research, Howard University.

Takagi, P. 1981. "Race, Crime and Social Policy: A Minority Perspective." *Crime and Delinquency* (January): 48–63.

Theodorson, G.A., and A.G. Theodorson. 1969. *Modern Dictionary of Sociology.* New York: Crowell.

Thio, A. 1978. *Deviant Behavior.* Boston: Houghton Mifflin.

Thrasher, F. 1936. *The Gang.* Chicago: University of Chicago Press.

Trojanowicz, R.C. 1978. *Juvenile Delinquency: Concepts and Control.* Englewood Cliffs, N.J.: Prentice-Hall.

U.S. Department of Justice. 1980. *Crime in the United States, 1979.* Washington, D.C.: Government Printing Office.

———. 1984. *Crime in the United States 1983.* Washington, D.C.: Government Printing Office.

U.S. Department of Labor. 1965. *The Negro Family: The Case for National Action.* Washington, D.C.: Government Printing Office.

Washington, V., and V. LaPoint. In press. *The Cultural Foundations of Black Children: Social Status, Public Policy, and Future Directions.* New York: Garland Publishers.

Wilkerson, K. 1976. "The Broken Family and Juvenile Delinquency: Scientific Explanations or Ideology?" In *Juvenile Delinquency.* Edited by R. Giallombardo. New York: John Wiley.

Williams, J.R., and M. Gold. 1978. "From Delinquent Behavior to Official Delinquency." In *The Children of Ishmael.* Edited by B.J. Knesberg and J. Austin. Palo Alto, Calif.: Mayfield Publishing Company.

Williams, R.L. 1980. "The Death of White Research in the Black Community." In *Black Psychology,* pp. 403–417. Edited by R.L. Jones. New York: Harper & Row.

Wolfgang, M.E. 1970. "A Sociological Analysis of Criminal Homicide." In *Crime in America.* Edited by B.J. Cohen. Itaska, Ill.: Peacock Publishers.

Wolfgang, M.E., and L.A. Curtis. 1972. "Criminal Violence: Patterns and Policy in Urban America." *International Review of Criminal Policy* 30:7–10.

Wolfgang, M.E., and J. Ferracuti. 1967. *The Subculture of Violence.* London: Social Sciences Paperbacks.

Woodsen, R.L. 1983. "Youth Crime Policies." In *Criminal Justice Reform: A Blueprint,* pp. 37–56. Edited by P.B. McGuigan and R.R. Rader. Illinois: Regnery Gateway.

Young, V. 1980. "Women, Race, and Crime." *Criminology* 18:26–34.

13
Stress Resolution among Middle-Aged Black Americans

Lena Wright Myers

Although family violence exists in all social classes, it is thought to be more prevalent in some groups than others because of the socioeconomic status of those groups. Black Americans, for example are confronted with racism in addition to the usual stressful events of everyday life, and they live under the continuous and varying stresses of oppression. Chester Pierce, a noted black psychiatrist, views blacks as living in a mundane, extreme environment, that is, an environment where racism and subtle oppression are ubiquitous, constant, continuing, and mundane rather than an occasional misfortune (Pierce 1975). The numerous sources of stress include poor employment prospects, ranging from unemployment to underemployment, and inadequate educational opportunities.

To survive in this environment, black families have had to adapt. Unfortunately, many studies have viewed black families as deviant and problem prone while ignoring the behaviors, attitudes, and coping mechanisms required to survive within the context of mundane extreme environmental stress (Peters and Massey 1983). Racism and a vast array of associated variables are realities for black families, and they render many blacks at risk for maladaptive behaviors (Hampton, Daniel, and Newberger, 1983).

In addition to racism, blacks, like other Americans, experience stressful life events. Family stress theories have traditionally examined how families react to and manage the stressful events that occur as part of the family's encounter with misfortunes such as a sudden loss of income, death of a family member, loss of limb, birth of a retarded or handicapped child, debilitating illness, or long-term absence of a parent (Peters and

Some of the data used in this chapter were analyzed and used in "Blacks Coping in White America: Challenges and Opportunities," presented at the American Sociological Association meetings, Detroit, Michigan, August 31–September 4, 1983. The data were funded by the National Institute of Mental Health. The author served as a member of the National Advisory Council to the Staff of the National Survey of Black Americans.

Massey 1983). Because such knowledge is already established, this chapter focuses on how middle-aged black Americans manage or resolve stressful life events in order to function in everyday life.

Data and Methods

From 1976 to 1980, the staff of the Black Research Program at the Institute for Social Research, University of Michigan, developed two major interrelated studies of black Americans aged 18 and older. The research attempted to address certain limitations in existing literature by means of a cross-sectional and a three-generational study. Each interview lasted two and one-half hours and focused on several major aspects of black American life. They included issues of personal adjustment, how black Americans cope with the rigors of day-to-day life, and the social and family support systems used to buffer stressful events.

To discover and delineate the stress resolution techniques used by middle-aged black Americans, a subsample of cases ($N = 1,456$) was examined. Middle-aged respondents were defined operationally as between 40 and 50 years of age. Five questions formed the basis for the preliminary analyses of stress and coping within this sample, but responses to only three of the questions are used in this chapter:

Is there a difference in the salient type of stress experienced by black men and black women?

Do middle-aged black men and women experience the same incidence of different types of stress?

What techniques do middle-aged black Americans use in stress resolution?

To describe accurately the stress resolution techniques used by middle-aged black Americans, specific attention was devoted to marital status and to female-male differences in techniques employed. The null hypotheses to be tested were that no significant differences existed in the modes of stress resolution employed by (1) black females versus black males and by (2) black married males and females versus black single males and females. Chi-square tests for contingency tables were used to test for differences in these analyses.

Results

The data in table 13-1 provide an overview of the types of stress experienced by the middle-aged respondents in the areas of health, money,

Table 13–1
Distribution of Types of Stress, by Sex

Salient Type of Stress Experienced	Men	Women
Health	36%	40%
Money	32	31
Jobs	2	4
Family or marriage	3	3
People outside the family	5	3
Children	3	3
Victim of crime	1	3
Police	2	1
Love life	2	1
Treated badly because of race	6	2
Illness or death of a family member	4	2
Other	3	2
Total	100	100
	(N = 508)	(N = 948)

jobs, marriage, and crime. Health-related stress was the most prevalent type reported by 36 percent of the men and 40 percent of the women.

Money or financial concerns constituted another prominent stressful condition in the sample for almost one-third of both male and female respondents. Only 4 percent of the males and 2 percent of the females reported stress resulting from the death of a family member.

How much stress did respondents report as related directly to their race? When asked if they were treated badly because of race, 6 percent of the males and 2 percent of the females stated that they felt some stress from this situation. This figure might seem lower than expected, but it can be explained in two different ways. First, racism can affect an individual directly in an identifiable manner, such as racial harassment at work or in the neighborhood. But it can also be expressed more subtly by institutions doing business as usual, and this form of racism may frequently go undetected. Second, in the light of the respondents' age, they may have developed strategies for coping with racism as an outgrowth of their previous experiences. In this case, racial stress is viewed as part of the larger environment; as such, the individual respondent may perceive of it as less salient than stress related to health, money, or children.

Table 13-2 presents data in response to the question, "Do middle-aged black men and women experience the same incidence of stress?"

Table 13–2
Incidence of Stress, by Sex

Salient Type of Stress	Men	Women
Health	36%	41%
Money	32	31
Other[a]	32	28
Total	100	100
$X^2 = .740$; $df = 2$; $p = $ NS	(N = 508)	N = 948)

[a]Includes jobs, family or marriage, people outside the family, children, victims of crimes, police, love life, treated badly because of race, illness or death of a family member.

Although females reported a slightly higher incidence of health-related stress than males (41 percent versus 36 percent), there appears to be no significant difference between the sexes in the type of stress experienced.

Table 13–3 presents data on several types of stress-producing problems and problem-resolving strategies that respondents used. These data reveal that both men and women relied most heavily on direct action to relieve the stress produced by most problems. For the purposes of this research, direct action comprises confronting the stressful situation with a specific plan of action, facing the situation head on, and not buckling under. To relieve the stress caused by economic problems, 44 percent of the men and 41 percent of the women chose direct action. Resignation ranked second in this category as the choice of 26 percent of the men and 31 percent of the women.

Direct action was also the preferred response to family problems. Thirty-three percent of the men and 42 percent of the women selected direct action, followed by 25 percent of the men and 17 percent of the women who selected resignation. Ten percent of the men and 15 percent of the women stated that religion was their strategy for coping with family problems.

Most respondents used the services of formal agencies to resolve the stress experienced by health-related problems. Both men (65 percent) and women (73 percent) reported this technique as their primary strategy.

It appears from the data that most of the respondents used traditional American methods for resolving stress. Few of the respondents (4 percent men and 6 percent women), for instance, chose religion as a way to resolve economic problems. Instead they relied heavily on direct action. Similarly, neither religion nor family was chosen frequently to resolve stress in response to family and health problems. It also appears that in some instances the choices overlapped, as when most of the respondents chose formal or authoritative techniques to resolve health problems. I

Table 13–3
Salient Stress Resolution Techniques, by Sex and Type of Problem

Stress Experienced and Resolution Technique	Men	Women
Economic problems		
Direct action	44%	41%
Family or informal network	3	4
Formal agencies or authorities	6	6
Religion	4	6
Resignation	26	31
Others	17	12
Total	100	100
	(N = 248)	(N = 441)
Family problems		
Direct action	33	42
Family or informal network	6	9
Formal agencies or authorities	12	10
Religion	10	15
Resignation	25	17
Other	14	7
Total	100	100
	(N = 52)	(N = 152)
Health problems Direct action	19	10
Family or informal network	0	1
Formal agencies or authorities	65	73
Religion	0	3
Resignation	5	5
Other	11	8
Total	100	100
	(N = 79)	(N = 178)
Other Direct action	25	20
Family or informal network	6	5
Formal agencies or authorities	13	19
Religion	6	11
Resignation	42	36
Other	8	9
Total	100	100
	(N = 138)	(N = 168)

believe that such a choice, which was offered in the study as an alternative response, is itself direct action.

The "other" category of problem, which includes crime, love life, people outside the family, and illness or death of a family member, yields different findings. In this category most respondents (42 percent of the men, 36 percent of the women) named resignation as a technique for resolving stress.

Table 13-4 shows the overall stress resolution techniques by sex. These data respond to the question, "What techniques do middle-aged black Americans use in stress resolution?" Both middle-aged men (34 percent) and women (31 percent) used direct action to resolve stress more frequently than any other technique. Resignation ran a close second; at

Table 13–4
Distribution of Stress Resolution Techniques, by Sex

Technique	Men	Women
Direct action	34%	31%
Family agencies or informal network	4	4
Formal agencies or authorities	18	21
Religion	4	8
Resignation	27	25
Other	13	11
Total	100	100
	(N = 508)	(N = 948)

least 27 percent of the men and 25 percent of the women in the sample relied on this method. It appears that at one end of the spectrum, middle-aged black men and women face stress head on with a clear-cut plan for resolving it, while at the other end, a significant number of men and women resign themselves to their stressful situations.

Table 13–4 also reveals that religion was employed less frequently than expected. Historically, religion has been the burden bearer for many black people. Blacks traditionally believe that faith and trust in the deity will lead to a better life in the hereafter.

In previous research (Myers 1980), black women aged 20 to 81 years revealed that the family was one of the most important supports. Most of the women felt that they could rely on family when they could count on no one else. The information presented in table 13–4, however, suggests that the black men and women in the present sample tended not to rely on family when faced with stress.

When we examine male-female differences in response to stress created by economic, health-related, and family problems, we find no significant differences (table 13–5).

Currently married men tended to rely more heavily than formerly married men (divorced, separated, or widowed) on direct action as a stress resolution technique (table 13–6). It is noteworthly that 33 percent of the formerly married men reported resignation as the next most frequently used technique, whereas only 20 percent of currently married men used this approach. In stress resolution techniques, however, there was no significant difference between these two groups.

A statistically significant difference in stress resolution techniques exists when married males are compared to never-married males. The latter group chose the following stress resolution approaches: resignation,

Table 13–5
Stress Resolution Techniques, by Sex and Type of Problem

Stress Experienced and Resolution Technique	Men	Women
Economic problems		
Direct action	44%	41%
Family, formal or informal	10	10
Resignation	20	31
Religion or other	26	18
Total	100	100
$X^2 = .648; df = 3; p =$ NS.	(N = 248)	(N = 441)
Family problems		
Direct action	33	42
Family, formal or informal	18	19
Resignation	24	17
Religion or other	25	22
Total	100	100
$X^2 = 2.496; df = 3; p =$ NS.	(N = 52)	(N = 152)
Health problems		
Direct action	19	10
Family, formal or informal	65	74
Resignation	5	5
Religion or other	11	11
Total	100	100
$X^2 = 3.376; df = 3; p =$ NS.	(N = 79)	(N = 178)

Table 13–6
Stress Resolution Techniques of Men, by Marital Status

	Marital Status		
Stress Resolution Technique	Married	Formerly Married	Never Married
Direct action	38%	27%	31%
Family or informal network	2	3	7
Formal agencies or authorities	21	19	10
Religion	5	5	4
Resignation	20	33	34
Other	14	13	14
Total	100	100	100
	(N = 262)	(N = 103)	(N = 147)

Married versus formerly married: $X^2 = 5.348; df = 5; p =$ NS.
Married versus never married: $X^2 = 11.135; df = 5; p < .04.$

34 percent; direct action, 31 percent; and other techniques, 14 percent. Married men selected direct action, 38 percent; formal agencies, 21 percent; and resignation, 20 percent.

Table 13–7
Stress Resolution Techniques of Women, by Marital Status

	Marital Status		
Stress Resolution Technique	*Married*	*Formerly Married*	*Never Married*
Direct action	38%	27%	35%
Family or informal network	3	4	7
Formal agencies or authorities	22	24	15
Religion	8	9	4
Resignation	23	24	29
Other	6	12	10
Total	100	100	100
	(N = 311)	(N = 416)	(N = 217)

Married versus formerly married: $X^2 = 4.172$; $df = 5$; p = NS.
Married versus never married: $X^2 = 6.072$; $df = 5$; p = NS.

A similar analysis was performed to determine whether differences existed among married women, formerly married women, and never-married women with respect to stress resolution techniques. The analysis (table 13–7) showed no significant differences among these groups.

Conclusions

From the subsample of middle-aged black Americans, I draw the following conclusions:

1. There is no statistically significant difference in the salient type of stress experienced by men and by women of this age group.

2. Both men and women of this age group relied more heavily on direct action than on any other techniques to relieve themselves of stress produced by their experiences.

3. Resignation ran a close second to direct action. At one end of the spectrum, middle-aged black men and women had a clear-cut plan for resolving stress. At the other end, a significant number stated they had resigned themselves to their stressful situation. Direct action, however, outweighed any other technique used for stress resolution.

4. Middle-aged black men and women experienced the same incidence of stress.

5. There is no significant difference between the modes of stress resolution used by married men and by formerly married men. Similarly,

there is no difference between the modes employed by married women and by formerly married women.

6. Although no significant difference existed between the stress resolution techniques used by married and by single women, a statistically significant difference did exist between married and never-married men.

This chapter does not suggest that family violence exists or does not exist among black Americans. It is fair to conclude, however, that some black Americans are just as capable as nonblacks of finding alternatives to violence for responding to stressful experiences of everyday life.

Although this nationally representative sample of middle-aged black respondents provides some valuable insights into the type of problems and coping strategies black Americans use, it does not allow us to assess the extent to which violence may have been part of their stress resolution techniques in the past or in the present. Future research is required to address stress resolution strategies among a younger sample. The research instrument must include questions regarding stress, violence, and stress resolution techniques.

References

Gelles, Richard J. 1985. "Family Violence." *Annual Review of Sociology* 11:347–367.

Gelles, Richard J., and Murray A. Straus. 1979. "Determinants of Violence in the Family: Toward a Theoretical Integration." In *Contemporary Theories about the Family*, 1:549–581. Edited by W.R. Burr, R. Hill, F.I. Nye, and I.L. Reiss. New York: Free Press.

Hampton, Robert L., Jessica H. Daniel, and Eli H. Newberger. 1983. "Pediatric Social Illnesses and Black Families." *Western Journal of Black Studies* 7:190–197.

Myers, Lena Wright. 1980. *Black Women: Do They Cope Better?* Englewood Cliffs, N.J.: Prentice-Hall.

O'Brien, John E. 1971. "Violence in Divorce Prone Families." *Journal of Marriage and the Family* 33, no. 4:692–698.

Peters, Marie F., and Grace Massey. 1983. "Mundane Extreme Environmental Stress in Family Stress Theories: The Case of Black Families in White America." *Marriage and Family Review,* nos. 1–2:193–217.

Pierce, Chester. 1975. "The Mundane Extreme Environment and Its Effect on Learning." In *Learning Disabilities: Issues and Recommendations for Research.* Edited by S.G. Brainard. Washington, D.C.: National Institute of Education.

14

A Developmental Perspective on Black Family Violence

Johnella Banks

he developmental or family life cycle model is the model least known and least applied to the study of Afro-American family life. To my knowledge, the literature contains no studies that use this longitudinal approach to Afro-American families, although some investigators have used family evaluation histories and cross-sectional and life-stage variants of the developmental model to discuss such issues as sexuality and extended family relations (Staples 1978; McAdoo 1978). This chapter will discuss the developmental theory in an attempt to provide researchers and helping professionals with an overview that might be useful for understanding some types of family violence.

The purpose of this chapter is to apply several important concepts emerging from a developmental perspective to the study of intrafamilial violence among blacks. Although families have been studied by many disciplines and from a variety of perspectives, the developmental approach is based on the observation that families are long-lived groups with a natural history or life cycle.

The Family Life Cycle

Like individuals, families go through successive stages of growth and development. Duvall and Hill (1948) suggested three criteria for establishing stages: changes in the number of members of the family, developmental stages of the eldest child, and retirement status of the husband-father. These criteria take into consideration events in the occupational and educational careers of family members, as well as normative changes in marital and parental careers, that add stress to customary interactions.

The beginning of each new stage represents a critical transition point in normal family development. These junctures, which have been called points of no return, lead to resolution and growth or to maladaptation and subsequent deterioration of the system (Rapoport 1963).

Although there are numerous ways to measure the family life cycle, this discussion will use a standard scheme found frequently in the literature and typified in the work of Duvall (table 14-1). Duvall (1977) takes the position, with which most other developmentalists agree, that the birth of the first child marks the end of the first stage and the beginning of a new stage. Because it is assumed that the role relationships within the family change as children mature, a number of stages are marked off according to the age of the eldest child. At all these stages, role prescriptions by age levels, which are coupled in some cases with biological changes, produce critical role transitions and lead to family change. When the child enters school, for example, parents must conform to school scheduling demands and accept the influence of a teacher and peers on their child's thinking and behavior (Aldous 1978).

Obviously not every family conforms to the normative family life cycle stages. Some never marry, some remain childless, some separate or divorce, and some follow an alternative life-style.

At each stage of the life cycle, families face developmental tasks. Some of these tasks are imposed by physical demands placed on all family members as bodies grow, develop, and mature. Other tasks are culturally imposed; the sociocultural system and the community create pressures on the family members to conform to numerous sets of expectations. Finally, each family may establish certain developmental tasks based on their unique goals, aspirations, and values.

A family developmental task can be conceptualized as one of the family functions necessary for its continuance at a particular stage. These functions, as outlined by Aldous (1978), include the following:

1. Physical maintenance of family members.
2. Socialization of family members for roles in the family and other groups.

Table 14-1
Family Life Cycle

Stage	Description
I	Beginning families (usually without children)
II	Early childbearing families (eldest child is an infant through 30 months)
III	Families with preschool children (eldest child is 30 months to 6 years of age)
IV	Families with school children (oldest child is 6–13 years old)
V	Families with teenagers (eldest child is 13–20 years old)
VI	Launching-center families (first child gone until last child leaves home)
VII	Families of middle years (empty nest to retirement)
VIII	Families in old age and retirement (retirement to death of both spouses)

Source: Duvall (1977, p. 179).

3. Maintenance of family members' motivation to perform family and other roles.

4. Maintenance of social control within the family and between members and outsiders.

5. Addition of family members through adoption or reproduction and their release when mature.

One challenge in family life is to meet each member's needs, as well as those of the entire family. The meshing of individual developmental needs and family tasks is not always possible. Because most families are not totally self-sufficient, a second challenge is to obtain extrafamilial resources or supports as needed for adequate functioning at each phase of the life cycle. Family members must interact with other individuals and institutions to meet their religious, economic, political, educational, and recreational needs.

Stage I: Beginning Families

Although relationships begin before marriage, marriage is still generally defined as the beginning of a new family. The socially accepted family of procreation is the predominant intimate relationship among both blacks and whites.

The three critical tasks of this period are establishing a mutually satisfying marriage, relating harmoniously to the extended family network, and family planning. The potential for interspousal violence increases when these tasks are not met successfully. A couple must make adjustments with respect to sexual and nonsexual roles.

It was once thought that the marriage license was a hitting license (Gelles 1974); violence between members of a couple was considered acceptable within marriage but not outside. New studies of courtship violence, however, show that for many couples, marital violence is simply the continuation of a pattern begun earlier in the relationship.

Violence is used frequently as an attempt to demonstrate one's power and adequacy. Working with couples to reduce their isolation, improve communication skills, and develop socially acceptable conflict-resolution tactics may also reduce the feelings of powerlessness and inadequacy often associated with violence.

Like members of other groups in the United States, blacks have been involved in nontraditional families. Couples involved in such relationships need as much help as—if not more than—those in traditional groups from family workers who may be asked to intervene during a crisis. At times, family workers are caught in the cross-fire between the couple's family of orientation and their family of procreation. In such a situation, the worker's role may include assisting both families to understand themselves and each other and working to relieve the crisis.

Family planning, or the lack of it, is crucial to families at stage I. The absence of informed, effective family planning has adverse effects on family health: maternal-infant morbidity and mortality, child neglect, child physical and emotional health, and marital discord. Informed, intentional family formation requires decisions regarding the circumstances and timing of marriage, pregnancy, and family size. In the ideal situation, a planned, uncrowded family has the desired number of children, timed in such a way that they minimize risks to the mother and other family members.

A number of factors contribute to the potential for family dysfunction and violence at this stage in the life cycle. Inadequate income, unemployment, crowded living conditions, substance abuse, and unplanned pregnancy may trigger interspousal violence. Although unplanned pregnancies are frequently cited as a risk factor in wife abuse, a planned pregnancy may also lead to violence (Gelles 1975). The violence may be a symptom of other relational dysfunctions.

Stage II: Early Childbearing Families

Stage II begins with the birth of the first child and continues through the infant's thirtieth month. The arrival of a child creates changes for family members in their relations with one another and with others outside the family. The birth of the first child has been viewed by at least one researcher as a family crisis (LeMasters 1957).

The family with a newborn child faces several important developmental tasks, related primarily to establishing a stable unit, reconciling conflicting developmental tasks of the various members, and jointly facilitating the developmental needs of mother, father, and child in ways that strengthen each other and the family as a whole. New roles must be learned as the family expands its functions and responsibilities.

The couple with an infant must allocate resources for his or her care and nurturance. Although there is some class variation in fulfilling these responsibilities, many black couples attempt a traditional gender role division of household labor. Black families, like other American families, attempt to cope with the normative stresses associated with infant care.

In addition to the normative stress that families with infants and toddlers experience, black families must cope with higher infant mortality rates (21.8 per 1,000 for blacks versus 11.4 per 1,000 for whites) and a higher incidence of infants who have a low birth weight (National Center for Health Statistics 1983). One of every 47 black infants dies during the first year of life.

More than half of all black infants born in 1982 were born into poverty. In 1982, 51.5 percent of all black children under the age of 3, 47.7 percent of all black children 3 to 5 years old, and 48 percent of all black children 6 to 13 years old were poor (U.S. Bureau of the Census 1983).

The often observed inverse relationship between marital duration and the probability of divorce is most apparent in black families. A high proportion of black families at this stage and the next stage undergo separation and divorce (Hampton 1982).

Black parents must deal not only with the usual developmental issues of parent-child bonding and attachment but also with some extraordinary survival issues. Poverty, maternal employment, and a high rate of divorce and separation distinguish many black families from other families in this stage.

Stage III: Families with Preschool Children

The third stage begins when the first-born is about 2½ and terminates when he or she is about 5 years of age. At this stage, the family is more complex and differentiated and faces new developmental tasks. Family life can be busy and demanding for parents. Most black mothers are employed outside the household; consequently, suitable child care arrangements must be made.

Because the family is growing in size and complexity, the need for young children to explore the world around them, as well as parents' needs for privacy, housing, and adequate space, often become major challenges. Preschoolers are frequently sick with minor infectious illnesses. These normative crises impose additional stress on parents and family resources.

Contrary to expectations, research has shown that the arrival of a second child into a family may have an even more deleterious effect on the marital relationship. Feldman (1969) reports that parental roles make marital roles difficult in the following ways: couples perceive negative personality changes in each other; they are less satisfied with the home; there are more task-oriented interactions; and they engage in fewer personal and more child-centered conversations.

Another issue during this period is how the family will expand to meet the demands placed on it by a new member while attempting to meet the needs of the older child or children. The displacement of a child by a newborn can be traumatic, but parental sensitivity to the older child's feelings, needs, and behavior can reduce the trauma. During this stage, sibling rivalry is expressed by frequently hitting or relating negatively to the newborn, by regressive behaviors, or by attention-getting activity. The sibling rivalry that develops during this stage often becomes sibling-to-sibling violence in later years.

Although researchers and practitioners suggest that both parents should maintain outside interests and contacts to reinvigorate themselves, this is often difficult. The lower-class parent may lack the opportunity, which may contribute to a greater sense of social isolation. The paucity of available resources and previous unsatisfactory associations with the wider community in health, recreational, educational, vocational, or social areas may contribute to their sense of alienation.

In 1982, 2.6 million or 40.6 percent of the 6.4 million black families in the United States were female-headed households with no husband present (U.S. Bureau of Census 1983). More than 13.2 percent of white preschoolers do not have a father present in their household; approximately 35.2 percent of black preschoolers do not have a father present. The role strain on the single parent is very great and is associated frequently with stress, depression, and injuries to children (Hampton, Daniel, and Newberger 1983).

Preschoolers suffer an appreciable number of injuries and illnesses, some inflicted upon them by their parents. It can be argued that

> child abuse and child neglect are catchall euphemisms for a variety of childhood injuries that derive from parental commission or omission. Abuse and neglect in reality are categories of illness in children which seem to derive from "social" or "interpersonal" causes. Child abuse, neglect, accidents, ingestions, and failure to thrive result primarily from the child's social interaction with his environment. These pediatric social illnesses account for a major share of the mortality of preschool children and often have significant physical and psychological consequences. (Hampton, Daniel, and Newberger 1983, p. 190).

In their study of ninety-four black children aged 4 or younger, Hampton, Daniel, and Newberger (1983) attempted to assess the extent to which distinctive patterns of parent-child, personal-historical, and environmental variables were associated with childhood accidents, ingestions, failures to thrive, child neglect, and child abuse. They found that economic isolation, family stress, maternal depression, and a parental history of maltreatment place children at risk for pediatric social illnesses but that no particular pattern distinguished among the illnesses.

Although child abuse may share some common correlates with other childhood maladies, it requires additional discussion. Fundamentally, the causal factors of child abuse consist of a cluster of interacting variables (Gil 1975). These variables exist at the individual, institutional, and societal levels and may involve society's attitude toward the use of force, including corporal punishment.

The tendency to resort to force to deal with conflicts and the readiness to use physical force for disciplinary objectives are endemic in U.S. society (Gil 1975). Whenever corporal punishment in child rearing is sanctioned and even subtly encouraged by a society, incidents of serious abuse and injury are inevitable, and conscious action on the part of the perpetrators or because of loss of self-control.

In general, abusive attacks on preschoolers tend to be triggered by stress and frustration. On the other hand, stress and frustration may facilitate abusive attacks even without causing a loss of self-control, as long as the use of force in child rearing is accepted as appropriate (Gil 1975). This point must be considered in assessing whether a disciplinary action in black families constitutes abuse. Most blacks approve of corporal punishment under the aegis of discipline.

Child abuse has many causes, notably stressful life events, such as the loss of a job or loved one, and stressful life conditions, such as inadequate housing or chronic unemployment (Newberger, Newberger, and Hampton 1983). Another contributing factor is inadequate knowledge of normal child development and inadequate understanding of the child and the parental role (Newberger and Cook 1983). The abuse of black infants and preschoolers is seldom the result of a single factor.

Stage IV: Families with School-Aged Children

A new stage begins when the eldest child enters elementary school. At this point parents are struggling with the twin demands of finding fulfillment in raising the next generation and being self-absorbed in their own growth, while school-aged children are working to develop a sense of industry (Erikson 1950). The normative developmental tasks and stresses differ somewhat from those of the preceding stages.

Promoting school achievement is one of the critical socialization tasks parents face. Black family members with middle-class aspirations invest heavily in education as a way of assisting their children (Willie 1983). Parents feel intense pressure from the outside community through the school system and other extrafamilial associations to see that their children conform to the community's standards. This pressure influences the black middle-class family to stress traditional values of achievement and productivity and causes some working-class families and many poor families to feel alienated and in conflict with school and community values.

Peer relations and outside activities play large roles in the life of the school-aged child, and conflicts often arise over divergent peer and family values. These conflicts are one of many variables causing the disproportionate number of black physical abuse cases in the 6- to 12-year-old age group. Hampton (chapter 1) reports that 60 percent of the physically abused black children in his sample were in this age group, while only 46 percent of the white and 53 percent of the Hispanic physically abused children fell into this category.

Sibling-to-sibling violence and child-to-parent violence are likely to increase at this time. Straus, Gelles, and Steinmetz (1980) found a strong positive correlation between the severity of violence that children suffered at the hands of their parents and violent acts between the children and their siblings. Their data tentatively support the idea that as physical punishment of children increases, physical violence against siblings also increases.

Although few studies have been conducted on violence toward parents, the data appear to indicate that the rates of parent abuse are related to the frequency of other forms of family violence. The more violence children experience or witness, the more likely they are to strike out at a parent (Gelles and Cornell 1985). These findings are consistent with the theory that families who regard violence as a legitimate means of conflict resolution are at a significantly higher risk for all forms of family violence, including parent abuse.

Child-to-parent violence is most likely to occur at this and the following stage of the family life cycle. Although no specific study has examined ethnic differences, I believe that majority and minority families follow a similar pattern in this regard.

Stage V: Families with Teenagers

This stage begins when the eldest child reaches adolescence. The overall family goal at this stage is to loosen family ties to allow greater responsibility and freedom, in preparation for releasing young adults in the making (Duvall 1977). Douvan and Adelson (1966) suggest that the period begins with the child almost entirely dependent on the family and ends with a young adult transformed into a person more free to make decisions, committed to his or her own beliefs and values, and looking beyond family boundaries for love and support.

Adams (1971) delineates three aspects of the adolescent process upon which much attention has been focused: emancipation, youth culture, and the generation gap. If the dominant family type is binding and closed, the adolescent's attempt to unbind himself or herself will be crisis producing for the family, at least for a time (Stierlin 1974). This struggle for independence can be functional for both parents and youth; it can also lead to potentially lethal conflicts within the household.

Black teenagers face difficulties in addition to the normative parent-child struggles during adolescence. An analysis of major social indicators shows that black youths are worse off in the 1980s than they were in 1960 in rates of unemployment, delinquency, substance abuse, teenaged pregnancy, and suicide (Gibbs 1984). The only improvement in more than twenty-five years is a reduction of high school dropout rates. This reduction, however, does not reveal the number of black high school graduates who are functionally illiterate or barely able to fill out a job application. All of these phenomena are interrelated and operate in combination to reduce the life chances for black youth, restrict their social mobility, and move them toward a permanently disadvantaged status (Gibbs 1984).

All parents face the critical developmental task of balancing freedom with responsibility as teenagers mature and emancipate themselves (Duvall 1977). Although open communication is needed between parents and children, it is often an ideal rather than a reality. Parents and adolescents often reject each other's values and life-styles. Parents in multiproblem families frequently reject and then disengage from their older children.

No simple cause-and-effect relationship exists between the withdrawal of parental support and youth involvement in antisocial behaviors. Many black parents, struggling to survive, find that they do not have the social, emotional, or financial resources to assist their children as they try to cope with the challenges of adolescence.

The probability for expressive and instrumental violence is quite high in many of these households. Whereas conformity to family values and standards by teenagers is a general issue that all households must address, the potential for family violence is greater among black urban youth who are worse off in several significant social dimensions than members of the dominant society.

Stage VI: Launching-Center Families

This phase of family life begins when the first child leaves the parental home; it ends with the empty nest, when the last child has left. The stage can be quite short or fairly long, depending on the number of children in the household and the timing of their departure.

Family developmental tasks are critical while the family is shifting from a household with children to a husband-wife pair. The major family goal is to reorganize the family into a continuing unit while releasing mature young people into lives of their own. During this stage, the marital pair become grandparents, another change in roles and self-image. Because of the relatively early ages at which black females give birth to their first children, black parents become grandparents at a younger age than members of many other groups in U.S. society.

Three-generation families, although not the usual pattern, are not uncommon among blacks. Most often the multigeneration family seems to develop when the nuclear family is disrupted by death or divorce, but financial expediency, child care needs, and teenaged pregnancy may also encourage such living arrangements. Three-generation households are not necessarily more stressful than two-generation households; they often reduce social isolation and increase social support. On the other hand, they may require some difficult physical and social adjustments.

As children disperse, parents must reestablish independence, and the marriage must be viable if the parents' needs are to be fulfilled. Parents must readjust their relationship to relate to each other as partners rather than primarily as parents. For this stage to be complete, children must be independent while maintaining ties and with parents.

Stage VII: Families of Middle Years

The seventh stage of the family life cycle begins when the last child leaves home and ends with the retirement or death of one of the spouses. The postparental couple is not usually isolated from kin and family and may be involved with four generations of relatives.

Maintaining physical health is a major preoccupation and may be considered one of the couple's major developmental tasks. A second task is strengthening the marital relationship. A third task is to sustain satisfying and meaningful relationships with aging parents and with children. By accepting and welcoming grandchildren into the family and promoting satisfying intergenerational relationships, the couple can find this stage highly rewarding.

Stage VIII: Families in Old Age and Retirement

This stage can be problematic for many families as once-independent individuals often gradually lose their independence. As the couple grows older and retires, a variety of stressors or losses confound the role transition:

1. *Economic:* Adjusting to substantially reduced income and later perhaps adjusting to economic dependency (family or government subsidy).
2. *Housing:* Often moving to smaller quarters and later perhaps being forced to move to an institution.
3. *Social:* Death of siblings, friends, and spouse.
4. *Work:* Mandatory retirement and loss of the work role.

These changes necessitate role modifications that may be accompanied by declines in self-esteem, status, and health. The multiplicity of losses creates this situation among many aged persons when they are depleted of the coping energies needed to meet the challenges and making the adjustments. Social isolation, depression, and other psychological problems are serious concerns.

Discussion

The developmental or family life cycle model emphasizes normative changes inside the family. Each of these changes is attended by normative stressors, the predictable or expected changes that all or most families experience. The level of stress associated with these changes is affected by the interplay of the individuals. Husbands, wives, sons, and daughters are simultaneously growing and changing, meeting the challenges of personal development while adapting to changes in others.

All families, functional and dysfunctional, experience stress at various times throughout the family life cycle. Some recover from the stress and become stronger; other families cannot cope and are caught in a downward spiral toward increasing dysfunction (Boss 1980). Developmental theory identifies several stage-specific sources of normative stress as a family attempts to meet several interrelated developmental tasks. Intrafamilial violence is often a symptom of family dysfunction as its members attempt to address developmental issues within a given stage. Family violence can also be a consequence of a family's failure to address developmental tasks adequately at an earlier stage. Violence may be a symptom of family dysfunction.

Black families must cope with both normative and nonnormative pressures within the context of prejudice and racism. The most oppressive source of stress for blacks continues to be the interplay of racism, discrimination, and economic isolation (McAdoo 1982), which is present throughout the family life cycle. This type of stress can affect black families directly and indirectly.

Operating together, family and individual changes may create psychological and interpersonal disturbances that require coping and adaptation. Legitimate culturally determined attitudes, values, and beliefs are generated among groups as a way of coping with their environments and normative life cycle changes. More knowledge and understanding of the developmental stages and adaptations of Afro-American families, seen as strengths, could be used for remedial and preventive physical and mental health programs, as well as to prevent domestic violence.

Without question, a primary contributing factor to the seemingly high rate of violence among blacks lies outside the family. Efforts to explain violence from a developmental perspective cannot ignore external stressors, such as unemployment, poor housing, poverty, and hunger among black Americans. When we look at the social ecology of black family life along with the developmental changes and demands encountered at each stage of the life cycle, we can gain a better appreciation of the type, nature, and intensity of the stress and of the type of culturally sensitive interventions that may be useful in preventing violence.

References

Adams, B.N. 1971. *The American Family*. Chicago: Markham Publishing.

Aldous, Joan. 1978. *Family Careers: Developmental Change in Families*. New York: John Wiley.

Boss, Pauline. 1980. "Normative Family Stress: Family Boundary Changes across the Life-Span." *Family Relations* 29:445–450.

Douvan E., and J. Adelson. 1966. *The Adolescent Experience*. New York: John Wiley.

Duvall, Evelyn M. 1977. *Marriage and Family Development*. 5th ed. Philadelphia: J.B. Lippincott.

Duvall, Evelyn M., and Reuben Hill. 1948. "Report of the Committee for the Dynamics of Family Interaction." Prepared for the National Council on Family Life.

Erikson, Erik H. 1950. *Childhood and Society*. New York: Norton.

Feldman, Harold. 1969. "Parent and Marriage: Myths and Realities." Paper presented at the Merrill-Palmer Institute Conference, November 21.

Gelles, Richard J. 1974. *The Violent Home*. Beverly Hills: Sage.

———. 1975. "Violence and Pregnancy: A Note on the Extent of the Problems and Needed Services." *Family Coordinator* 24(January):81–86.

Gelles, Richard J., and Clair P. Cornell. 1985. *Intimate Violence in Families*. Beverly Hills: Sage.

Gibbs, Jewelle T. 1984. "Black Adolescents and Youth: An Endangered Species." *American Journal of Orthopsychiatry* 54, no. 1:6–21.

Gil, David 1975. "Unraveling Child Abuse." *American Journal of Orthopsychiatry* 45:346–356.

Hampton, Robert L. 1982. "Family Life Cycle, Economic Well-being, and Marital Disruption in Black Families." *California Sociologist* 5, no. 1:16–33.

Hampton, Robert L., Jessica H. Daniel, and Eli H. Newberger. 1983. "Pediatric Social Illnesses and Black Families." *Western Journal of Black Studies* 7, no. 4:190–196.

LeMasters, E.E. 1957 "Parenthood as Crisis." *Marriage and Family Living* 19(November):352–355.

McAdoo, Harriette P. 1978. "Factors Related to Stability in Upward Mobile Black Families." *Journal of Marriage and the Family* 40:761–776.

———. 1982. "Levels of Stress and Family Support in Black Females." In *Family Stress, Coping and Social Support*, pp. 239–252. Edited by Hamilton McCubbin, A. Elizabeth Cauble, and Joan M. Patterson. Springfield, Ill.: Charles C. Thomas.

National Center for Health Statistics. 1983. "Advance Report of Final Mortality Statistics." *Monthly Vital Statistics Report* 32, no. 4:xxx.

Newberger, Carolyn, and Susan Cook. 1983. "Parental Awareness and Child Abuse and Neglect: Cognitive-Developmental Analysis of Urban and Rural Sample." *American Journal of Orthopsychiatry* 53:512–524.

Newberger, Eli H., Carolyn M. Newberger, and Robert L. Hampton 1983. "Child Abuse: The Current Theory Base and Future Research Needs." *Journal of the American Academy of Child Psychiatry* 22, no. 3:262–268.

Rapoport, Rhonda. 1963. "Normal Crisis, Family Structure, and Mental Health." *Family Process* 2, no. 1:68–80.

Staples, Robert E. 1978. "Black Family Life Development." In *Mental Health: A Challenge to the Black Community*, pp. 73–94. Edited by Lawrence E. Gary. Philadelphia: Dorrance.

Stierlin, H. 1974. *Separating Parents and Adolescents*. New York: Quadrangle.

Straus, Murray A., Richard J. Gelles, and Suzanne K. Steinmetz. 1980. *Behind Closed Doors*. Garden City, N.Y.: Doubleday.

U.S. Bureau of the Census. 1983. "Money, Income, and Poverty Status of Families and Persons in the United States: 1982 Advanced Report." *Current Population Reports* P-60 (140). Washington, D.C.: Government Printing Office.

Willie, Charles. 1983. *A New Look at Black Families*. New York: General Hall Publishers.

Subject Index

Author Index

About the Contributors

Jo-Ellen Asbury is an assistant professor of psychology at the College of Wooster, Wooster, Ohio.

Johnella Banks is an associate professor of nursing, College of Nursing, Howard University, Washington, D.C.

Debra D. Cobb is executive director, Shelter for Help and Emergency, Charlottesville, Virginia.

Jessica H. Daniel is a staff psychologist at the Children's Hospital Center and the Judge Baker Guidance Center, Boston, and a lecturer on child psychiatry at Harvard Medical School, Boston.

Regina T. Dolan is a graduate student in psychology at George Washington University, Washington, D.C.

Aaron Ebata is a doctoral candidate in the College of Human Development, Pennsylvania State University, University Park.

James Garbarino is president of the Erikson Institute for the Advanced Study of Child Development, Chicago.

Pamela V. Hammond is an assistant professor of nursing, School of Nursing, Hampton University, Hampton, Virginia.

Darnell F. Hawkins is an associate professor of sociology and black studies at the University of Illinois, Chicago.

Velma LaPoint is an assistant professor of human development, School of Human Ecology, Howard University, Washington, D.C.

Ruby F. Lassiter is an assistant professor of social work, Department of Social Work, New Mexico State University, Las Cruces.

Coramae Richey Mann is an associate professor, School of Criminology, Florida State University, Tallahassee.

Lena Wright Myers is a professor of sociology, Jackson State University, Jackson, Mississippi.

Eli H. Newberger is an assistant professor of pediatrics, Harvard Medical School, and director, Family Development Study, Children's Hospital Center, Boston.

Lois H. Pierce is an assistant professor of social work, University of Missouri—St. Louis.

Robert L. Pierce is an associate professor, George Warren Brown School of Social Work, Washington University, St. Louis, Missouri.

Maurice C. Taylor is an associate professor of sociology, Hampton University, Hampton, Virginia.

Melvin N. Wilson is an assistant professor of psychology, the University of Virginia, Charlottesville.

About the Editor

Robert L. Hampton, Ph.D., received the A.B. degree from Princeton University and the M.A. and Ph.D. from the University of Michigan. He is an associate professor of sociology, Connecticut College, New London, Connecticut, a research associate in the Family Development Program, Children's Hospital Center, and lecturer on pediatrics (sociology), Harvard Medical School, Boston. He has published extensively in the area of child maltreatment. His research interests include interspousal violence, family homicide, stress and coping, and the institutional processing of victims and perpetrators.